Cotton was King

Indian Farms
to
Colbert - Franklin County Plantations

Alabama Plantation Series

Rickey Butch Walker

First Edition

ISBN - 978-1-949711-08-0

Library of Congress Control Number: 2018957400

Bluewater Publications
BWPublications.com

Published in the United States by Bluewater Publications.
Printed in the United States of America.

This work is based on the authors' personal interpretation of research.

Cover Photo Provided by: Photo of Belle Mont Mansion, 1569 Cook Lane, Tuscumbia, AL 35674, provided by Belle Mont Mansion. Historic Belle Mont is a museum property of the Alabama Historical Commission. Use of this photograph does not imply endorsement of this or any publication by the Alabama Historical Commission or by the Colbert County Historical Landmarks Foundation, which operates the museum. For more information about Belle Mont, visit www.bellemontmansion.org.

Acknowledgements

My sister, June Reed, was very helpful in editing the book, "Cotton was King," Volume II. She spent many hours making corrections, and I greatly appreciate her help and dedication in getting this book finished.

Yoland Morgan Smith, a local historian, was also very helpful in the completion of this book. She did an edit and provided family information on many of the cotton planters of Franklin County (present-day Colbert), Alabama. Her work was very valuable in the development of *"Cotton was King, Indian Farms to Colbert – Franklin County Plantations; Alabama Series Book Two."*

I also thank Ninon Parker and the staff of Belle Mont for helping with the texts concerning the Winston family.

I also must thank my wife, Mary Anne Walker, for putting up with all the hours I spent in writing on this book. She was very understanding and provided much encouragement to which I am extremely grateful.

Bluewater Publications
books by
Rickey Butch Walker

Cotton Was King - Lauderdale County – Alabama Plantation Series, ISBN 978-1-934610-99-2, $19.95

Appalachian Indians of the Warrior Mountains: History and Culture, ISBN 978-1-934610-72-5, $19.95

Appalachian Indian Trails of the Chickamauga: Lower Cherokee Settlements, ISBN 978-1-934610-91-6, $19.95

Celtic Indian Boy of Appalachia: A Scots Irish Cherokee Childhood, ISBN 978-1-934610-75-6, $19.95

Chickasaw Chief George Colbert: His Family and His Country, ISBN 978-1-934610-71-8, $19.95

Doublehead: Last Chickamauga Cherokee Chief, ISBN 978-1-934610-67-1, $19.95

Hiking Sipsey: A Family's Fight for Eastern Wilderness, ISBN 978-1-934610-93-0, $19.95

Soldier's Wife: Cotton Fields to Berlin and Tripoli, ISBN-978-1-934610-12-1, $19.95

Warrior Mountains Folklore: American Indian and Celtic History in the Southeast, ISBN 978-1-934610-65-7, $24.95

Warrior Mountains Indian Heritage-Teacher's Edition, ISBN 978-1-934610-27-5, $39.95

Warrior Mountains Indian Heritage-Student Edition, ISBN 978-1-934610-66-4, $24.95

Contents

Franklin County Cotton Plantations

Introduction

The first cotton farmed in North Alabama was grown by the black slaveholders of the Lower Cherokee and Chickasaw Indian tribes along Muscle Shoals of the Tennessee River. Indian people inhabiting the area referred to the Muscle Shoals as "Chake Thlocko" which means Great Crossing Place or Big Ford. The Muscle Shoals formed great barriers to navigation of the Tennessee River, but the shallow areas of the shoals provided many river crossings of Indian trails during low water periods. These shoals provided early Southeastern American Indians a staple diet of freshwater mussels of some 80 species and an abundance of wildlife. Evidence of large prehistoric Indian populations still exists in the huge shell middens along the shoals of the Tennessee River.

The Muscle Shoals of northwest Alabama stretched from the vicinity of the mouth of Fox's Creek on the present-day county line of Lawrence and Morgan Counties westward through Franklin (Colbert) and Lauderdale Counties to the Mississippi State line. Beginning upstream, the shoals of the Tennessee River included Elk River Shoals, Big Muscle Shoals, Little Muscle Shoals, Colbert Shoals, Bee Tree Shoals, and Waterloo Shoals.

The northern border of the original Franklin County included Little Muscle Shoals, Colbert Shoals, Bee Tree Shoals, and Waterloo Shoals. Franklin and other North Alabama counties adjacent to the Muscle Shoals were open to white settlement by the September 1816 Turkey Town Treaty. These 1816 land cessions from the Chickasaw and Cherokee Indians included Franklin (western Colbert), Lawrence (eastern Colbert), Lauderdale, Limestone, Morgan and the southwest half of Madison Counties.

Adjacent to the Muscle Shoals of North Alabama was very fertile alluvial bottomlands that were ideal for growing cotton and corn. Corn was a staple in the diet of historic Indians living along the river. Cotton produced by slave owning Indians became an important economic product of the Cherokee and Chickasaw in the late 1700's and early 1800's.

1

Cotton farmed by the Indians in the Tennessee Valley along the shoals was reported as growing taller than an average person; therefore, these Indian lands became highly sought after by the white eastern cotton planters of North Carolina and Virginia. Prior to the white takeover of the North Alabama area after the Turkey Town Treaty of September 1816, the black slaves of the Cherokee and Chickasaw people were the primary growers of cotton along the fertile lands adjacent to the Muscle Shoals of the great bend of the Tennessee River Valley.

By the late 1700's, both the Lower Cherokee and Chickasaw Indians of the Muscle Shoals owned black slaves which they used to farm large tracts of cotton. These black slaves were acquired by the Chickasaw and Cherokee Indians by various methods. Slaves of the Indians were stolen during raids on white settlements, taken from vessels using the Mississippi and Tennessee Rivers, escaped slaves that run away to Indian Territory for freedom, and later, slaves traded to Doublehead for large land leases in his Tennessee River reservation at the Muscle Shoals. From 1770 through the 1807 time period, the Chickamauga faction of the Lower Cherokee Indians occupying the Muscle Shoals was under the leadership of Doublehead.

The Chickasaws were primarily under the leadership of James Logan Colbert and his half blood Chickasaw sons-William, George, and Levi. Chickamauga Cherokee Chief Doublehead, the half blood Chickasaw sons of Scots Irish James Logan Colbert, and Creek Chief Alexander McGillivary were related through intermarriage. George Colbert was the double son-in-law of Doublehead, and George's oldest half-brother General William Colbert was the brother-in-law of Creek Chief Alexander McGillivary.

Beginning after the treaty of Sycamore Shoals in 1775, the warriors of these Native American tribes of the Lower Cherokee, Upper Creek, and Chickasaw Indian Nations were participants in Chickamauga Confederacy. The tribes formed the strongest Indian alliance to ever inhabit North Alabama and fought together in the Chickamauga War that lasted from 1775 to 1794. After the war, the Chickasaw and Lower Cherokee basically controlled all of the cotton growing and trade along the Tennessee River until the early 1800's.

Chickasaw Colberts

The Chickasaw Colberts controlled the cotton farming in Franklin County (present-day Colbert); later, George Colbert would enter large tracts of land in Franklin County, Alabama. George and his siblings were half white from their father James Logan Colbert, a Scotsman. According to historical records, it appears that James Logan Colbert begin living among the Chickasaws by 1742 and eventually married three Chickasaw women who bore him nine children. Chickasaw interpreter Malcolm McGee said in 1841, "William Colbert had the old man's property. William's first war exploits was in the Red Nation; had joined the Cherokees and aided in their warfare against the whites, under Dragging Canoe in 1776 at the Tatum Flats; then about 16 and his father was along".

In order to prevent white settlement on Chickasaw territory, James Logan Colbert and his sons supported and fought in the Chickamauga War (1775-1794) with

the Lower Cherokee. In 1781, James Logan Colbert led a siege of Fort Jefferson which had been built on Chickasaw land without their permission. The building of the fort by whites was a direct invasion on Chickasaw Territory with the intent of taking Indian lands for future settlement and eventually cotton plantations.

On July 5, 1782, a declaration was made by Spanish merchant Silbestre Labadie who had been a captive of James Logan Colbert in the spring of 1782 when his boat, slaves, and goods were captured at Chickasaw Bluff on the Mississippi River. Labadie stated that James Logan Colbert "was about 60 years old, possessed of good health, and a strong constitution. An active man, despite his years, he had a violent temper, and was capable of enduring the greatest hardship. He had lived among the Chickasaws for 40 years and boasted that he was owner of a fine house and some 150 blacks. He said he had several sons by Chickasaw women, who were very important chiefs in that nation."

During a trip toward his home after meeting with his friend and ally Creek Chief Alexander McGillivary, James Logan Colbert died on January 7, 1784. His black slave Cesar claimed that James Logan Colbert was thrown from his horse, but his sons' believed that Cesar killed their father. Prior to his death, James Logan Colbert owned some one hundred fifty black slaves.

After he died, James Logan Colbert's black slaves were divided among his mixed blood Chickasaw children. James Logan Colbert's two Chickasaw Celtic sons Levi and George Colbert became very wealthy using their black slaves to carry on the farming operations.

James Logan Colbert and his Chickasaw sons fought to prevent white settler encroachment on Chickasaw territory until it was eventually taken by the United States in a series of treaties. Shortly after James Logan Colbert's death in 1784, Chickasaw Chief Piomingo led the Chickasaw Nation in the first treaty negotiations with President George Washington on January 10, 1786. As a result of the treaty, the United States recognized the Chickasaw ownership of lands from the mouth of Flint River south of Huntsville, Alabama, west to the Mississippi River even though the Muscle Shoals was occupied by the Chickamauga faction of Lower Cherokees at that time.

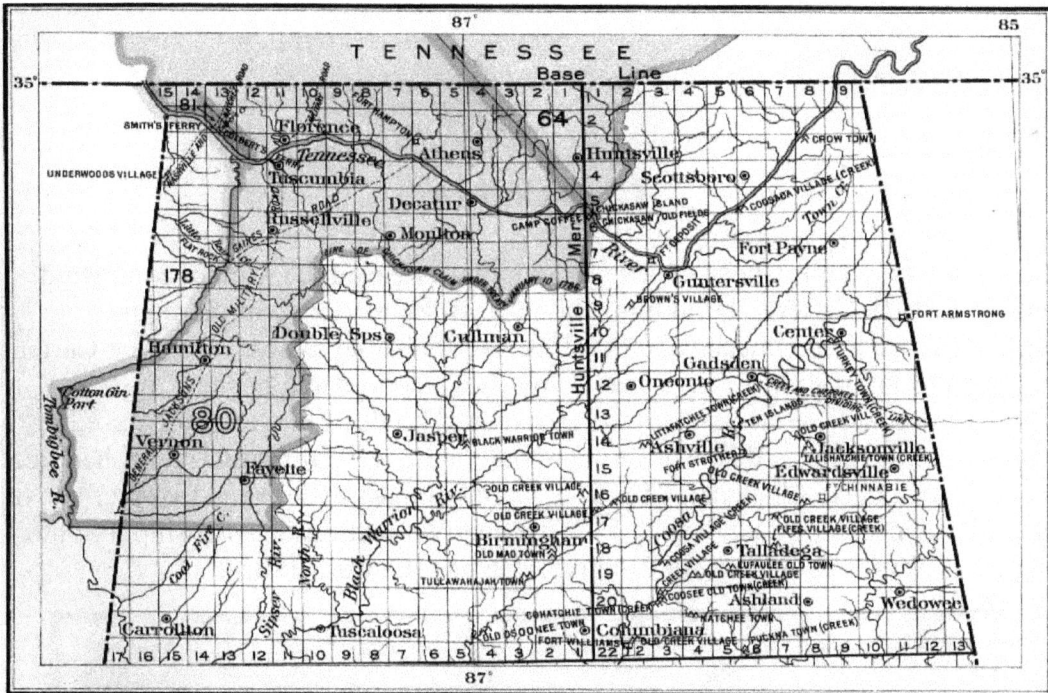

Chickasaw Claims 1/10/1786

Article One of the treaty required all black slaves taken during the Chickamauga War be returned to the citizens of the United States as follows: "They (Chickasaws) shall restore all the Negroes, and all other property taken during the late war from the citizens, if any there be in the Chickasaw Nation, to such person, and at such time and place, as the Commissioners of the United States of America shall appoint." However, most of the black slaves of the Colbert family had been taken prior to their involvement in the war; therefore, the black slaves of the Colbert family remained property of the Chickasaws.

Levi Colbert

Levi Colbert, whose Chickasaw name was Itawamba Mingo, contracted with Kilpatrick Carter to build him a home at Buzzard Roost Spring on the Natchez Trace in present-day Colbert County, Alabama. Later, Kilpatrick Carter became the son-in-law of Chickasaw Chief Levi Colbert and nephew of Chickasaw Chief George Colbert. Carter owned 45 black slaves that he used on his farm land at Buzzard Roost Spring about a mile west of present-day Cherokee in Colbert County, Alabama. Kilprtrick Carter entered and owned two sections of land in Township 3 South, Range 14 West and two sections inTownship 3 South, Range 13 West in old Franklin County, Alabama (Cowart, 1985).

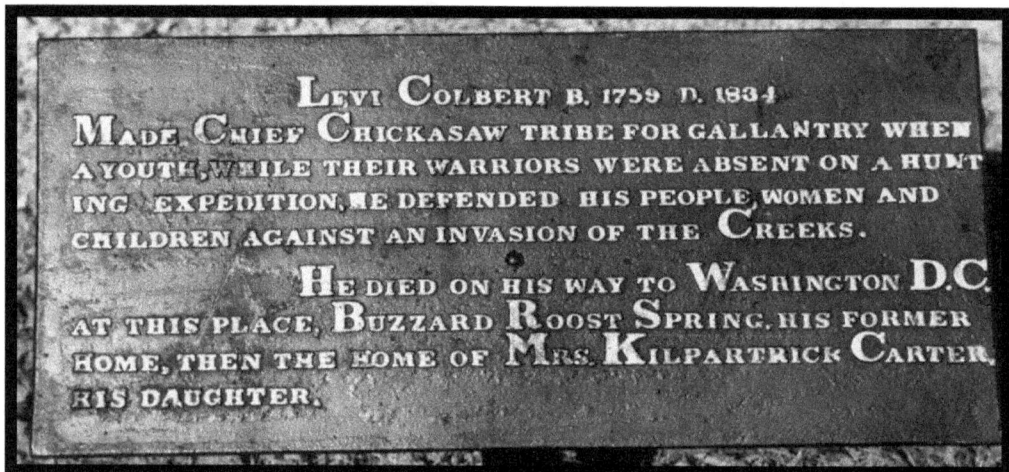

LEVI COLBERT B. 1759 D. 1834
MADE CHIEF CHICKASAW TRIBE FOR GALLANTRY WHEN A YOUTH, WHILE THEIR WARRIORS WERE ABSENT ON A HUNTING EXPEDITION, HE DEFENDED HIS PEOPLE, WOMEN AND CHILDREN AGAINST AN INVASION OF THE CREEKS.

HE DIED ON HIS WAY TO WASHINGTON D.C. AT THIS PLACE, BUZZARD ROOST SPRING, HIS FORMER HOME, THEN THE HOME OF MRS. KILPARTRICK CARTER, HIS DAUGHTER.

Supposedly during the construction of the home, Levi's daughter Phalishta "Pat" Malacha Colbert fell in love and married Carter. Levi told Carter if he would build him another house at Cotton Gin Port that he would give his daughter and Kilpatrick Carter the home at Buzzard Roost Spring which he did. After he gave his home, Levi Colbert moved from Buzzard Roost Spring near the small Town of Cherokee to Cotton Gin Port on the Tombigbee River in Mississippi.

Cotton Gin Port was located at major Chickasaw trail crossings of the Tombigbee River close to the home of Levi Colbert.

The large Chickasaw town located at the Cotton Gin Port crossing site was situated on the bluff west of the river. One trail which crossed the Tombigbee River at Cotton Gin Port was Gaines Trace which was surveyed from Melton's Bluff on the Tennessee River in present-day Lawrence County, Alabama, by the Captain Edmund Pendelton Gaines of the United States Army beginning in December 1807. Another fork of Gaines Trace ran to the home of George Colbert at Colbert's Ferry on the Tennessee River in Franklin County (present-day Colbert), Alabama. One fork of the High Town Path crossed at Cotton Gin Port and led to the Mississippi River at Chickasaw Bluffs near the mouth of the Wolf River.

After the passage of the Indian Civilization Act in 1801, the United States government established a cotton gin on the west side of the Tombigbee River at Cotton Gin Port. This action was an attempt to convert the Chickasaws into peaceful farmers and to win the support of the tribe that had long been allied with the English. According to one legend, the cotton gin was a gift from President George Washington to the Colbert Chickasaws to encourage their growing of cotton. Many think that the cotton gin was given to enhance the acceptance of the treaty with the Chickasaws of December 1801 authorizing the Natchez Trace.

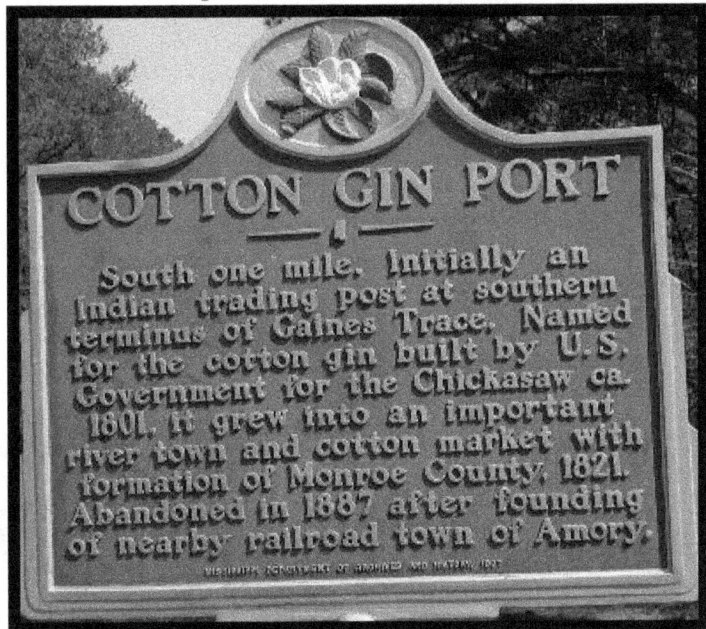

COTTON GIN PORT

South one mile, initially an Indian trading post at southern terminus of Gaines Trace. Named for the cotton gin built by U.S. Government for the Chickasaw ca. 1801. It grew into an important river town and cotton market with formation of Monroe County, 1821. Abandoned in 1887 after founding of nearby railroad town of Amory.

With the help of his black slaves, Levi Colbert became one of the wealthiest and most powerful of the Colbert family. He lived just west of Cotton Gin Port located in Monroe County, Mississippi. He owned four thousand cattle, five hundred horses, a large herd of sheep, and several head of swine. Major Levi Colbert was born in 1759, and he died on June 2, 1834, at his daughter's home near Buzzard Roost Spring in old Franklin County (now Colbert County), Alabama, at 74 years of age.

George Colbert

George Colbert was a planter and owner of huge cotton plantations that utilized black slaves. His farming operations were around Colbert's Ferry on the Tennessee River before he moved his cotton plantation near Tupelo in northeastern Mississippi. Most of the black slaves belonging to the Colberts were taken on Chickasaw raids of Spanish and French vessels on the Mississippi River by their Scots Irish father James Logan Colbert. At one time, the French referred to the Mississippi River as "Riveria de Colbert" or River of Colbert.

George Colbert became the double son-in-law of Doublehead when he married two of Doublehead's daughters-Tuskiahooto and Saleechie. George and his Cherokee wives lived at the crossing of the Natchez Trace in Franklin (Colbert) County, Alabama, until the death of his primary Cherokee wife Tuskiahooto in 1818. George then moved with his Cherokee wife

George Colbert's Home on Natchez Trace

Saleechie to his plantation near Tupelo where he continued his cotton farming operations.

The Treaty with the Chickasaws on May 24, 1834, allowed individual Chickasaw Indian people to own their reservations or tracts of land they lived upon and improved in Franklin County, Alabama. This allowed them to receive compensation on the quality of their farm land and for their improvements. Many of these land entries for individual Chickasaw Indians are listed in the early land records of Franklin (Colbert) County and include Chickasaw Chief George Colbert and his son Pitman Colbert. Other Chickasaw Indian land owners in western Franklin County, Alabama, included John McLish, Pamela Reynolds, Tookishishtubby, Betsy Colbert, Robert Colbert, James Colbert, Weeyanachat, Wehaplaumly, Bahnowwah, Enockthapahtubby, Kilpatrick Carter (son-in-law of Levi Colbert), Eyicochar, Mushhetubby, TushKahsueKa, AhlaKintubby, and ShetowiKa (Cowart, 1985).

On October 6, 1840, George Colbert owned all the land in Sections 1, 2, 11, and 12 of Township 3 South and Range 14 West in Franklin County, Alabama. Pitman Colbert owned Sections 13 and 24 and Sections 7, 8, 17, and 18 of Township 3 South and Range 13 West (Cowart, 1985). Pamela Colbert Reynolds, daughter of George Colbert and wife of Francis Reynolds son of Indian agent Benjamin Renolds, entered land in six sections in Townships 2, 3, 4 South and Ranges 13, 15 West; she owned three entire sections. Other Colbert family members also entered land in Franklin (Colbert) County. A section of land is equivalent to 640 acres or one square mile with a full township containing 36 square miles.

After George and his family were forced west on November 14, 1837, he continue his large scale farming of some three to five hundred acres of cotton with the labor of his one hundred fifty black slaves. He raised cotton, corn, and other farm products on the rich bottomlands near Doaksville, Arkansas.

According to The Five Civilized Tribes by Grant Foreman (1989), "A number of wealthier half-breeds settled on the rich bottom lands near Fort Towson where they engaged on a large scale in raising cotton and other farm products. One of them Colonel George Colbert, the first year after his arrival prepared to plant from three to five hundred acres of cotton with the labor of his

150 slaves." On November 7, 1839, Chickasaw Chief George Colbert died near Fort Towson, and he was said to be ninety-five years old.

Members of the Colbert family were some of the largest slave holders in the Chickasaw Nation. By the time of Chickasaw Indian removal in 1837, the Chickasaw Indian people numbered about 4,914, and they owned 1,156 black slaves.

At the time of Chickasaw Indian removal from Franklin County, Alabama, some families of black slaves had been living and working among the Chickasaws for several generations. The black Chickasaw slaves became known as Chickasaw Freedmen. From the time of their freedom after the Civil War, the Chickasaw Freedmen were not considered to be citizens of either the United States or the Chickasaw Nation.

After the Civil War, Colbert County was formed from the north part of Franklin County and the northwestern portion of Lawrence County. The county was named in honor of the Colbert family of the Chickasaw Nation.

Cotton Plantations and Slave Owners

The Tennessee River was being used as early as 1764 as a water route by white settlers who were heading for the Natchez District of West Florida which had been opened up for settlement by a proclamation made in 1763. Most of these early emigrants from Virginia and North Carolina traveled by land to Southwest Point (present-day Kingston, Tennessee) at the junction of the Clinch River and Tennessee River. These white settlers ventured down the Holston, Tennessee, Ohio, and the Mississippi Rivers to their new homes.

The 1760's time period was prior to the Chickamauga War that started with the signing of the Treaty of Sycamore Shoals in 1775. The Chickamauga War slowed the Natchez District migration to a trickle; however, the flood gates of migration became wide open with the ceding of Indian lands along the Muscle Shoals of northwest Alabama.

The Turkey Town Treaty of September 16 and 18, 1816, ceded most of the Indian lands in northwest Alabama which included Franklin (western portion of Colbert) County, Lawrence (eastern portion of Colbert), and Morgan Counties on the south side of the Tennessee River, and the counties of Lauderdale, Limestone, and the southwest portion of Madison on the north side of the river. A wedge shaped section of Madison County was ceded by the Chickasaws during the Chickasaw Treaty of December 1801, which started at a point at the mouth of Flint River and ran about 45 degrees toward the Tennessee state line.

After the Turkey Town Treaty of 1816, Madison County was squared up with its western boundary beginning at the Tennessee state line and running perpendicular to the Tennessee state line to the Tennessee River. The 1816 treaty was ratified by congress in July 1817, after which the federal government opened up these Indian lands for purchase starting in 1818.

Prior to the federal sale of Indian lands in September 1818, General Andrew Jackson purchased Indian land from half blood Cherokee David Melton on November 22, 1816; therefore, Jackson became the first legal white landowner of the Turkey Town land cessions. Jackson's Muscle Shoals plantation was called Marathon and was located at Melton's Bluff in Lawrence County, Alabama. After the Indians were removed, the federal sale of Cherokee and Chickasaw lands began in 1818.

The sale of Indian farms along the Muscle Shoals led to a land rush called "Alabama Fever." The cotton planters primarily from North Carolina and Virginia had depleted the nutrients in their soil and wanted the rich farm land of the great bend of the Tennessee River. They had been told of cotton growing higher than a man on the rich alluvial bottoms of the Tennessee River Valley.

Groups of slave owning cotton farmers from the original colonies along the eastern seaboard came into North Alabama to claim the Indian cotton lands. From the colonial states of Virginia, Carolinas, and Georgia, cotton planters organized as groups to make a wagon train trek across the Appalachians to obtain the rich fertile Indian lands along the Muscle Shoals for their farming activities. Some wagon trains consisting of forty to fifty families with their black slaves traveled over rough mountainous terrain to newly acquired Indian lands of northwest Alabama in order to purchase their cotton plantations. Many cotton planters were already established in the northeastern portion of the original Madison County which was formed about 1806 becoming the first county in North Alabama.

During the federal sale of Indian lands at the Muscle Shoals in 1818, there was a mass migration of wealthy cotton planters and their slaves to previous Indian owned farm lands along the Tennessee River. After Indians were removed from their lands, cotton planters with their slaves poured into the western portion of the Big Bend of the Tennessee River Valley. Most of these cotton planters coming to North Alabama seeking new lands had exhausted their colonial farms through the over-cultivation of cotton. They were drawn to the Muscle Shoals of the Tennessee River Valley by stories of the rich soil where "Cotton was King."

The wealthy eastern planters that came to the Muscle Shoals area brought with them many black slaves to use in the labor of reaping the wealth through the planting, working, and picking the cotton. Their plantation system was readily transplanted from the poor lands of the eastern colonial states to the rich river bottom lands adjacent to the Muscle Shoals of northwest Alabama. The steady demand for cotton made this product the nation's leading export during the first half of the 1800's; it also made the slave owning plantation holders wealthy and powerful people with a sense of self-importance. Prior to the Civil War, the large slave holding planters enjoyed a time when "Cotton Was King."

Most of the wealthy cotton planters in the Franklin County area sent their children to the LaGrange academic schools for a formal education. LaGrange College was the first college in Alabama; the school was on Lawrence Hill on LaGrange Mountain in Franklin County, Alabama. In association with LaGrange, Lafayette Academy for girls was opened shortly after LaGrange College. In 1863, the schools were destroyed by being burned to the ground by the military forces under the command of Union General Grenville Mellen Dodge.

Before the end of the Civil War, the wealthy cotton planters of the Muscle Shoals that depended on slave labor experienced a disastrous decline in their money and power. Many of these slave owning planters lost everything during and after the Civil War. According to an article titled Lauderdale County,

Black People picking cotton while overseerer watches on horseback
Unknown photographer 1895

Alabama, History of the Shoals and published in the Times

13

Daily, Thursday, February 25, 1999, by Harry E. Wallace, "The Civil War brought great destruction to the Counties of the Tennessee Valley. Almost all transportation, communication, and industry were destroyed. Education facilities ceased to operate and the "cotton kingdom" was virtually destroyed. Post-war recovery would be long and painful."

After the Civil War, a few of the very wealthy plantation and former slave owners were able to hold on to vast tracts of Turkey Town cession lands that were passed down to their future generations by placing their lands in a trust. Today within the Tennessee Valley of northwest Alabama, many families still enjoy these large land holdings that they were able to gain through the free labor of their black slaves.

Franklin (Colbert) County

On February 4, 1818, Franklin County, Alabama, was created from the Bureau of Land Management by the Alabama Territorial Legislature at St. Stephens. In 1818, shortly after Franklin County was created, former Chickasaw and Cherokee territory came open for white settlers except the Chickasaw Nation west of Cane Creek. After the Civil War, Colbert County was created out of portions of north Franklin and northwestern Lawrence Counties.

Most of the first wealthy cotton planters came into Franklin County, Alabama, from North Carolina, and Virginia. They followed old Indian trails many of which that had been upgraded to wagon roads. Beginning with the federal land sales in 1818, these cotton barons begin claiming the fertile lands that lay to the south of the Tennessee River in Franklin County. Before the arrival of the white cotton planters, these were some of the same lands that the Cherokees and Chickasaws had already been farming cotton with the help of their black slaves.

For the first few years after the Indian land cessions of 1816 and government land sales of 1818, wagon trains regularly rolled out of Virginia and North Carolina headed to the northwest Alabama area of the Tennessee Valley; many planters would wind up in Franklin County, Alabama. Wealthy cotton

14

barons with their families, all their belongings, and sometimes hundreds of black slaves traveled for weeks and months along rough Indian trails to reach the rich flat valley lands along the Muscle Shoals of the Tennessee River.

Ferry Crossings of the Tennessee River

The Cherokee Indian territory east of Madison and Morgan Counties did not open to white settlement until after Indian removal in 1838. Therefore, before the late 1830's, most of the cotton planters coming to Franklin County had to avoid passing through Indian territory unless they possessed a passport or permit. The most direct route without passing through occupied Indian Territory was south from Nashville to one of the many Tennessee River ferry crossings.

Many of the first white planters had already arrived in the northeast half of Madison County which was created in 1806 by the Indian land cession of the Chickasaw Treaty of December 1801. From Madison County, cotton barons migrated west into Franklin County to claim the new cotton country by way of the many ferries along the Muscle Shoals of the Tennessee River.

Other planters arrived in Franklin County and other counties opened for settlement after the 1816

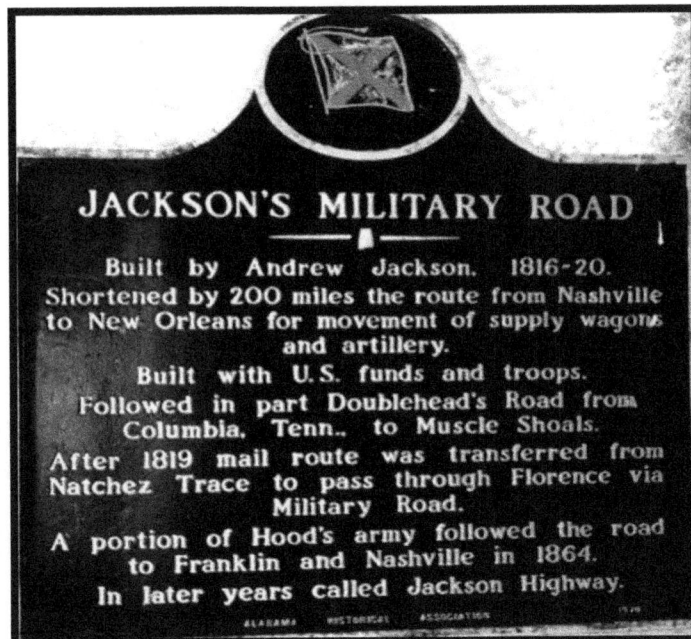

JACKSON'S MILITARY ROAD

Built by Andrew Jackson. 1816-20. Shortened by 200 miles the route from Nashville to New Orleans for movement of supply wagons and artillery.
Built with U.S. funds and troops.
Followed in part Doublehead's Road from Columbia. Tenn., to Muscle Shoals.
After 1819 mail route was transferred from Natchez Trace to pass through Florence via Military Road.
A portion of Hood's army followed the road to Franklin and Nashville in 1864.
In later years called Jackson Highway.

ALABAMA   HISTORICAL   ASSOCIATION

Indian land cessions by way of Nashville, Tennessee. They would follow the Indian path known as the Great South Trail, later called the Old Huntsville Road, leading from Nashville to Big Spring in Huntsville. Some planters would fork off the Old Huntsville Road at Columbia, Tennessee, to follow Doublehead's Trace, later called Jackson's Military Road, to the Tennessee Valley where they would cross the river. At Loretta, Tennessee, Doublehead's Trace forked with one route to the mouth of Bluewater Creek at the Bluewater Ferry and the other fork near Florence to Campbell's Ferry at Bainbridge, and then the planters would continue into Franklin County.

Campbell's Ferry east of Florence at Bainbridge was another widely used crossing along an alternate route of Doublehead's Trace which was a later crossing of the Byler Road. The Byler Road started at the south end of Jackson's Old Military Road Bridge crossing of Shoals Creek at Samuel Craig's place. Today, the original limestone pillars are still in the middle of Shoals Creek and mark the original site of the beginning of the Byler Road. The Byler Road in present-day Colbert County became the County Line Road through Leighton and White Oak. One original section of Doublehead's Trace and the old Byler Road in present-day Colbert County can be found on Bainbridge Loop.

John Lamb, a Cherokee Indian, established Lamb's Ferry on the Indian path crossing of the Tennessee River known as the Sipsie Trail, later McCutcheon's Trace, or Lamb's Ferry Road, in the early 1800's. Travelers would leave the Old Huntsvile Road at Columbia and head to Lamb's Ferry which was located between Elk River Shoals upstream and Big Muscle Shoals downstream. The Lamb's Ferry Road would lead planters to Courtland, a major hub for the wealthy cotton barons in Lawrence County, Alabama. Many of these planters would eventually buy lands in Franklin County, Alabama, and move west along the Muscle Shoals.

By the time of the Battle of Talladega in 1813, Browns Ferry was used as an early Cherokee Indian ferry crossing of the Browns Ferry Road connecting Hunt's Spring (Huntsville) to Gourd's Settlement (Courtland, Alabama). The Browns Ferry crossing of the Tennessee River was south of Athens with the route leading to Courtland, Alabama. Half blood Cherokee Captain John Brown ran the ferry prior to moving to Otali which is present-day Attalla. For a short period after John Brown left, his stepdaughter Betsy who married a Cox ran the ferry that was then called Cox's Ferry; however, the ferry reverted back to the name Brown's Ferry.

Rhodes Ferry at Decatur was also an early ferry across the Tennessee River that was used by cotton planters. The eastern terminal of the Tuscumbia-Decatur Railroad was near Rhodes Ferry. By 1820's, several other minor ferrys were in operation along the Tennessee River within the North Alabama counties opened to white settlement by the 1816 Indian land cessions.

George Colbert's Ferry was a Tennessee River crossing of the Natchez Trace. The Natchez Trace was major Chickasaw Indian ferry which connected Lauderdale and Franklin Counties, and it was established by the Chickasaw treaty of December 1801. However, the Chickasaw Nation still controlled and lived in the area until 1837. Therefore, the western part of Franklin County west of Cane Creek was not available for white settlement until Chickasaw Indian removal was completed in 1837.

Franklin Planters

For several years after Indian removal, a mass influx of wealthy white cotton planters continued to arrive in Franklin County of the Tennessee Valley after the Indian land cessions. The 1820, 1830, 1840, 1850, and 1860 census included many individual slave owners and black slaves living and working in Franklin County, Alabama, that are not included in this book.

According to the 1830 Franklin County, Alabama, United States Census, there were a total of 11,078 inhabitants in the county. Of those enumerated in Franklin County, there were 6,069 white people, 4,988 black slaves, 12 free black males, and nine free black females. According to the 1830 census, John Davis owned 150 black slaves, and Alexander Williams Mitchell, first owner of Belle Mont Plantation, owned some 115 black slaves. The 1830 Franklin County census was hand written and many times very difficult to read the names of the heads of households. This census is online.

The following alphabetical listing is the slaveholders owning 15 or more slaves and numbers of slaves as found in the Franklin County, Alabama, census records. This is as best as could be read and interpreted of the hand written census records. Sometimes, the writing style was almost illegible. Nearly every slave holder over several census periods had their names spelled different, misspelled, or written so badly that it was hard to read. Not only microfilm of the original documents, but other records used to interpret Franklin County census documents included RootsWeb, Ancestry, Alabama Genealogical Register, Old Land Records of Franklin County by Margaret Cowart, and information transcribed by Tom Blake from NARA microfilm records.

It appears that some slaveholders are listed twice, but persons of the same name maybe father and son or uncle and nephew with the same name; therefore, both are listed. For example, Isaac Winston had a son Isaac Winston, Jr. and both were slave owners. In addition, Isaac also had an uncle named Isaac Winston, and the family came to Franklin County, Alabama. Another Winston brother, William Henry Winston had a son named William Henry Winston and also an uncle named William Winston that settled in Franklin County.

During the 1820s through the 1860s, there were many black slaves living in Franklin County that were not listed in the following tables because their owner had less than 15 servants. The vast majority of the black slaves were owned by wealthy cotton planters from North Carolina and Virginia, who came during Alabama Fever caused by the release of thousands of acres of Indian land cessions.

According to the 1850 slave census of old Franklin (Colbert west of County Line Road) County, Alabama, there were a total of 545 slave owners with some 110 cotton planters that owned 20 or more black slaves. There were 55 of the 545 slaveholders that were females who owned 596 slaves. Only eight women owned more than 20 slaves in 1850 and include Amanda Barton (155), Elizabeth Cockburn (25), Martha Harris (33), Minerva Tazewell Jones Harris (26), Lucinda Mhoon (65), Mariah Murphy (25), Polly Towns (68), and Anne Sherrod (wife of Fredrick O. A. Sherrod) (84).

The listing below does not include families that owned less than 15 slaves; therefore, the slaveholders that had smaller numbers of black slaves are not listed. The following alphabetical listing is the slave owners and numbers of slaves according to the 1820 through 1860 Franklin County, Alabama, slave records.

Franklin County Slave Owners	1820	1830	1840	1850	1860
Abernathy, John Townsend			19	56	91
Abernathy, Richard Towns					19
Aldridge, Thomas		72			
Alexander, James W.					15
Alexander, John				24	20
Alexander, William R.					29
Allen, Lindsey					28
Alsobrook, William B.		16	36	62	50
Anderson, F. H.			9		21
Anderson, H. S.		15	6		
Armstead, Peter Fountain II			20	39	41
Armstrong, James			8	34	
Atkinson, Calvin			21		
Bailey, C. C.				31	
Bailey, Joseph J.			18		36
Barnett, John W.					20
Barton, Amanda C.				155	106
Barton, Armstead		5	21		
Barton, Arthur C.				45	72
Barton, Henry C.					62
Basden, George					15
Bean, Nancy	9	2	22		
Bell, John J.		31	40		
Bell, Robert E.					15
Blockey, Sarah			42		
Bowlin, William E.				25	
Bowman, James			47		
Boyd, William			26		
Bradley, William S.					21
Bullock, Francis	5	15			
Bunson, Robert	45	45			

Franklin County Slave Owners	1820	1830	1840	1850	1860
Burgess, Nancy					18
Burgess, William	9	11			17
Burris, John	20	20			
Burt, James S.					33
Bynum, Drury Sugars		22			
Bynum, Fredrick W.		20	68	133	
Byrd, William				24	
Carlock, John			16		19
Carloss, H. P.					25
Carroll, DeRody				25	
Carroll, George W.		28	88	137	
Carter, H.		38			
Carter, John C.		15			
Carter, Kilpatrick		45			
Caswell, George		25			
Cauchon, Robert T.					29
Cheatham, Littleton B.			18		
Christan, A S			39		
Clair, George				20	
Clarbour, Phil W.			23		
Clark, John			30		
Cleary, William					17
Cleere, George D.					18
Cobb, Asa			23	37	19
Cockburn, Elizabeth				25	
Cockburn, George		15	22		
Cockburn, Theophilus A. W.	16				
Cockburn, William		28			
Cockrill, G. L.			33		
Cockrill, John		73	75		
Cockrill, Sterling R.			44	156	

Franklin County Slave Owners	1820	1830	1840	1850	1860
Cole, Willis		26			
Cook, William Henry	8	16			
Coons, Samuel W.				32	
Cooper, L. B.			4		29
Cooper, William			97	34	17
Cox, Henry	22	22			
Cox, John A.		31			
Cox, Joshua		23			
Cox, Patin	35	43			
Cranton, Joseph			18		
Crawford, James		5		21	
Crofs, William				42	
Cross, William C.					70
Dancy, William E.			20		
Davis, Gurley				41	
Davis, John	43	150			
Davis, Major		23			
Delony, E. B.				43	21
Deshler, David			24		
Dickson, Hugh			25		
Dickson, William			14	66	83
Donelson, E. E.			42		
Donelson, John		30			
Downs, W. W.				56	
Drake, James William		20		20	22
Drenning, Charles			23		
East, Thomas			8	35	42
Elam, John W.			17		
Elliott, Edmund				31	38
Elliott, Robert				32	
Ellis, Richard	23	51			

Franklin County Slave Owners	1820	1830	1840	1850	1860
Fant, Sarah		30			28
Featherstone (Fetherson), Lewis	14	37			
Felton, Elizabeth					18
Forter, M. L.			43		
Foster, Davie		88			
Foster, John		32			
Franklin, Mrs. Cawken			22		
Freeman, Jane M.			16		20
Garner, Argy Leander				110	86
Garrett, Lewis G.			6	36	
Gay, L. P.					25
Gholston (Golston), Francis (es)	2	17	29		
Gholston, Susan					20
Gist (Gest), A. G.		18	33		
Gist (Gest), Levi J.	9	29			
Goodloe, David Short		88			
Goodloe, John Calvin			14	101	102
Goodloe, Robert Atlas			23	78	157
Gorman, Thomas					23
Greenhill, Samuel				22	34
Gurley, Davis			20		
Guy, Albert				36	
Guy, E.		23			
Guy, Joseph A.					25
Guy, Lewis M.			19		
Guy, Lorenzo				22	
Hailey, James T.				62	80
Hannigan, Ambrose				20	
Harrington, S. J.				43	
Harris, Benford			50		
Harris, Benjamin		30	69	80	

Franklin County Slave Owners	1820	1830	1840	1850	1860
Harris, Clinck					17
Harris, Edward		15			
Harris, H. M.			17		
Harris, James		7	12		
Harris, John C.					14
Harris, John W.			15		36
Harris, Martha				33	32
Harris, Minerva Tazewell Jones				26	
Harris, Nancy					14
Haslep, Joseph	44	44			
Heygate, Joseph			21		
Heygate, Thomas			26		
Hobbs, Presley H.					30
Hobgood, William					42
Hobgood, Davis S.			83		
Hobgood, Elijah			33	43	
Hobgood, John			23	55	48
Hogan, A. L.		63			
Hogan, A. S.		46	51		
Hogan, James	14	24	28		
Hogan, John	3	46	62	126	
Hogan, John H.				40	
Hogan, Sarah W.					36
Hogan, Smith	30	46			
Hollingsworth, Henry (O.)			11		16
Hooks, Callen		17	38		
Hooks, Curtis	15		18		
Hooks, Warren		15	37		
Hopson, A. S.		43			
Horn, Josiah		3			16
Houston, Nathan J.			6		27

Franklin County Slave Owners	1820	1830	1840	1850	1860
Hudson, Benjamin		24	7		
Hudson, C.			38		
Hurley, Jesse					21
Hutson, James M.					46
Hutson, Nathan				38	
Hyde, Henry			15		
Isbel, Ellis		10		30	29
Jack, William P.					18
Jackson, George					56
Jackson, James		2	9		19
Jackson, John C.		6	22	29	18
Jackson, William M.					59
Jarman, W. H.					21
Johnson, Jacob Vanpool	3	14	22	34	45
Johnson, John				29	26
Johnson, Rufus			51		
Jones, Arthur		42			
Jones Benjamin A.		57			
Jones, Nel B.			36		
Jones, Richard		37			
Jones, Samuel		46			
Jones, William S.	30	44	53	42	70
Jower, William A.		22			
Kalley, Mary T.			35		
Keller, David		49			
Keller, John					26
Kelly, J. O.			51		
Kennener, James C.			45		
Kerlock, John				31	
King, H. R.					25
Kirk, F. S.					17

Franklin County Slave Owners	1820	1830	1840	1850	1860
Kirk, James M		10	25		25
Kulaw?, John		25			
Lane, Isaac			57	106	
Lee, William			16		
Leigh, Robert H.		21			
Lewis, John McClanahan		24	46		
Little, Edward			12	26	
Lockhart, James B.		28	39		
Long, James D.			19		
Lucas, William W.	11	32			38
Mahom, James			90		
Malone, Alexander		2	52	27	25
Malone, E. M.		51			
Malone, Goodloe Warren	0		30	116	
Malone, John Lewis				109	
Malone, John S.					49
Mann (Mame), Richard			17	46	46
Martin, Peter	1	32			
McCulloch, Elijah		13	21	37	
McCulloch, Phebe					22
McCulloch, Thomas E.		6			15
McDonald, Elizabeth A.		57	54		
McDonald, James	20	20			
McIntire, N.		16			
McKeirnan, Bernard		37	28	92	
McKeirnan, Charles B.					22
McKiernan, M. C.					23
McKiernan, M. F.					16
McRea(Mckae), John L.		41	11		
McReynolds, R. S.					69
Merredith, Elisha		23			

Franklin County Slave Owners	1820	1830	1840	1850	1860
Merredith, Samuel			41		
Messenger, Asa				22	27
Mhoon, James George			90	100	
Mhoon, Lucinda A.				65	25
Mitchell, Alexander Williams	51	115	9		
Moody, Appe		96			
Moore, J. B.					15
Moore, William S.			33		
Moorman, Mary S.			19		
Morton, Quin		18			
Mullens (Mullins), Matthew		25			
Mullens (Mullins), William	5	18	35	22	
Murphy, James O.					30
Murphy, Mariah				25	
Murphy, Spenser			20		
Napier, Charles		27			
Napier, John		32			
Nelson, O. O.					33
Newsom, Whitmill R.					82
Niosoy, K.		107			
Nooe, John B.	20	43			
Oats, David Cannon					123
Oats, Samuel Kinnard			61	96	
Owen(s), Thomas		27	26		
Pace, S. S.		24			
Parsons, William H.					45
Patterson, James A.	1				42
Payne, Armstead					28
Payne, James			20		
Payne, Robert			24		
Payne, William W.		35			

Franklin County Slave Owners	1820	1830	1840	1850	1860
Pearsall, Edward	13		47	62	
Pearsall, P.					16
Pearson, Gowd?		27			
Peden (Peeden), Warren W.		7	20	31	33
Peete (Peele), William A.			1		40
Penick, Edward			16		
Perkins, William O.	19	64	90	95 E	
Personett, William H.				21	
Peters, John				29	
Petman, William			16		
Plant(es), William Jackson				34	
Pope, Thoe. M.	18				
Prent, R. N.		25			
Price, R. W.					57
Pride, Edward Mitchell		3	12 E		
Pride, Halcote (Hawk) J.				45	41
Pride, James E.					25
Pride, John Fletcher		4	53	112	53
Pride, Joseph P.					89
Pride, Nathaniel Jones		1	20	31	48
Pride, William H.		8	29	27	
Prince, S. P.		24			
Prout, H. W.				39	46
Pruit, P. H.		25			
Ragland, Samuel J.		9	14	53	
Rand, John Walter			27	40	75
Rand, Parker Nathaniel Greene					19
Reed, Clement (Clemons)				22	23
Reed, John J.		30			
Reynolds, Benjamin		3	26		
Reynolds, Frances M.			33		

Franklin County Slave Owners	1820	1830	1840	1850	1860
Reynolds, Gamml M.			18		
Ricks, Abraham		49	104	209	
Ricks, Abraham, Junior					132
Ricks, Charlotte Bryan					58
Ricks, William Fort					86
Rictor (Rector), John		27			
Riley, Susannah E.		40			
Robert(s), Henry		36		30	
Robert(s), James			17	32	
Robert(s), John		36			
Robinson, Moses					22
Ross, Elizabeth					16
Roy, John S.		15			
Rutland, John W.		36	12	36	48
Rutland, Whitman		58	44	58	
Sam, Isaac					124
Sanford, James T.	10	53			
Sargent, Oran					29
Sargent, Temple	3	23	24	23	
Sheffield, Joseph			24		14
Sheron, Samuel W.			57		
Sherrod, Benjamin					53
Sherrod, F O A			66		
Sherrod, Anne				84	
Shines, John G.			27	54	35
Sledge, Joshua				26	
Sledge, Marlin					23
Smith, Benjamin J.					23
Smith, James		21			
Smith, John N.		21			
Smith, William E.			17	21	35

Franklin County Slave Owners	1820	1830	1840	1850	1860
Southall (Southell), Augustus H.			5		39
Sugg, Elizabeth J.					37
Sugg, Thomas	10		5		20
Sugg, William C.	3		20	28	18
Symington (Simington), Henry	8	22			
Tarver, M.			23		
Thompson, Lawrence (Sammie)				64	73
Thompson, Taley D.		11	20		
Thompson, William J.					15
Thornton, L. B.					23
Tompkins, William					20
Toney, Charles Augustus		50	46	52	64
Towns, E. D.				35	
Towns, John L.			74		
Towns, Polly S.				68	
Towns, William A.		22			
Underwood, A. J.					19
Vincent, P.		31			
Vinson, Drury		31	42	107	
Vinson, Fletcher Curtis					54
Vinson, John E.					42
Waddle, John		19			
Walker, L. Peter			18	46	
Warren, Hugh M.		22		25 E	
Warson, Nancy E.			54		
Washington, A. B.			79		
Watkins, R. S.					17
Weaver, Joseph M.				22	46
White, Robert L. (M.)		15	18	39	
White, Thomas					15
Williamson, E. M.					23

Franklin County Slave Owners	1820	1830	1840	1850	1860
Wilson, Benjamin					18
Wilson, Bryce			8	27	35
Winston, Anthony		87			
Winston, Joel Walker		87			
Winston, John Jones		81			
Winston, John M.		20			15
Winston, Isaac		31	62	99	114
Winston, Stephen				24	
Winston, Thomas		22			9
Winston, William		32	46	84	
Winston, William Henry		74			
Winston, William O.		21			
Winter, B. R.					16
Winter, T. W.					28
Winton, L. W.				33	

After the Civil War, the original Franklin County was subdivided in 1867 into Colbert County from the Tennessee River in the northern valley portion where wealthy planters once resided. Franklin County remained most of the southern hill country where mostly poor subsistence farmers lived.

Colbert County originally included all the land west of the Byler Road which later became the County Line Road. Prior to these names, the road was one route of Doublehead's Trace leading south. Another route of Doublehead's Trace was Highway 101 which is east of the present-day County Line Road.

The territory east of the County Line Road to the center of stream known as Town Creek, and to the south bank of the Tennessee River was added to Colbert County in 1897. One reason given for the annexation of the Lawrence County portion was the failure of Lawrence county officials to maintain a good bridge connecting to the areas west of the stream called Town Creek.

Since Lawrence County did not properly maintain the bridge crossings of Town Creek, the people in the portion Lawrence County west of Town Creek to the County Line Road petitioned to be added to Colbert County. Therefore, the area from the eastern corner of Franklin and Colbert Counties and west of Town Creek to the County Line Road was annexed from Lawrence County and added to Colbert County in 1897. The 1897 addition included a small portion of the northeast corner of Franklin County. Therefore, Colbert County records prior to the Civil War were listed as either Franklin County or Lawrence County.

Tuscumbia

The Town of Tuscumbia was the principal economic center of the slave holding plantation owners of the old Franklin County, Alabama. Big Spring in Tuscumbia was a popular referenced site in early historical records. The spring provided an abundance of fresh water to support the large community which sprang up nearby. Not far from the town center, the Tennessee River was navigable downstream, but the treacherous rapids of the Muscle Shoals prevent upstream travel by way of the river. The Town of Tuscumbia was also the western terminus and considered the beginning of the first railroad west of the Appalachian Mountains.

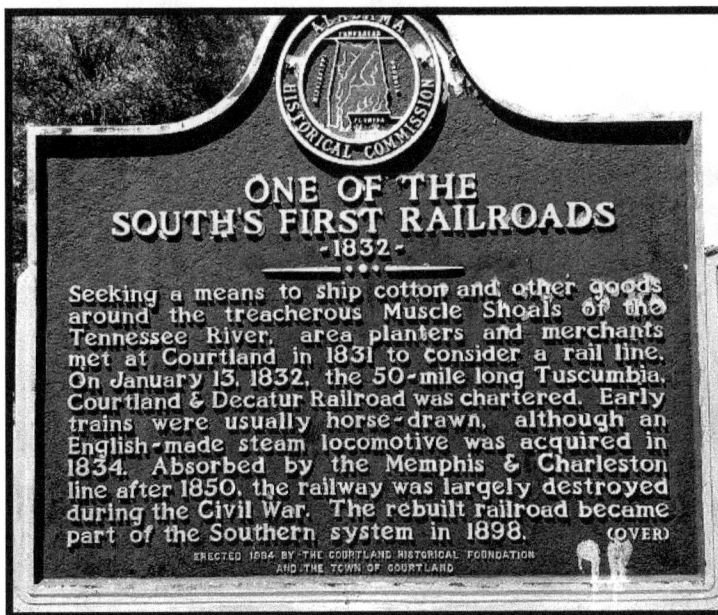

ONE OF THE
SOUTH'S FIRST RAILROADS
-1832-
•••
Seeking a means to ship cotton and other goods around the treacherous Muscle Shoals of the Tennessee River, area planters and merchants met at Courtland in 1831 to consider a rail line. On January 13, 1832, the 50-mile long Tuscumbia, Courtland & Decatur Railroad was chartered. Early trains were usually horse-drawn, although an English-made steam locomotive was acquired in 1834. Absorbed by the Memphis & Charleston line after 1850, the railway was largely destroyed during the Civil War. The rebuilt railroad became part of the Southern system in 1898. (OVER)
ERECTED 1994 BY THE COURTLAND HISTORICAL FOUNDATION
AND THE TOWN OF COURTLAND

Tuscumbia Landing was the off loading site and western end of the first railroad west of the Appalachian Mountains. The rail line ran from Decatur to just west of Tuscumbia at Tuscumbia Landing. The landing was at the mouth of Spring Creek on the Tennessee River where cotton could safely be transported to New Orleans and other export sites. From the landing toward the west, the river was deep enough and the remaining rapids of the Muscle Shoals were not a threat to navigation of flatboats and keel boats to Waterloo. At Waterloo, the rapids of the lower Muscle Shoals ended and the river could support steamers which could transport cotton to many ports. From Tuscumbia Landing upstream to Decatur, the Little Muscle Shoals, Big Muscle Shoals, and Elk River Shoals were to dangerous to allow safe water passage.

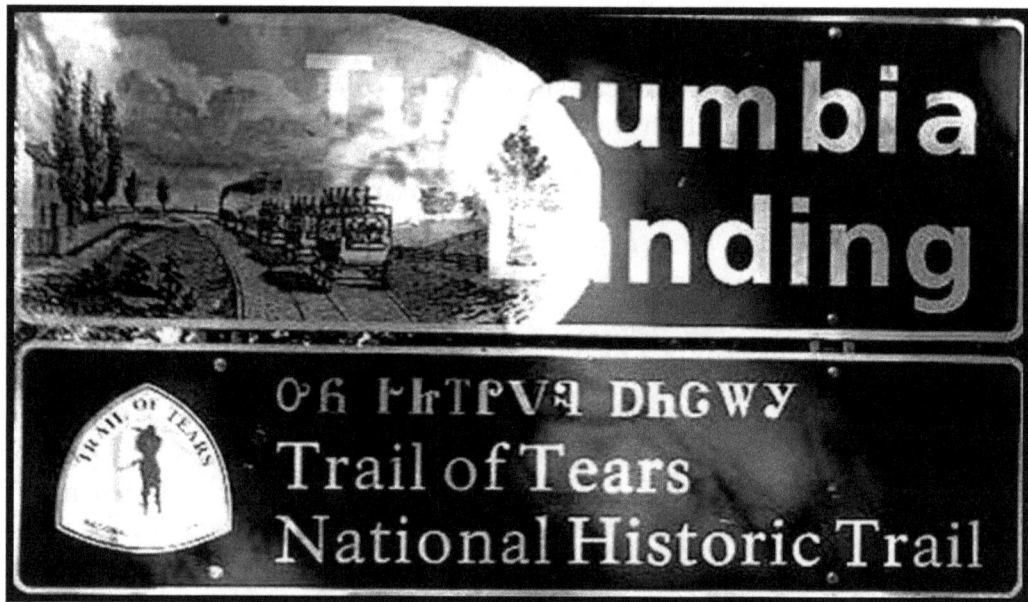

The reason that the section on Franklin County includes Colbert west of County Line Road is that all the pre-Civil War records that exist for Franklin County covers the area that became Colbert County. After the Civil War, Colbert County was originally formed out of the northern portion of Franklin County from the County Line Road that runs through Leighton and White Oak west to the Mississippi state line. Colbert was originally established on February 6, 1867, after it was split from Franklin County over political issues after the Civil War. It was abolished eight months later on November 29, 1867, by an Alabama constitutional convention and then reestablished on February 24, 1870.

Map[4] showing location of town of COLD WATER (TUSCUMBIA)

Signed by John Coffee, Surveyor. Darkened area reads "TOWN - To be laid off for a to See Letter of Sec. of Treas. of 3 Feb 1819." Map dated 6 Mar 1820.

4. Huntsville Land Office Plat Book, p. 91. Alabama Dept. of Archives and History, Montgomery, Alab

According to an article titled Lauderdale County, Alabama, History of the Shoals and published in the Times Daily, Thursday, February 25, 1999, by Harry E. Wallace, "No plantation study has yet been done for Franklin County but the names of planters include: Henry King, John Rand, Edward B. Delony, Col. James Fennel, Thomas Lyle, Drury Vinson, Elisha Madding, Richard Preuit, Isaac Winston, Peter Fontaine Armistead, William Winston, A. S. Christian, Col. William M. Jackson, Bernard McKiernan, Armstead Barton, William Dixon, Henry Hyde, William Lucas, Winter Payne, Thomas Winston, John Thompkins, John W. Rutland, Isaac Lane, David Goodloe, James Barton, Captain Monoah Hampton, William A. King, Robert King, George Carroll, F. W. Bynum and John G. Shine." Some of the planters mentioned in the article are not found in the 1850 Slave Schedule of Franklin County, Alabama.

Cotton Planter Profiles

The following profiles are stories and history of some of the larger slave holders of old Franklin (Colbert) County, Alabama. It was not possible to include all the slave holders or to find information about their cotton plantations.

Abernathy, John Townsend

John Townsend Abernathy and his family probably came to Madison County, Alabama, around 1818 or earlier. His first land entry was about six miles west of Town Creek and some six miles south of the Tennessee River near the County Line Road between Leighton and Ford City in present-day Colbert County, Alabama. On September 16, 1818, he entered 79.71 acres of land in the west ½ of the southwest ¼ of Section 6, Township 4 South, and Range 9 West. In addition, he entered some 950 acres of land most of which was originally part of Lawrence and Franklin Counties, Alabama (Cowart, 1985). The 1820 census of Lawrence and Franklin Counties does not list any Abernathys, but records show that John T. Abernathy married in Madison County in 1822; therefore, he was probably living in Madison County during the 1820 census.

According to Ancestry.com, "John T. Abernathy was born on December 8, 1799, in Virginia. He married Sarah Elliott (1806–1841) on December 7, 1822, in Madison County, Alabama. His father was David Abernathy (1772–September 5,

1845), and his mother was Lavinia Towns (1776–March 13, 1843)." John T. Abernathy later married Eliza J. Wright Abernathy (1819-1895). He had half brothers Richard Locke Abernathy (1797-1875) and Lunenberg C. Abernathy (1800-1849).

Remains of the brick Abernathy House
February 1959

In 1830, John T. Abernathy is listed in the census records of Lawrence County, Alabama. It appears that his parents, wife, and four young sons accompanied him to Lawrence County. According to the 1830 Lawrence County, Alabama Census of John T. Abernathy, there are three white males from 0-5 years old. There was one white male from 5-10 years old which was probably Robert Townes Abernathy (1824–1895) who was born on November 22, 1824, in Lawrence County, Alabama. There was one white male between 20-30 years old which is probably John T. Abernathy, and one white male between 60-70 which is probably his father David Abernathy. One white female between 20-30 was probably John T. Abernathy's wife Sarah Elliott. One white female between 40-50 was probably John's mother Lavinia. In addition, listed in his household are a total of 18 black slaves with 13 black males and black five females.

In the 1850 Lawrence County, Alabama Slave Census of District 7, John T. Abernathy owned 56 slaves. The 1850 Franklin County, Alabama, Agricultural Census does not have John T. Abernathy listed in either Lawrence or Franklin County. As found on page 213 of the 1860 Franklin County, Alabama Largest Slaveholders, John T. Abernathy owned 91 black slaves. Ancestry.com lists John T. Abernathy's residence in two locations in 1860; one source has him in Franklin County Eastern Subdivision, and another source has him in Lawrence County, Northern Division.

The 1860 Census Lawrence County, Northern Division, Alabama, lists "John T. Abernathy as age 60, head of household, birthplace Virginia, and occupation as a planter. He was living with his second wife, Eliza J. who was age 40, birthplace Alabama; daughter, Mattie age 26, birthplace Alabama; son, John age 20, birthplace Alabama; daughter, Harriet age 12, birthplace Alabama; daughter, Sallie J. age 9, was born on March 16, 1851, in Alabama, and died in 1892; and son, Emmet age 3, birthplace Alabama."

John T. Abernathy died on July 27, 1869. His obituary was given in the Moulton Advertiser on August 6, 1869 as follows: "Colonel John Townsend Abernathy, Birth: December 8, 1799, Death: July 27, 1869. We learn with deep regret of the sudden death of Colonel John T. Abernathy at his home, near Leighton, yesterday morning about 2 o'clock." The obituary was reprinted in Footprints In Time, Volume 1.

According to the North Alabamian and Times on July 28, 1869, "We learn with deep regret of the sudden death of Colonel John T. Abernathy at his home near Leighton yesterday morning about 2 O'clock. On Monday afternoon, Colonel Abernathy was out in his field attending to the thrashing of his wheat. About 5 O'clock, he suddenly fell, and, with the exception of making one or two efforts to speak was insensible until the time he died. He was one of the oldest and most respected citizens of North Alabama; was a man of influence and irreproachable character, a good citizen and devoted friend. We earnestly join our community in the profound sympathy if feels for his son, Dr. Robert Abernathy, our fellow citizen, and the other members of the family of the deceased in this their great affliction."

Colonel John Townsend Abernathy (December 8, 1799-July 27, 1869) is buried in the Abernathy Cemetery, near Leighton in Colbert County, Alabama. The inscription on his tombstone reads: "John T. Abernathy, Born Dec.8, 1799, died July 27, 1869. Strong in Faith, Diligent in business, Fervent in Spirit, He filled the measure of ever trust was loved and honored of men, and died as he had lived A CHRISTEN." The cemetery is located off Sixth Street east of County Line Road in Colbert County, just north of the City of Leighton (Find a Grave Memorial Number 76633064). Others buried in the Abernathy Cemetery include:

1) John Abernathy, January 30, 1836-November 6, 1838;
2) Laura Ann Abernathy, November 1838-September 1839;
3) Richard A. Abernathy, March 1, 1826-July 26 1846;
4) Sarah A. Abernathy, March 1806-1841, daughter of R. Elliott and Consort of John T. Abernathy;
5) Eliza Wright, August 19, 1819-May 28, 1875, wife of John T. Abernathy;
6) Lavina Abernathy, 1776-March 13, 1843, consort of David Abernathy, 1772-September 5, 1846;
7) Emmett Abernathy, February 21, 1857-September 5 1872;
8) William W. _____, December 11, 1851-May 19, 1857;
9) Mattie Abernathy, June 5, 1852-July 1880;
10) James William Abernathy, November 24, 1827-May 8, 1890;
11) Little Baby, October 10, 1885-June 10, 1886.

Abernathy, James William

James William Abernathy was born in Alabama on November 24, 1827, to John Townsend Abernathy and Sarah A. Elliott Abernathy. He married Mattie A. McGregor on June 13, 1855, in Lawrence County, Alabama. Mattie A. McGregor Abernathy was born on February 5, 1838; she was the daughter of William and Elizabeth McGregor.

James William Abernathy (November 24, 1827-May 8, 1890) and Robert Townes Abernathy (1824-1895) were two of John T. Abernathy and Sarah A. Elliott Abernathy's (March 1806-1841) sons who also owned black slaves. According to the 1860 census of the largest slaveholders in Franklin County, Alabama, James William and his brother Robert Townes Abernathy owned 51 black slaves. These two Abernathy brothers were listed on page 213B next to their father John T. Abernathy who owned 91 slaves; therefore, the father and sons owned some 142 black slaves in 1860.

According to the 1850 Franklin County, Alabama Slave Census, James Abernathy owned 11 slaves. As reported in the 1850 Franklin County, Alabama Agricultural Census, James Abernathy owned 350 acres of improved land, 290 acres of unimproved land; his farm value was $8,000 with implements worth $250 and livestock at $1200.

In the 1860 Eastern Subdivision of Franklin County, Alabama, United States Census, James W. Abernathy is listed as a white male 33 years of age born in Alabama along with Martha A. Abernathy who is a 23 year old white female born in Alabama. The 1870 Leighton, Colbert County, Alabama Census gives James Abernathy's real estate value as $4,000.00 and personal estate value is $1,800.00. In 1870, he is listed as a 42 year old white male with Martha Abernathy a 32 year old female born in Alabama, John Abernathy a 29 year old white male born in Alabama, and Sarah Abernathy a 20 year old white female born in Alabama.

According to the 1870 census, Phillip Abernathy and his family lived in household number 66. Phillip was black man and probably a slave of James before 1865; he lived three houses from James Abernathy. Philip was 52, his wife was 34 and they had six children. None of this household could read or write and his personal value was $100.00.

James William Abernathy died on May 8, 1890. According to The Moulton Advertiser on Thursday May 22, 1890, "Captain James W. Abernathy died at Leighton on the 15th, in the 62nd year of his age." The Moulton Advertiser on Thursday May 29, 1890, stated, "James W. Abernathy was born November 24, 1827, and died May 8, 1890. He was 62 years old." This obituary was reprinted Footprints In Time, Volume 1. He is buried in Abernathy Cemetery, Leighton, Colbert County, Alabama (Find a Grave Memorial # 76609035).

James was the husband of Mattie A. McGregor Abernathy (1838-1875). They were married June 13, 1855, in Lawrence County, Alabama. The Moulton Advertiser reports the death of Mattie Abernathy on Friday, October 22, 1875, "Died at her home in Leighton, on the 7th inst., of hemorrhagic malarial fever, Mrs. Mattie A. Abernathy, wife of James W. Abernathy, in the 38th year of her age." The obituary is reprinted in Footprints In Time, Volume 1. She was buried in the Abernathy Cemetery (Find a Grave Memorial Number 37544975).

Alsobrook, William Brantley

According to The Heritage of Colbert County, Alabama (1999), "In the early1800's, William B. Alsobrook I and his family moved into the Spring Creek community of eastern Franklin County, Alabama. Spring Creek was located approximately 20 miles east of the Franklin County seat of Russellville. At Spring Creek, William I and Alice built a very fine home, with cabins in the back of the great house for the Negroes."

William B. Alsobrook, Senior, was born on December 16, 1774, and he died on July 20, 1843, in Franklin County, Alabama. William married Alice Sessums on February 19, 1797. She was born on December 1, 1771, in Edgecomb County, North Carolina, and she died on September 28, 1847, in Franklin County, Alabama. William B. and Alice had the following nine children that were born in Halifax County, North Carolina:

1) Lunsford Long Alsobrook was born on November 14, 1799;
2) Kindred N. Alsobrook was born on February 1, 1801;
3) Jacob S. Alsobrook was born on April 8, 1803;
4) Lewis Dickson Alsobrook was born on August 21, 1805;
5) William Brantley Alsobrook was born August 15, 1807;
6) Martha Ann Alsobrook was born April 15, 1809;
7) Harry B. Alsobrook was born May 12, 1811;
8) Henry R. Alsobrook was born February 28, 1813;
9) Mary Eliza Alsobrook was born on April 24, 1815.

Lunsford Long Alsobrook

Lunsford Long Alsobrook is a fascinating person and the oldest son of William B. and Alice Alsobrook. He was evidently very smart and schooled to be an attorney; however with his wife, he does not seem to be as intelligent as evidenced in the following information.

According to The Tuscumbian on October 6, 1824, "Lunsford L. Alsobrook, Attorney and Cousellor at Law, having removed from Russelville, his former place of residence, to Tuscumbia, will transact all business committed to his management with strict attention. His Office is on Dickson Street, where he will generally be found unless when absent on professional business."

In 1826, Lunsford Long Alsobrook married Temperance B. Eaton who was from Warren County, North Carolina. According to Petition Analysis Record 20184526, State of Alabama, Sumter County, 1845, "Prior to their marriage in 1826, Temperance B. Eaton and Lunsford Long Alsobrook signed a premarital agreement placing Temperance's eight slaves in a trust estate for her sole and separate use. However, in 1838, Temperance asserts, the slaves were "wrongfully and illegally" taken out of her possession and sold at auction "under a certain Deed in Trust made by her said husband." One slave, Dick, was sold to Richard Inge, then to Thomas Tart. When Tart died, Dick came into the possession of Tart's estate administrator, William H. Pratt of Mobile County. Temperance Alsobrook sues Pratt as well as her husband, a "lunatic" from whom she is separated in bed and board, for "the value and amount of the hire and services" of Dick. She argues that Dick is worth fifteen hundred dollars with a yearly hire worth two hundred dollars."

Lewis Dickson Alsobrook

Lewis Dickson Alsobrook was the fourth child of William Brantley and Alice Alsobrook. From Nina Leftwich's book Two Hundred Years at Muscle Shoals (1935), "In the mid 1820's, according to family tradition, Chief George Colbert of the Chickasaws offered Lewis Alsobrook one of his barrels of silver if he would marry one of his daughters." According to Richard Sheridan in Times Daily on April 6, 2008, Lewis Dickson Alsobrook was a partner with Pitman Colbert, son of Chief George Colbert. Prior to Chickasaw removal west in 1837, Lewis and Pitman sold their trading post to E. P. Carloss; however, Lewis had already fell in love with Pitman's sister Susan Colbert.

Susan (Sukey or Susie) Colbert was born to Doublehead's daughter Saleechie (Standing Fern) and Chief George Colbert about 1810. Lewis Alsobrook followed the Colbert family west to Indian Territory; however, Susan was not so enthralled with her suitor and refused to accept his attentions and proposal. Susan eventually married John McLish and later Robert McDonald Jones; she died at Hugo in the Choctaw Nation on January 13, 1860.

When he was rejected by the spirited daughter of Chief George Colbert, Lewis decided to return home to Alabama. Prior to coming home, Pitman gave Lewis D. Alsobrook his father's peace medal as a token of esteem and friendship he felt for him. After arriving home, Lewis gave the medal to his nephew William Brantley Alsobrook III and the medal remained with the family for many years.

41

The silver peace medal stayed in the Alsobrook family until it was sold to Dr. George W. Huckaba for $875.00 in an estate sale and auction at the Colbert County Courthouse in 1969. In 1995, Huckaba donated the medal to the Chickasaw Nation and it was placed in their museum. The silver peace medal originally belonged to Chickasaw Chief George Colbert and was eventually passed to his son Pitman. During the Treaty of Chickasaw Bluffs on October 24, 1801, the medal was presented to George Colbert from President Thomas Jefferson as a mark of appreciation for services rendered by the chief in helping the American colonies secure freedom from the British during the Revolutionary War.

William Brantley Alsobrook II

William Brantley Alsobrook, II was born in Halifax County, North Carolina, on August 15, 1807, and he died on October 14, 1857. William was the son of William Brantley Alsobrook I and Alice Sessums Alsobrook. William B. Alsobrook II married Caroline Allen (1822-1856) and their children were William Brantley Alsobrook III (1850-1913) and Henry Edgar Alsobrook (1852-1875).

According to the 1850 slave census of Franklin County, Alabama, William B. Alsobrook II owned 44 slaves at one place and 18 at another place for a total of 62 slaves. In the1850 Franklin County, Alabama, Agricultural Census, William B. Alsobrook owned 900 acres of improved land and 1220 acres of unimproved land for a total of 2,100 acres. From February 1830 to February 1833, he had entered some 400 acres, most of which was in Township 5 South and Range 11 West (Cowart, 1985).The cash value of his farm was $18,000 with the value of implements and machinery at $1000 and livestock valued at $3400.

In the Franklin County, Alabama, United States Census of 1850, William B. Alsobrook is listed as a 42 year old white male with household number 112. Also listed in the 1850 census was Parnectin Alsobrook a 28 year old white female born in North Carolina, Wilantina Alsobrook a four year old white female born in Alabama, Mary Livis Alsobrook a three year old white female born in Alabama, and William Alsobrook a one year old male born in Alabama.

During the 1860 Western Division, Franklin County, Alabama Census, William B. Alsobrook was a 45 year old white male with Willintina Alsobrook age 15, Mary Alsobrook age 13, William B. Alsobrook age 11, Henrey E Alsobrook age 9, and Peter B. Pride a 24 year old white male born in Alabama. The household identification number was 299.

William B. Alsobrook died on October 14, 1857, in Franklin County, Alabama. He is buried in the Allsboro Cemetery, Colbert County, Alabama, (Find a Grave Memorial Number 36282542).

Armistead, Peter F. II-Melrose Plantation

Peter Fontaine Armistead II came to Lauderdale County, Alabama, with his parents Peter Fontaine Armistead I and Martha Henry Winston Armistead. Peter II was born May 6, 1810, in Culpepper County, Virginia. Peter Fontaine Armistead II married Mary Susan Winston in December 1839. Shortly after their marriage, Peter II and Mary moved to Franklin County, Alabama, and established their plantation called "Melrose."

Mary Susan Winston was born on December 16, 1822, in Alabama, and died on December 29, 1879. Mary Susan was the daughter of Isaac Winston (1795-1863) and Catharine Baker Jones Winston (1798-1884). Mary Susan Winston Armistead had a brother Isaac Winston (1829-1863) and a sister Catherine Baker Winston Burt (1832-1876).

Peter II and Mary had twelve children who were:

1) Catherine Winston Armistead McFarland (1843-1920);
2) Peter Fontaine Armistead III (1846-?);
3) Henry Coles Armistead (1848-1932);
4) George Washington Armistead (1850-?);
5) Johnnie Walker Armistead (1851-1856);
6) Martha Henry Armistead (1854-?);
7) Mary V. Armistead (1857-?);
8) Medora Virginia Armistead Bugg (1858-1954);
9) Isaac Winston Armistead (1860-?);
10) Robert Lee Armistead (1862-1888);
11) John Anthony Armistead;
12) Mattie Armistead (1866-1886).

Mary Susan Winston Armistead
12/16/1822-12/29/1879

According to the 1850 Franklin County, Alabama Slave Schedule, Peter Fontaine Armistead II owned 39 black slaves. According to page 211B of the 1860 Franklin County, Alabama Slave Schedule, Peter Fountain Armistead owned 68 black slaves.

In the 1850 Franklin County, Alabama, Agricultural Census, Peter owned 850 acres of improved land, 350 acres of unimproved land. His land was valued at $20,000.00 with farming equipment valued at $500.00 and livestock valued at $4000.00.

On July 18, 1855, Peter Fontaine Armistead II entered an additional three tracts of land containing some 240 acres in Franklin County, Alabama, in Section 33 of Township 4 South and Range 11 West. On January 11, 1858, he entered 40 acres in Section 4 of Township 5 South and Range 11 West (Cowart, 1985).

According to page 85 of the 1860 Eastern Subdivision of Franklin, Alabama, United States Census, Peter Fountain Armistead II was a 50 year old white male who was born in Virginia about 1810. In the 1860 census, other white individuals born in Alabama were M. J. Armistead a 38 year old female, C W Armistead a 16 year old female, P. F. Armistead a 14 year old male, A. E. Armistead a 12 year old male, G. W. Armistead a 10 year old male, M. H. Armistead a six year old female, M. V. Armistead a three year old female, J. W. Armistead a one year old male, and A. V. Armistead a 11 year old female born in Mississippi.

In the 1870 Franklin County, Alabama, United States Census, Peter Fountain Armistead II was a 61 year old white male born in Virginia. The members of his household 171 included his wife Mary Susan Armistead who was a 48 year old female, Peter Fountain Armistead a 24 year old male, Henry C. Armistead a 22 year old male, George W. Armistead a 20 year old male, Martha Armistead a 15 year old female, Madora Armistead a 13 year old female, Isaac W. Armistead a 10 year old male, and Robert Armistead a seven year old male.

The death date of Peter Fontaine Armistead II is given on his tombstone as February 7, 1908. However, the following is the obituary of Peter Fontaine Armistead II as given in The Florence Standard Journal of February 11, 1898. "Peter Fontaine Armistead, one of the oldest citizens in North Alabama, died at his home four miles south of Tuscumbia, Monday night at 9 p.m., after a brief illness. His remains were interred in the Winston Cemetery, Tuesday afternoon at 3 p.m. Reverend Henry Kingham conducted the funeral services. Mr. Armistead was born at Culpepper, Virginia in 1800, and while a small boy removed with his parents to Lauderdale County, settling in what is known as the "Armistead Place," six miles northwest of Florence. In December 1839, he married Miss Mary Susan Winston, removing shortly afterward to Franklin, now Colbert County, where he has since resided. To the union twelve children were born, only four of whom survive him, G. W. and H. C. Armistead of Colbert County, Mrs. R. T. Bugg of Winchester, Tennessee, and Mrs. Kate McFarland of Florence. He has one brother surviving, George Armistead, a resident of Arkansas."

Peter Fontaine Armistead II death date differs in his obiturary and his tombstone. He is buried in the Winston Family Cemetery located in Tuscumbia, Colbert County, Alabama (Find a Grave Memorial Number 37637265). Mary Susan Winston Armistead (12/16/1822-12/29/1879) is also buried in the Winston Family

Cemetery in Tuscumbia, Colbert County, Alabama (Find a Grave Memorial Number 37641426). According to the Lauderdale County, Alabama, Obituaries found inThe Lauderdale News from December 31, 1879 through December 29, 1880, is the following listing: "Armstead, Mary Wife of Fountain A. Armisted, Sr. 7 Jan 1880."

Armistead, Peter Fontaine III

Peter Fontaine Armistead III was the son of Peter Fontaine Armistead II and Mary Susan Winston Armistead. According to the Florence Times, Journal 1 of October 1, 1873, Peter F. Armistead III married Elizabeth Baker on September 17, 1873, at St Paul's Church by the Reverend Doctor Bannister.

Barton, Hugh-Barton Hall Plantation

Dr. Hugh Barton was born in Frederick County, Virginia, on May 17, 1775. He was the son of Roger Barton who was born July 9, 1747, in Frederick County, Virginia. Hugh's mother was Margaret Galbreath who was born in Ireland in 1748 and died about 1828. Roger and Margaret were married in 1770 in Frederick County, Virginia. Roger Barton died June 24, 1826, at Clinton, in Anderson County, Tennessee.

Dr. Hugh Barton married Mary Magdalene (Polly) Shirley in January 1799 at Greenville in Greene County, Tennessee. Mary was born on April 11, 1780. Hugh and Mary had 11 children who were:

1) Armstead Barton was born on August 2, 1800, in Knox County, Tennessee, and he died in 1847 in Franklin County, Alabama.
2) Roger Barton was born on October 20, 1802, and he died March 4, 1855.
3) Elizabeth Barton Dickson was born on November 15, 1804, in Knox County, Tennessee. She became the wife of William Dickson and died on December 25, 1885, at Chisca in Colbert County, Alabama.
4) Arthur Crozier Barton was born in 1806, and he died about 1891 or 1892.

5) Hannah Barton was born in 1809, and she died in 1809.
6) Margaret Ann Barton Rutland was born May 7, 1813. She married John W. Rutland in 1833 and died October 3, 1855, and is buried in the Rutland Cemetery.
7) Hannah Marie Barton was born March 29, 1815, and she died in 1891.
8) Hugh Barton was born on January 3, 1817, and he died in 1891.
9) John Barton was born Feburary 2, 1819, and he died in 1886.
10) Louisa Vance Barton was born March 10, 1822, and she died in 1901.

Armstead Barton
8/2/1800 – 5/29/1847

11) James Shirley Barton was born at Clinton in Anderson County, Tennessee, on April 2, 1826, and he died in 1890.

Dr. Hugh Barton died in Franklin County, Alabama, on February 19, 1853 (Find a Grave Memorial Number 105550364). Mary Magdalene (Polly) Shirley Barton died on December 27, 1852, at Buzzard Roost in Franklin County, Alabama (Find a Grave Memorial Number 105550400). Hugh and Mary Magdalene (Polly) Shirley Barton are buried in graves marked with stone crypts in the Rutland Cemetery at Cherokee in Colbert County, Alabama. The inscription on his crypt says, "Dr. Hugh Barton, born in Frederick County, Va, May17, 1775, died in Franklin County, Ala, February 19, 1853."

Armistead Barton

Armstead Barton, the oldest son of eleven children of Dr. Hugh and Mary Barton, was born on August 2, 1800. He married Amanda Catherine Cook who was born in Sumner County, Tennessee, on June 4, 1809. Armstead and Amanda had four children:

1) Henry Cook Barton (1832-1911);
2) James Armistead Barton (1841-1921);
3) Josephine Shelton Barton (1841-1845);
4) Emma Shirley Barton Aldridge (1843-1907).

Armstead became the Governor of the Mississippi Territory; in that position, he became a friend to the Colberts, who were leaders of the Chickasaw Indians. Through friendship with influential Chickasaws, he came into possession of a large amount of the land in the western part of what is now Colbert County.

Amanda Catherine Cook Barton
6/4/1809 – 7/7/1884

Beginning in 1836, Armstead Barton began entering land in Franklin (Colbert) County. Some Chickasaw Indians still owned large tracts of land in the western part of old Franklin (now Colbert) County, Alabama, while other tribal members were moving west to Indian Territory in Oklahoma. It was during this time on October 5, 1836, that Armstead Barton entered his first tracts of land some of which were adjacent to property owned by Chickasaw Indians. Much of the land being entered was west of Caney Creek which was the eastern Chickasaw boundary line that was established during the Turkey Town Treaty in September 1816.

From 1836 through 1844, Armstead Barton entered some 8,400 acres of land in Franklin (Colbert) County, Alabama, that a few years earlier were Chickasaw Indian Territory. The land Armstead entered lay in Townships 2,3, 4, 5, 6, 7 South, Ranges 12, 13, 14, 15 West much of which was within the Chickasaw Boundary lines of 1816 and in close proximity to land owned by George and Pitman Colbert (Cowart, 1985 and 1986). Armstead Barton and Isaac Lane shared the entry of a few tracts of land next to sections of land that belonged to the Chickasaw Chief George and his adopted son Pitman Colbert.

Several settlers developed good relations with their Chickasaw neighbors which give them an advantage in securing these Indian holding after removal in 1837. Armstead Barton also benefitted from the fact that his family's business was next to Pitman Colbert's trading post in Tuscumbia.

Between October 1838 and March 1851, Arthur Crozier Barton, younger brother of Armstead, entered some 1600 acres of land around Barton, Alabama, most of which was in Township 4 South, Range 13 West. Much of the land in and around the Cherokee and Barton area was entered by the Richard Wallace Anderson, Armstead Barton, William Dickson, Isaac Lane, William Henry Saunders, the Pride family, the Thompson family, and the Rutland family.

According to the 1850 Franklin County, Alabama, Slave Schedule, Arthur C. Barton owned 45 black slaves, and Amamda Barton owned 155 black slaves. According to the 1860 Franklin County Slave Schedule, Amanda C. Barton owned only 106 black slaves, and Henry C. Barton owned 62 black slaves.

Armstead and Amanda Barton are buried in the Rutland Cemetery in Colbert County, Alabama. Armstead Barton, who died May 29, 1847 (Find a Grave Memorial Number 28947337), has a white marble tombstone that is the tallest in the cemetery. His marker was made in St. Louis and shipped down the river by boat; the stone was pulled from the Tennessee River to the cemetery by a team of horses. Amanda Barton died on July 7, 1884 (Find a Grave Memorial Number 28947221).

According to an article contributed by Fred Smoot in 1999 to Colbert County, Alabama, History about Barton Hall, "About 1840 Mr. Armistead Barton built his mansion down in the "Nation" on the Natchez Trace, near the town of Buzzard Roost. The old mansion still standing is two stories high with roof garden which was used as an observatory for watching the Negroes on the plantation. Underneath is a solid stone foundation. The porch is of solid stone with large columns extending to the second floor. The floors of the double parlors and hall are of solid black walnut and at the time they were laid were two inches thick; but when the home passed out of the hands of the original owners these planks were removed, sawed in two, the one inch planks replaced and the other half sold. The floors in these rooms were laid "log cabin style" and were very attractive. The windows for these rooms cost $100 each.

Barton Hall Plantation Mansion

The timber for the mansion was selected in Mississippi and was drawn by oxen for a distance of two hundred miles and sawed by hand. Around the walls of the double parlors was a molding of pure gold leaf, which also was removed long since. There was a double winding stairs leading to the roof garden. In its original state, the home had a very large and beautiful lawn with box-bordered walks to the gate, a distance of a quarter mile, and drives on each side shaded with cedars. At the rear was a barn large enough to accommodate fifty horses. The vegetable and flower gardens were in keeping with other surroundings. The orchard containing all kinds of luscious fruits covered twenty acres of land (From: "Two Hundred Years at Muscle Shoals" by Nina Leftwich, 1935)."

Bynum, F. W.-Hawkins Springs Plantation

Frederick W. Bynum was born circa 1815 in Nash County, North Carolina. He was the son of Drewry Sugars Bynum and Susan Peabody Bynum. Drewry was born about 1786 in Greensville County, Virginia, but he was raised in Northampton County, North Carolina. Drewry later moved to Nash County,

North Carolina; Drewry was there during the 1810 census with his 35 black slaves. In the 1820 census, Drewry owned 38 black slaves.

By December 29, 1828, Drewry and his family were living in Lawrence County, Alabama. On April 26, 1830, Drewry S. Bynum entered 80 acres, and on April 26, 1831, he entered 120 acres near the south bank of the Tennessee River some five miles west of mouth Town Creek in Section 7 of Township 3 South and Range 9 West in present-day Colbert County (Cowart, 1985). Drewry and Susan will be discussed in another book that includes planters of Lawrence County, Alabama.

Before his death on October 22, 1837, Drewry Sugars Bynum left his son Frederick the Hawkins Springs Plantation located in Franklin County, Alabama. While in Alabama, Frederick and his wife Cornelia had the following children who were Robert (Robin) Bynum (born circa 1846), Frederick Bynum (born circa 1849), Harry Bynum (born circa 1853), Florence Bynum (born circa 1856), and Belle Bynum (circa 1862) was probably born in Desha County, Arkansas.

In the 1840 census of Franklin County, Alabama, Fred Bynum is listed as resident and owner of 68 slaves. In the 1850 census, Frederick W. Bynum is listed as a 36 year old white male, with wife Cornelia and two children less than four years old.

According to the 1850 slave census of District 5 in Franklin County, Alabama, F. W. Bynum is listed twice. The first listing shows him owning 77 black slaves; and, he is shown as owning 56 black slaves with Joseph Askew as manager for a total of 133 slaves.

The 1850 agricultural census of Franklin shows him as the owner of 1270 acres of improved land and 907 acres of unimproved land for a total of 2,177 acres. The cash value of his plantation home and land was valued at $35,000 with implements and machinery valued at $3000 and livestock valued at $5000 for a net worth of $43,000.

Between 1855 and 1860, as did many other plantation owners seeking better and more fertile lands, Frederick W. Bynum moved his family and slaves west in Desha County, Arkansas which was established in 1838. The county is located on the Mississippi River in the southeastern part of Arkansas. According to the 1860 census of Desha County, Arkansas, Frederick W. Bynum owned 133 slaves, and he was listed as one of largest slave owners in county.

According to the 1870 United States Census of Desha County, Arkansas, Frederick W. Bynum was a 54 year old white male. His wife Cornelia Bynum is listed as a 43 white female who was born in North Carolina. Living in the household was Robert Bynum a 22 white male, Harry Bynum a 17 year old male, Florence Bynum a 14 year old white female, Belle Bynum an eight year old white female, and Robert Rice a 21 year old male born in Arkansas. Between 1870 and 1880, Frederick W. Bynum died. According to the 1880 census of Desha County, Arkansas, Cornelia, his widow, was living in the household with her son Robert Bynum. Robert (1846-1936) and his sister Florence Bynum Grinder (Died 1955) are buried in Memphis, Tennessee.

Carroll, G. W.-Johnson's Woods Plantation

George W. Carroll was born in Maryland on March 4, 1800, to his parents Charles John Carroll and Jennette Brown Carroll; George was related to two signers of the Declaration of Independence. According to the Franklin County, Alabama, marriage records, George W. Carroll married Lucy Lockhart in 1828; Lucy was born in Virginia on August 7, 1809. George and Lucy had the following children:

1) Caledonia Carroll Abernathy;
2) Georgie Carroll Hooper;
3) Araminta Brooke Carroll Nowland;
4) Kattie Carroll Baker Ashley;
5) Hibernia Carroll Armstrong;
6) Charles Carroll;
7) John Carroll;
8) Catherine Carroll;
9) Lucy Carroll.

According to the 1820 Franklin County, Alabama Census, George W. Carroll owned 28 black slaves. Also living in his house was one white male under five, one white male 15 to 20, one white male 20 to 30, two white females under five, and two white females 20 to 30.

On March 3, 1828, George W. Carroll entered 160 acres in northeast ¼ of Section 3 in Township 4 South, Range 11 West in Franklin County, Alabama. On January 18, 1843, George W. Carroll entered 80 acres in the west ½ of the southeast ¼ in Section 27 of Township 3 South, Range 11 West (Cowart, 1985).

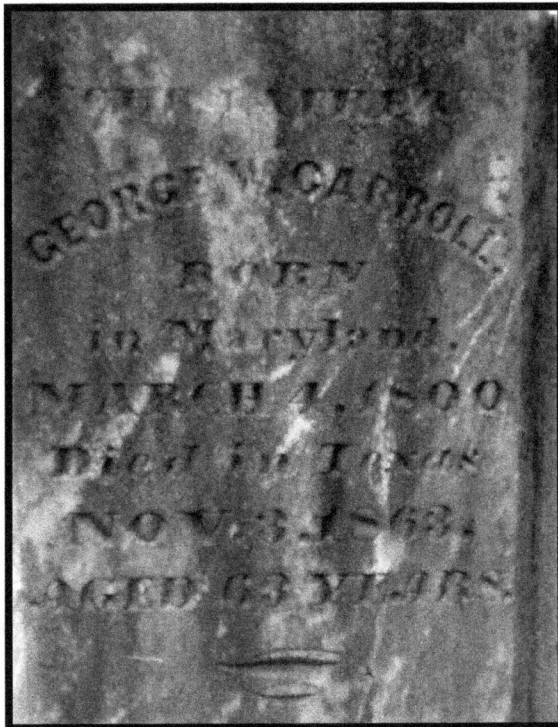

According to the 1850 Franklin County, Alabama Agricultural Census, George W. Carroll owned a 3,000 acre farm known as Johnson's Woods Plantation that included 1,800 acres of improved land and 1,200 acres of unimproved land. The land was valued at $60,000.00 with the livestock and farm equipment valued at $11,000.00.

As listed in the 1850 Franklin County, Alabama, Slave Schedule, George W. Carroll owned 157 black slaves. Sometime between 1855 and 1860, George sold his plantation to William Mahoon and moved with his family to Arkansas.

George died in November 3, 1863, in Texas; and Lucy died at Little Rock on April 7, 1876. They are buried at Mount Holly Cemetery in the City of Little Rock in Pulaski County, Arkansas.

The Franklin County plantation of George W. Carroll became known as Johnson's Woods. The plantation home was placed on the National Register of

Historic Places on May 4, 1988, with reference number 88000511. The home's architectural style was considered early classical revival. The George W. Carroll House is located on 801 East North Commons Street in Tuscumbia, Alabama.

George W. Carroll Plantation House
Alex Bush-July 13, 1935, Library of Congress

Cobb, Asa

Asa Cobb was born on August 7, 1805, in Roane County, Tennessee; his wife was Adeline Ligon (1826-1882). On November 3, 1818, Asa Cobb entered 160 acres in Section 31 of Township 3 South and Range 9 West in Franklin (present-day Colbert) County, Alabama. Also in 1818, Asa Cobb entered 80 acres in Section 1 of Township 6 South and Range 10 West in Franklin County, Alabama (Cowart, 1958 and 1986). At the time he entered the land, Asa would have been only 13years old; therefore, Asa may have also been the name of his father.

By 1830 United States Census, Asa Cobb was living in Lawrence County, Alabama. He was listed as head of the household with one white male between 60 and 70, two white males between 20 and 30, two white males between 10 to 15, and one white male 5 to 10. Also in the household of Asa Cobb were one white female 60 to 70, one white female 10 to 15, and one white female under five.

By 1840, Asa Cobb's family including his sister Mahuldah Cobb Williams and her children were living in Franklin County, Alabama. Mahuldah Cobb married Reuben Williams in Roane County, Tennessee on December 7, 1819. Reuben died about 1835 in Morgan County, Tennessee, leaving children Joseph Miller Williams, Asa Cobb Williams, Robert T. Williams, Deborah R. Williams, Reuben Williams and Francis Williams.

In the 1850 census of Franklin County, Asa Cobb was listed with one male under 21, one male over 21, one male between 18 and 45, one female under 21, and one female over 21. Also in 1850, Asa had 36 black slaves and three free persons of color. According to Familysearch.org, Asa Cobb owned 107 black slaves in 1850.

According to the 1850 agricultural census of Franklin County, Alabama, Asa Cobb had 200 acres of improved land and 300 acres of unimproved land. His property was valued at $5,000 for his land, $500 for his farm equipment, and $2,200 for his livestock.

According to the 1850 Slave Schedule for Franklin County, Alabama, Asa Cobb owned 37 black slaves and had one free person of color living in the household. Asa's neighbors in the slave schedule were cotton planters James Alexander and William Winston.

In addition, Asa Cobb is found in the 1855 state census of Franklin County, Alabama, which lists three males under 21, three males over 21, two females under 21, and one female over 21. With an additional four white inhabitants in just five years, in all probability, it appears that some of his sister's children are living in Asa's household. During the 1855 census, Asa has 37 black slaves and one free person of color.

After 1855, as with many cotton planters, Asa Cobb moved his family west to the fertile lands along the Mississippi River and settled near Friars Point in Coahoma County, Mississippi. Friars Point was founded in 1836 and was situated at a bend on the Mississippi River. Prior to the Civil War, the town flourished as the largest shipping center for cotton south of Memphis. The area was ideal for slave holding planters such as Asa Cobb, to grow and ship their cotton to market.

According to the United States Census taken on August 11, 1860, Asa and his family were living near Friars Point in Coahoma County, Mississippi. Asa is listed as a 54 year old white male farmer with a real estate value of $54,000 and a personal value of $60,000.   Living in his household is Adeline a 30 year old female born in Tennessee, Thomas a 13 year old male born in Alabama, Georgian an 11 year old female born in Alabama, Abner an eight year old male born in Alabama, Mary a six year old female born in Alabama, and Robert a four year old male born in Alabama.

According to the 1870 United States census of Friars Point in Coahoma County, Mississippi, Asa Cobb was a 64 year old white male born in Tennessee. Asa probably died at Friars Point in Coahoma County, Mississippi, on November 20, 1875.

Cockrill, Sterling Roberston

Sterling R. Cockrill was son of John Cockrill III who married Elizabeth Bibb Harding Underwood about 1803; she was born on January 3, 1783, and died on Feburary 7, 1824, near Tuscumbia, Alabama. Sterling was named after his uncle and was born in 1804 near Nashville, Tennessee.

Major John Cockrill II

John Cockrill III was the oldest son of Major John Cockrill II and Ann Roberston Cockrill. His father John Cockrill was born on December 19, 1757, in Richmond County, Henrico County, Virginia; John died on April 11, 1837, in Nashville in Davidson County, Tennessee. John married Ann Robertson in 1781 in Nashville, Tennessee; she was born on February 10, 1757, in Johnston County, North Carolina, and died in October 1821, near Nashville, Tennessee. John and Ann Roberston Cockrill had nine children:

1) John Cockrill III was born on July 8, 1781, at Roberstons Ford in North Carolina and died on August 12, 1841, at Tuscumbia in Franklin County, Alabama.
2) Nancy Ann Cockrill was born on February 1, 1783, in Davidson County, Tennessee.
3) Sterling Roberston Cockrill was born March 17, 1785, in Davidson County, Tennessee.
4) James Cockrill was born on January 28, 1787, at Johnson's Lick in Davidson County, Tennessee.
5) Mark Robertson Cockrill was born on December 2, 1788, in Nashville, Tennessee.
6) Susanna Cockrill was born on December 2, 1788, in Nashville, Tennessee.
7) Ann Cockrill was born on September 2, 1790, in Davidson County, Tennessee.
8) Sarah Cockrill was born on May 15, 1794, in Nashville, Tennessee.
9) Martha Cockrill was born on November 5, 1800, in Tennessee.

Sterling's father John Cockrill III was first found in Franklin County, Alabama, when he entered a lot in Coldwater (Tuscumbia) on October 27, 1820. On March 3, 1823, he purchased lots four and five containing 10 acres each in Section 4, Township 4 South, and Range 11 West. On September 29, 1830, John

59

entered 160 acres in Section 36, Township 3 South, Range 11 West, and again on January 16, 1834, he enterd 640 acres of Section 1, Township 4 South, Range 11 West.

According to the 1820 Franklin County, Alabama Census, John Cockrill owned 73 black slaves. In addition, John Cockrill III's brother, Mark R. Cockrill, enter two lots in Coldwater on October 24, 1820, and another lot on Octobert 25, 1820 (Cowart, 1985).

Sterling Roberston Cockrill married Ann Henrietta McDonald and they had a son whom they named Sterling Roberston Cockrill, Jr. Sterling Jr. was born on September 26, 1847, and died January 12, 1901a. Sterling Jr. served as Chief Justice of the Arkansas Supreme Court from 1884 until 1893; he has a huge tombstone at Mount Holly Cemetery in Little Rock, Arkansas.

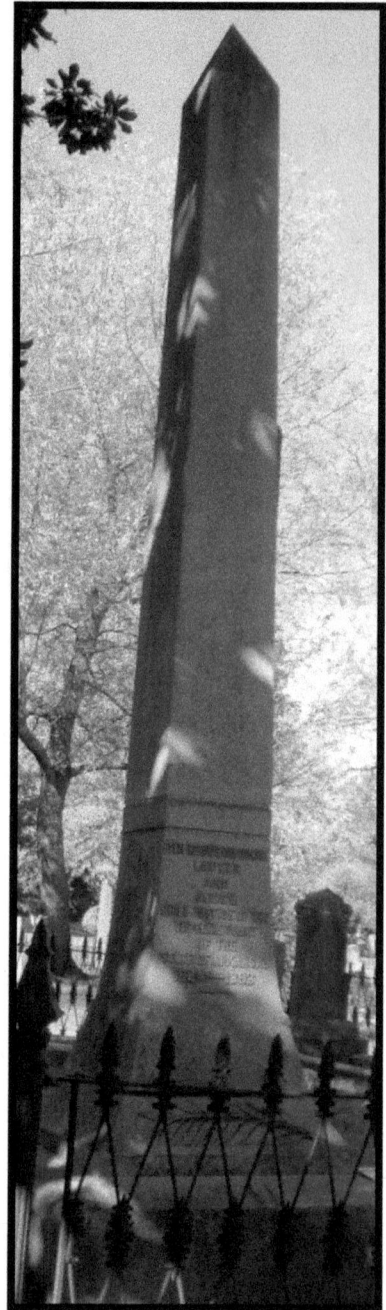

On January 13, 1832, a state law was approved for Sterling R. Cockrill to be appointed a trustee of the Tuscumbia Academy in Franklin County, Alabama.

According to the 1850 slave census of Franklin County, Alabama, Sterling Cockrill owned 156 black slaves. In 1850 agricultural census, he owned some 1,700 acres of land with 700 acres in row crops with his plantation valued at $45,000, farm equipment at $500, and livestock at $3,500.

In 1855, Sterling and Ann Cockrill moved to Pine Bluff in Jefferson County, Arkansas. The county was created on November 2, 1829, and the area was known as the Arkansas Delta that extended to the Mississippi River. In addition, the Arkansas River which passed through the area would occasionally flood leaving rich alluvial deposits of soil. Large plantations were developed which fronted the rivers for transportation of cotton. Since the planters were dependent on slave labor, the population of the county was comprised of a majority of black folks prior to the Civil War.

Sterling Roberston Cockrill moved west as many other planters to farm the rich delta soils. Since Sterling had some 156 black slaves, he could make a fortune on the rich delta soil. Sterling died on July 18, 1891, at Mt. Nebo, Arkansas. He and his wife are buried in the Bellwood Cemetery at Pine Bluff in Jefferson County, Arkansas (Find a Grave Memorial Number 101675215).

Delony, Edward Brodnax

Shortly after the land in Franklin, Lawrence, Lauderdale, Limestone, Morgan, and southwest Madison County was taken from the Indians, many cotton planters and their slaves migrated into the Muscle Shoals area of the Tennessee Valley. It appears that many planters came in family groups and small wagon trains with their black slaves to claim the fertile lands along the Tennessee River that were opened up after the Turkey Town Treaty of September 1816. These planters followed early Indian trails and roads to make their way into North Alabama. Edward Brodnax Walker Delony was one of those wealthy planters from Virginia and North Carolina who came into the area to make his fortune with slave labor in cotton farming.

Some believe that Edward Brodnax Walker Delony migrated into the area of Lawrence County, Alabama, in the mid 1820's, but official land records indicate he first purchased land in the late 1830's. From the story of Burchet Curtis King 1785-1872 by Peggy A. Bowling (2005), "In 1826, an important event occurred when 15 wagons arrived from Wake County, North Carolina, carrying prominent planters looking for new land. They were led by Henry King and included John Rand, Edward B. Delony, Col. James Fennell, Thomas Lyle, Drury Vinson, Elisha Madding and Richard Preuit."

Edward Broadnax Walker Delony (1784-1858) and Margaret Bonner Fox (1793-1863) were from Virginia. The 1850 census of Lawrence County, Alabama, lists Edward Delony as a 68 year old from Virginia living in the household of J. E. Delony. Based on the census record, the Edward B. W. Delony was probably born about 1782; he is listed in the 1840 census of Lawrence County, Alabama. His household had one white male between 50 and 60 years old, one male between 20 and 30 years old, two males between 15 and 20 years old, one male between 10 and 15 years old, three males between five and 10 years old, one male under five years old, and one white female between 40 and 50 years old.

On February 1, 1837, Edward B. W. Delony entered some 444 acres in present-day Colbert County, Alabama. On February 2, 1837, he entered some 285 acres in present-day Lawrence County, Alabama (Cowart, 1985 and 1996). The land Edward entered lay near Town Creek which is the present-day county line between Colbert and Lawrence Counties, Alabama.

Edward Brodnax Walker Delony and his wife Margaret had a son; they named him Edward Brodnax Delony. He was born on October 5, 1813, in Northampton County, North Carolina. The young Edward became a medical doctor, and in 1845, Doctor Edward Brodnax Delony married Nancy Emily Smith in Lawrence County, Aabama. She was born on December 29, 1818, in Lawrence

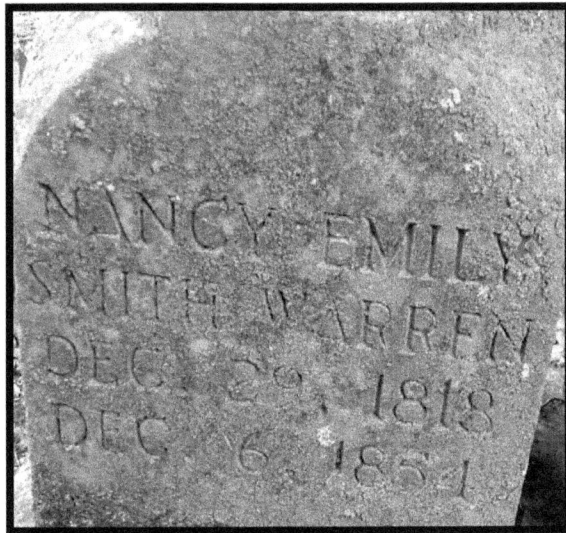

County, Alabama, and died December 6, 1854, in Franklin County, Alabama. Doctor Delony later married Susan Amelia Jones Delony (1830-1895).

As found in the Colbert County Banner on May 9, 1895, "Mrs. S. A. Delony, for a long time a resident of Colbert County, died at the home of her brother-in-law, Mr. P. H. Hobbs near South Florence, on Saturday Morning, May

4, 1895, in the 64th year of her age. Mrs. Delony came to Alabama from South Carolina, and was at one time principle of the high school at Tuscumbia, at which place she was married to Dr. E. B. Delony. Her husband died in Colbert County in August 1868. For a long time she taught school successfully in Leighton, and there are still many of her old pupils here who will deeply regret to hear of her death. In 1894 the old homestead, near Leighton, where she so long resided was destroyed by fire, and since that time she made home with the family of Mr. Hobbs. She was a devoted Christian mother, and leaves behind her noble sons and daughters to morn their loss. She was the mother of Messrs. Woodruff and Angelo Delony, Mrs. Tom Lile, Mrs. E. C. King, and Mrs. J.W. C. Smith, and stepmother of Mrs. James and Luto Spangleer of this place, and Judge Fox Delony and John Delony of Tuscumbia…The remains were interred at Oakwood Cemetery (Tuscumbia) Sunday evening at 3 o'clock."

Dr. Edward Brodax Delony's children include:

1) Caroline (Carrie) Delony, born about 1843, and she married Wesley M. Smith.
2) Rebecca Delony Fennel was born on September 6, 1846 in Leighton of Franklin County, Alabama, and she died on September 20, 1903, in Colbert County, Alabama.
3) Nancy (Nannie) Emily Delony was born on September 12, 1849, and she died on October 30, 1895. Nancy married James H. Spangler.
4) Fox Delony was born on February 14, 1848, and he died on December 3, 1905, in Tuscumbia, he married Katie Jarmon.
5) Margaret Delony Spangler was born on January 17, 1853, and she died on August 22, 1899, in ColbertCounty, Alabama.
6) John Edward Delony was born on November 6, 1854, and he died on February 14, 1942, in Tuscumbia.
7) Gazelle Delony King was born on February 6, 1859, and she died on April 24, 1923.
8) Woodroof Delony was born on August 6, 1860, and he died on August 22, 1946.
9) Octaiva Delony was born in 1865, and she died in 1957. Octavia married Jim W. D. Smith.
10) Angola Davis Delony was born in 1865 and died in1928. He married Mamie Phillips.

11) Sue Delony Lile was born in 1869 and died in 1901.

A few years prior to the Civil War, Dr. Edward B. Delony entered several acres of land. On February 2, 1857, he entered 40 acres in Section 17 of Township 5 South, Range 9 West. On May 1, 1858, he entered 240 acres of land in Township 5 South, Range 10 West. On December 1, 1859, he entered 79.62 acres in Section 10 of Township 5 South, Range 10 West, in Colbert County, Alabama (Cowart, 1985). Dr. Delony and his father entered a total of nearly 1,100 acres of land in Lawrence and present-day Colbert Counties of North Alabama.

According to the 1850 Franklin County, Alabama Census, District number five, E. B. Delony owned 43 slaves. In addition, the 1850 Lawrence County, Alabama, Slave Census indicates that Edward Delony owned 11 slaves; since Dr. Deloney's father died in 1858, this may have been slaves of Sr. Delony.

In the 1860 slave schedule of Lawrence and Franklin Counties, Alabama, Edward B. Deloney owned 81 black slaves. His real estate value was $35,000.00, and his personal estate value was $50,000.00. Shortly after the Civil War, he was listed in the 1866 Alabama State Census of Franklin County, Alabama.

Dr. Edward Brodnax Delony died August 28, 1868, at Leighton in Colbert County, Alabama. His remains are interred and still lie buried in the Delony Cemetery, but his orginal tombstone was moved to the King Cemetery in Colbert County, Alabama, near the west bank of Town Creek (Find a Grave Memorial Number 95304464).

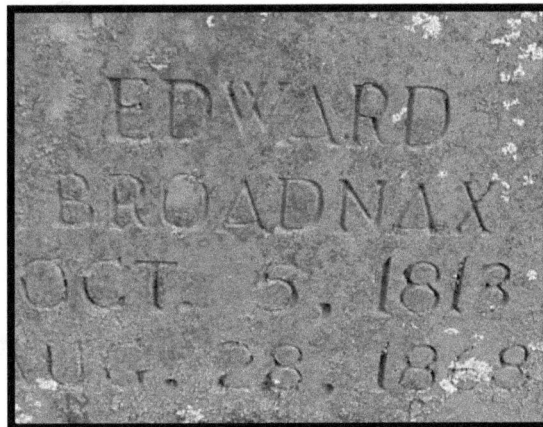

Dickson, William

William Dickson became a planter and slave holder in Franklin County, Alabama. William's father was Reuben Dickson who was born on March 7, 1774, in Orange County, North Carolina, and Reuben died on January 21, 1848, in Franklin County, Alabama. William's mother was Elizabeth Moore Dickson who was born on September 7, 1768, in Orange County, North Carolina, and Elizabeth died on September 26, 1859, in Franklin County, Alabama. William Dickson was born on July 13, 1798, in Orange County, North Carolina. According to the Old Land Records of Lauderdale County, Alabama, William Dickson entered 160.57 acres on March 30, 1818 (Cowart, 1996); however, beginning in the 1839, he entered over 10,000 acres in Franklin County, Alabama.

William Dickson married Elizabeth Barton who was born on November 15, 1804, in Knox County, Tennessee; she died on December 25, 1885, at Chisca in Colbert County, Alabama. Elizabeth Barton Dickson's parents were Hugh Barton (May 17, 1775-February 19, 1853) and Mary Magdalene Shirley Barton (April 11, 1780-December 27, 1852). Elizabeth's siblings were Armistead Barton (1800-1847) and Margaret Ann Barton Rutland (1813-1855). Elizabeth Barton Dickson's inscription on her tombstone says, "Dau of Dr. Hugh & Mary Barton." She is buried in the Rutland Cemetery near Cherokee in Colbert County, Alabama (Find a Grave Memorial Number 84535118). William and Elizabeth Barton Dickson's children include:

1) Elizabeth Dickson Rivers was born on February 2, 1830, and died December 3, 1852. On her tombstone is written, "In Memory of; wife of Thomas Rivers; dau of William & Elizabeth Dickson; A more lovely romance never lived; A better Christian never died."

2) Mary Dickson was born on October 1, 1831, in Madison County, Alabama, and died June 22, 1851, in Franklin County, Alabama. On her tombstone is the following, "Precious in the sight of the Lord, Is the death of his saints, Rest here blest saint till from his throne, The morning break and pierce the shadow, Break from his throne illusturous morn, All end on earth his soveriegn word, Restore thy trust a glorious form, Shall then arise to met the Lord."

3) William Dickson was born on October 6, 1838, in Franklin County, Alabama, and he died on October 1, 1852.

William Dickson Plantation Mansion

According to the 1840 census of Franklin County, Alabama, William Dickson owned 14 black slaves and had a total of 26 inhabitants. By the 1850 Franklin County, Alabama, United States Census, William Dickson was listed as a 52 year old white male who was born about 1798 in South Carolina with house number 392. His wife Elizabeth Dickson was listed as a 46 year old white female from South Carolina. Also enumerated in the census was Elizabeth Dickson a 20 year old female born in South Carolina; Mary Dickson an 18 year old female born in South Carolina; Barton Dickson a 14 year old male born in North Carolina; William Dickson a 12 year old male born in North Carolina; Margaret Dickson a six year old female born in North Carolina; Louisa Dickson a four year old female born in North Carolina; Elizabeth Dickson an 82 year old female from North Carolina; William Coats a 25 year old male born in Tennessee; and, John Henry a 20 year old male born in Alabama.

The 1850 census of Franklin County, Alabama gives William Dickson's value as $29,000.00. In addition, the 1850 Franklin County Slave Schedule reported that William Dickson owned 66 black slaves.

According to the 1860 census, William Dickson's real estate value was $90,000.00 and his personal estate value was $85,000.00. In addition, the 1860 Franklin County Slave Schedule indicates that William Dickson owned 83 black slaves. His two storied plantation home is shown as a huge mansion.

The 1860 census of the Western Division of Franklin County, Alabama, lists Wm Dickson as a 62 year old white male born in Tennessee. Also listed is Elizabeth Dickson a 56 year old female born in Tennessee; Barton Dickson a 23 year old male born inTennessee; M. J. Dickson a 16 year old female born in Tennessee; and, M. L. Dickson a 16 year old female born in Tennessee.

Dickson Rifles

In 1861 at the outbreak of the Civil War, William Dickson, Owen Nelson (an attorney from Tuscumbia), and Lewis Sadler (a physician) started a rifle making enterprise called the Shakanoosa Arms Company. William Dickson, one of the original founders of the company, was owner of a large slave plantation; he had entered some 10,500 acres of land around Cherokee in Franklin (Colbert) County, Alabama (Cowart, 1985). The firearms were originally made at the first manufacturing plant just west of the present-day Town of Cherokee at Buzzard Roost in Colbert County, Alabama.

In the summer of 1862 the Shakanoosa Arms Company was forced to move its operation to Rome, Georgia, because Union forces were operating along the Tennessee River not far from the factory in Franklin (Colbert) County,

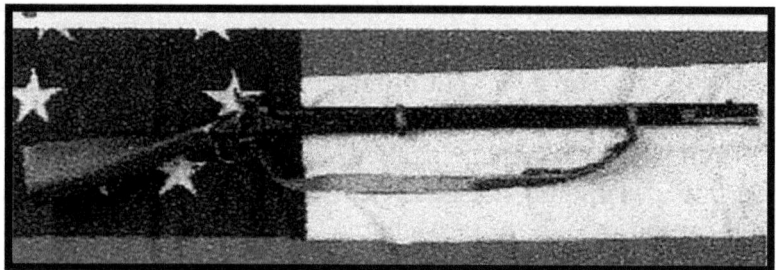

Alabama. The name of the company was changed to Nelson Dickson Gun Factory.

In 1863, the Nelson Dickson Gun Factory received $7,000.00 to manufacture the 1841 United States Model of the Mississippi type rifles for the State of Alabama. The 1841 Model Mississippi Rifles were made under the supervision of inspecting officer, Captain B. J. McCormick. The 58 caliber rifles had 33 inch barrels and 48 inch stocks with brass hardware which included a

straight butt plate, two piece trigger guard, barrel bands and nose cap. Only a few thousand of the rifles were made for the Confederate Army.

While in Rome, the rifle company buildings were destroyed by fire, and the company moved to Adairsville, Georgia, under the name Dickson, Nelson, and Company. Finally in February of 1864, the company was moved to its final home in Dawson, Georgia.

Based on the Rutland Cemetery tombstones in present-day Colbert County, Alabama, it appears that some of the Dickson family followed the rifle factory to its final location in Dawson, Georgia. The following is an inscription found on a Rutland Cemetery tombstone, "Dickson, Lizzie 28 Sep 1864-18 Oct 1871 b Dawson, Terrill County, GA, d Dickson, Colbert County, AL, dau of Barton & Nellie Dickson." It appears that Barton and Nellie Dickson followed the factory to Dawson, Georgia, where their daughter was born. Prior to the death of their daughter in 1871, Barton and Nellie moved back to Cherokee in Colbert County, Alabama.

Post Civil War

In the 1870 census of Colbert County, Alabama, William Dickson was listed as a 71 year old white male born in North Carolina. Also listed in 1870 was Elizabeth Dickson a 66 year old female born in Tennessee; Luttie Dickson a 24 year old female born in Alabama; John Strong a 27 year old male born in

69

Mississippi; Margaret Strong a 24 year old female born in Alabama; Mattie Strong a 15 year old female born in Mississippi; William Bell a 43 year old male born in Alabama; Mary Dickson a 30 year old black female domestic servant born in Virginia; Reuben Dickson a four year old mulatto male born in Alabama; Martha Riveras a 45 year old mulatto female domestic servant born in Tennessee; Rosa Dickson a 13 year old black female domestic servant born in Alabama; Harriet Dickson a 11 year old black female domestic servant born in Alabama; and, Cole Strong a 13 year old black male domestic servant born in Arkansas.

The 1870 census noted William Dickson's real estate value was $20,000.00, and his personal estate value was $1000.00. After the Civil War, William Dickson's real eastate value dropped $70,000, and his personal estate value dropped $84,000. As evidenced by the official census record, the Civil War had a devastating impact on the wealth of previous slave holding owners of large cotton plantations.

William Dickson, Sr. died on July 3, 1880, at Chisca in Colbert County, Alabama. William Dickson Sr. is buried in the Rutland Cemetery near Cherokee in Colbert County, Alabama (Find a Grave Memorial number 84533954).

Downs, William Woods

William Woods Downs was the second of three children born to William and Sarah (Downs) Downs on August 12, 1802, at Weldon in Halifax County, North Carolina. William married Henrietta (Sparks) in 1823; she was born in Morgan County, Georgia, on July 20, 1808. They had twelve children:

1) John Thomas Downs, 1825-1825;
2) James Mortimor Downs, 1826-1852;
3) Fernando DeCoella Downs, 1828-1863;
4) William Pinkney Downs, 1830-1860;
5) Isabella Virginia Downs Mullens, 1832-1878;
6) Mahala Annie Downs Maddin, 1835-1915;
7) John Wesley Downs, 1838-1917;
8) Oscar J. Downs, 1840-1877;

9) Thomas Lucius Downs, 1844-1876;
10) Josephine Downs Marshall,1846-1917;
11) Alice Henrietta Downs Parrott, 1848-1896;
12) Charles M. Downs, 1851-1887.

William W. Downs entered land in Lawrence and Franklin (Colbert) Counties of North Alabama from November 2, 1831, through May 20, 1851. He entered some 250 acres in Lawrence County, 400 acres in present-day Franklin County, and 600 acres in Township 5 South and Range 10 West in present-day Colbert County (Cowart 1985, 1986, and 1991).

According to the 1850 Franklin County, Alabama, Slave Schedule, William Woods Downs owned 56 black slaves. Also in 1850, he owned some 1,250 acres with 600 acres of improved land and 400 acres of unimproved land in Franklin County which at that time included Colbert County. The cash value of his farm was $15,000 with farm equipment being valued at $500. In addition, William Woods Downs had livestock which were valued at $3,000.00.

Shortly after 1850, William Woods Downs went to Texas seeking new cotton lands. By 1854, he was a plantation owner on the Brazos River south of Waco. In the Waco area, the flood plains of the Brazos River provided fertile lands suitable for growing cotton. William W. Downs decided that his Brazos plantation would be the place where he could make a fortune growing cotton and sugar cane with the help of his black slaves.

William Woods Downs died on September 22, 1882, in Waco, Texas, (Find a Grave Memorial Number 13247201). His wife Henrietta Sparks Downs died on April 28, 1886 (Find a Grave Memorial Number 13247252). William and Henrietta are buried in the Oakwood Cemetery at Waco in McLennan County, Texas.

According to the Waco Daily Examiner in 1882, "Sat. Sept. 23, Major William Wood Downs died Friday morming, Sept. 22, aged 80 years. Funeral today from the residence of Col. R. B. Parrott; burial at Oakwood Cemetery. Born Weldon, North Carolina, Aug. 12, 1802. To Morgan Co., Ga., as a child, with the family. Married Miss Henrietta Sparks, who survives. In 1837, to Lawrence Co., Ala. To Waco in 1854. Purchased land in Waco and a planatation on the Brazos south of Waco. Of 10 children, 5 survive: Mrs. J.W. Maddin, wife of Dr. Maddin of Nashville, Tenn.; Mrs. R. B. Parrott; Mrs. John F. Marshall; Major J. W. Downs; and C. M. Downs."

According to the Waco Daily Examiner in 1886, "Thu. Apr. 29: Mrs. Henrietta Downs had lived in Waco 32 years. Nee Sparks. Was born in NC Aug. 28, 1808. Married to W. W. Downs at Salem, Geo. Aug 10, 1823. In 1838 to Alabama with husband and children, then to Texas. To Waco in 1854. Col. R. B. Parrott is her son-in-law. Her husband Rev. W. W. Downs died several years ago. Was mother of 13 children. Five survive: Maj. J. W. Downs, founder of the Examiner; C. M. Downs; Mrs. R. B. Parrott; Mrs. John F. Marshall, and Mrs. Maddin of Tennessee. Funeral was yesterday, with burial at Oakwood Cemetery."

Elliott, Robert

Robert Elliott was probably born in Ireland about 1797 since he had two older brothers Andrew and David Elliott born in Ireland and a younger brother brother James C. Elliott born in Ireland; however, census records indicate he was born in South Carolina. Robert was the third child of nine children born to his parents John B. Elliott and Jane Kerr Elliott who came from Ireland and settled near Athens in Limestone County, Alabama.

John B. Elliott was born March 17, 1769, in Enniskillen, Fermanagh County, Ireland, and died November 11, 1855. He is buried in the Old Athens City Cemetery in Athens, Limestone Co, Alabama (Find a Grave Memorial Number 62812303). He married Jane "Mother Elliott" Kerr in Enniskillen, Fermanagh County, Ireland. Jane was born December 24, 1768, in Enniskillen, Fermanagh County, Ireland, and died on September 8, 1853. She is also buried in Athens, Alabama (Find a Grave Memorial Number 62812216).

As found in "Lure & Lore of Limestone County" written by John Tanner of his memories of Athens in 1876, "Old Mother Elliott was formerly an old Presbyterian, and if there are degrees in heaven, she is high up in glory in that happy land. She lived one mile from town on the Huntsville Road, and was quite an old lady when I was but a boy, but I shall never forget her regular attendance at church, night and day, and almost regardless of weather with her lantern of dark nights, and generally alone...She was ever on errands of mercy, to delight the sick and afflicted, and her chief delight was to do good...Would that we all were imitators of Mother Elliott!"

Children of John B. Elliott and Jane Kerr Elliott are:

1) Andrew M. Elliott was born on May 4, 1791, in Ireland, and he died on November 27, 1841, at Athens in Limestone County, Alabama.
2) David M. Elliott was born on December 6, 1794, in Ireland, and he died December 6, 1854, in Athens, Alabama.
3) Robert Elliott was born circa 1797.
4) Reverend James "Uncle Jimmy" C. Elliott was born on August 15, 1799, at Enniskillen in County Fermanagh, Ireland, and he died on June 5, 1875, at Athens in Limestone County, Alabama.
5) John Henderson "One Eye" Elliott was born on November 9, 1800, at Murfreesboro in Rutherford County, Tennessee, and he died on June 14, 1894, in Athens, Alabama.
6) Mary Elizabeth Wilson Elliott was born on April 6, 1806, in Murfreesboro, Tennessee, and she died on January 15, 1875, in Athens, Alabama.
7) Margaret D. Elliott was born about 1816 in Rutherford County, Tennessee.
8) Jane Wilson Elliott Locke was born on October 11, 1826, in Athens, Alabama and died on August 29, 1897, in Rockwall, Texas.
9) Prewet Elliott died on May 12, 1874.

According to the probate record of Limestone County, Alabama, on December 7, 1855, Book D, page 219, "The will of John B. Elliott was presented by his sons James C. Elliott and David Elliott residing in Texas, and Robert Lafayette Elliott residing in Tennessee. Citations were issued to Robert Elliott, John H. Elliott, Elizabeth W. Higgins and husband Hiram Higgins, David M. Elliott, Prewet Elliott, Margaret Brackeen and husband Josiah Brackeen, Elizabeth Stephenson, Jane W. Locke and William Locke her husband, and James Elliot. John Jackson is appointed guardian of William Anthony, Elizabeth, George, and Robert Elliott, infant heirs of said deceased."

In 1822, Robert Elliott married his first cousin Elizabeth Elliott, daughter of Samuel T. Elliott and Jane Randolph. In 1860, Samuel T. Elliott was owner of the Boxwood Plantation containing 1,300 acres and 92 black slaves in Lawrence County, Alabama. He was believed to be the brother of John B. Elliott the father of Robert. Robert Elliott and Elizabeth Elliott had a son Robert Kerr Elliott.

According to the 1850 United States Census of Franklin County, Alabama, Robert Elliott was a 53 year old white male born in South Carolina about 1797, his wife Elizabeth was 46 years old born in Tennessee. Robert and Elizabeth Elliott had five children living in their household: Mary was 22; Robert was 21; Nathan was 13; David was 11; and, John was four; they were all born in Tennessee.

According to the 1850 Franklin County, Alabama Slave Schedule, Robert Elliott owned 20 Slaves. The 1850 Franklin County, Alabama Agricultural Census states that Robert Elliott owned 1,000 acres of improved land and 503 acres of unimproved land. The cash value of his farm was $20,000 with equipment valued at $300 and livestock valued at $300.

From July 7, 1852, through December 4, 1855, Robert Elliott entered some 440 acres in Township 4 South and Range 11 West in present-day Colbert County, Alabama (Cowart, 1985). On December 9, 1846, he entered 80 acres in Township 1 South and Range 9 West in Lauderdale County, Alabama (Cowart, 1996). From April 10, 1833, through December 1, 1846, he entered some 320 acres in Lawrence County, Alabama (Cowart, 1991).

Robert Elliott is listed in the 1855 Alabama State Census of Franklin County, Alabama, and he is not found in North Alabama records afterward. He may have moved west as other North Alabama cotton planters did.

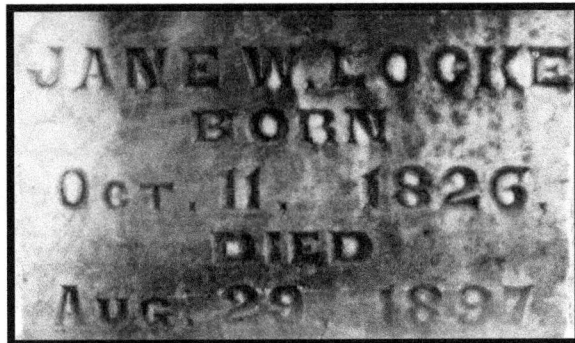

In 1855, Robert's brother David M. Elliott lived in Texas.

Robert's sister Jane Elliott Wilson Locke died in Rockwall, Texas, on August 29, 1897, and she was buried in Rockwall Memorial Cemetery. Jane had married Calvin Locke on February 22, 1844, in Limestone County, Alabama (Find a Grave Memorial Number 32746609). It is very probably that Robert Elliott moved to Texas prior to his death.

Garner, Argy Leander

Argy Leander Garner was the son of Revolutionary War soldier Sturdy Garner and Sarah Smith (1770-1846). Sturdy was born in Fauquier County, Virginia, on May 9, 1762, and he died in Madison County, Alabama, on March 4, 1845. Sturdy Garner is shown in the 1809 census in what was then the Mississippi Territory, before Alabama was a state. Sturdy and Sarah Smith Garner had nine named children. In addition, there were four other sons who died young.

1) Samuel Garner was born in 1789 and married Rachel Pugh who died in 1840.
2) Sarah Garner was married to Thomas Chennualt.
3) Robert Craig Garner was born in South Carolina on October 5, 1796.
4) Argy Leander Garner was born in Madison County, Alabama, in 1802, and he married Sharah M. Burton.

In Memory of
ROBERT CRAIG
GARNER
Born Oct. 5, 1796
Departed this Life
Franklin County, Ala.
June 19, 1846
Age 49 yrs. 8 mos. 12 days

5) Daniel H. Garner was born in 1806 and married Catherine Drinkwater.

6) Milton C. Garner was thought to be the father of Robert Milton Garner of Colbert County, Alabama. Robert bought his first land from Argy Garner located three miles south of Tuscumbia, Alabama.
7) Sturdy F. Garner.
8) William L. Garner.
9) Elizabeth Garner married Lawrence Nobles.

There is a tombstone in the Barton Cemetery in present-day Colbert County that reads, "In memory of Robert Craig Garner. Born: October 5, 1796. Departed this life in Franklin County, Alabama, June 19, 1846. Age 49 years, 8 months and 12 days. Born in South Carolina, Pendleton District, October 5, 1796. Robert Craig Garner was the son of Sturdy Garner and Sarah his wife. Sarah Garner was born July 22, 1770, and departed this life October 11, 1846."

It appears that Argy Leander Garner moved with his family to North Alabama at an early age and settled in Madison County, Alabama. He entered land in Lawrence County, Alabama, around 21 years of age since census records indicate he was born around 1807. By the late 1840's, Argy was entering land in present-day Colbert County, Alabama, where he eventually had a large cotton plantation and many black slaves.

From April 28, 1828, through April 28, 1830, Argy Leander Garner entered 240 acres in Township 7 South, Range 6 West in Lawrence County, Alabama. Most of the land he entered in Lawrence County was originally entered by Nicholas Johnson (Cowart, 1991). Between October 16, 1846, and December 21, 1852, Argy Leander Garner entered some 1,320 acres in present-day Colbert County, Alabama. Of this large tract, 1,120 acres was in Township 4 South and Range 13 West, 160 acres in Township 5 South and Range 14 West, and 40 acres in Township 4 South and Range 12 West (Cowart, 1985).

According to the 1850 Franklin County, Alabama United States Census, Argy Leander Garner was estimated to have been born in 1807 in South Carolina. He was listed as a white male age 43 in the 1850 census.

According to the 1850 Franklin County Slave Schedule, Argy L. Garner owned 110 black slaves that worked his cotton plantation. In the 1850 Franklin County, Alabama Agricultural Census, A. L. Garner owned 1,500 acres of improved crop land and 1,861 acres of unimproved land valued at $67, 220. Argy L. Garner owned some land south west of Tuscumbia, Alabama, and northeast of Barton, Alabama.The estimate of his crops and livestock were valued at $1,500.00 and $10,860.00 respectfully.

At the age of 57 in 1859, Argy L. Garner married Sarah M. Burton who was thirty-six years old. Sarah died during childbirth in 1861, but her baby Betty Sally Garner lived.

According to the 1860 Franklin County, Alabama United States Census, Argy Leander Garner was estimated to have been born in 1807 in South Carolina. He was listed as a white male age 53 in the 1860 census. The 1860 Franklin County, Alabama, Slave Schedule, he is listed as owing 76 black slaves.

In May 2004, Lewis C. Gibbs, Jr. had an article on Argy Leander Garner in Colbert County, Alabama Biographies. The following is a portion of that article, "On the fourth day of March, 1864, he made his will. His wishes were that his estate be kept together for the good of his slaves. The profit was to go to the children of Sturdy F. Garner and Daniel H. Garner in the amount of one hundred dollars a year per child. The remainder was to go to the children of Alexander Malone, Goodloe W. Malone and John S. Malone to be divided equally. This was in case his daughter Betty Sally died. This was to be in effect for fifty years. However we know that when the war ended the slaves were freed so this would change this arrangement.

In the last days of the war when the carpet-baggers came through they found Mr. Garner apparently in good financial condition because of the land and slaves he owned. They demanded to know where his gold was hidden and his answer was that he did not have any. Because he would not tell them they took him to the river bluff and hung him from a tree, not enough to kill him but enough to make him think they were going to kill him. He never did tell them. All he would say was that it was hid where the wild hog jumped off the bluff. They choked him so long that he had a mental problem for the rest of his life. A black man was hired to care for him the remainder of his life. The man's name was Dick Garner probably one of his former slaves. Dick Garner reported that his mind would go and come for the rest of his life. It was thought that two or three thousand dollars was the amount of gold hidden.

Mr. A. L. Garner died and his will was probated in 1867. The court appointed Mr. Willie J. Carlous, William Inman, J. Petree and Samuel Greenhill to appraise his real and personal property. Their decision was that his property value was $27,211.75.

In his will he did not want his daughter, Betty Sally, raised by any of his relatives. He wanted a dependable woman hired to take care of her until she reached legal age. For this service the woman was to be paid a salary and be taken care of the rest of her life. We have no record of what became of Betty Sally.

Mr. John D. Inman was made administrator of the estate. The first block of land was sold to the Bayless family. This was section 2, township 4 and range 13…In 1875 Mr. J. E. Gibbs bought the mountain land from Mr. John D. Inman…In 1870 Mr. Robert Garner bought the back and east part of this estate consisting of a part of section 36 and the east half of section 35, township 3 and range 13…In 1878 A. Judson Gilbert bought the west half of section 35, township 3 and range 13 for the sum of nine hundred, sixty dollars.

A Mrs. Catherine Inman bought eighty acres, Mr. Tom William's eighty acres, Tom King's forty acres and Richard Garner's forty acres. The last two were probably slaves of the Garner family.

When Mr. Arthur C. Barton willed section 3 township 4 and range 13 to his nieces and nephews, the children of James S. Barton, he states in the deed that one acre of this land had been sold to A. L. Garner for burial ground. There were cut stone corner and gate post put there and a cedar tree planted. There is still one grave marker that is readable dated 1817. The cemetery was first known as the Garner Cemetery, but I believe it was changed after the community of Barton was established. Because of this grave marker we know that the cemetery dates back to 1817."

Goodloe, David Short-Myrtle Hall Plantation

David Short Goodloe owned a cotton farm in Franklin (Colbert) County, Alabama, known as the Myrtle Hall Plantation. David S. Goodloe was born in Granville County, North Carolina, on July 26, 1776. He died on October 13, 1845, at Cherokee Station in Franklin County, Alabama, at 69 years of age. He was buried in Oakwood Cemetery in Tuscumbia, Alabama.

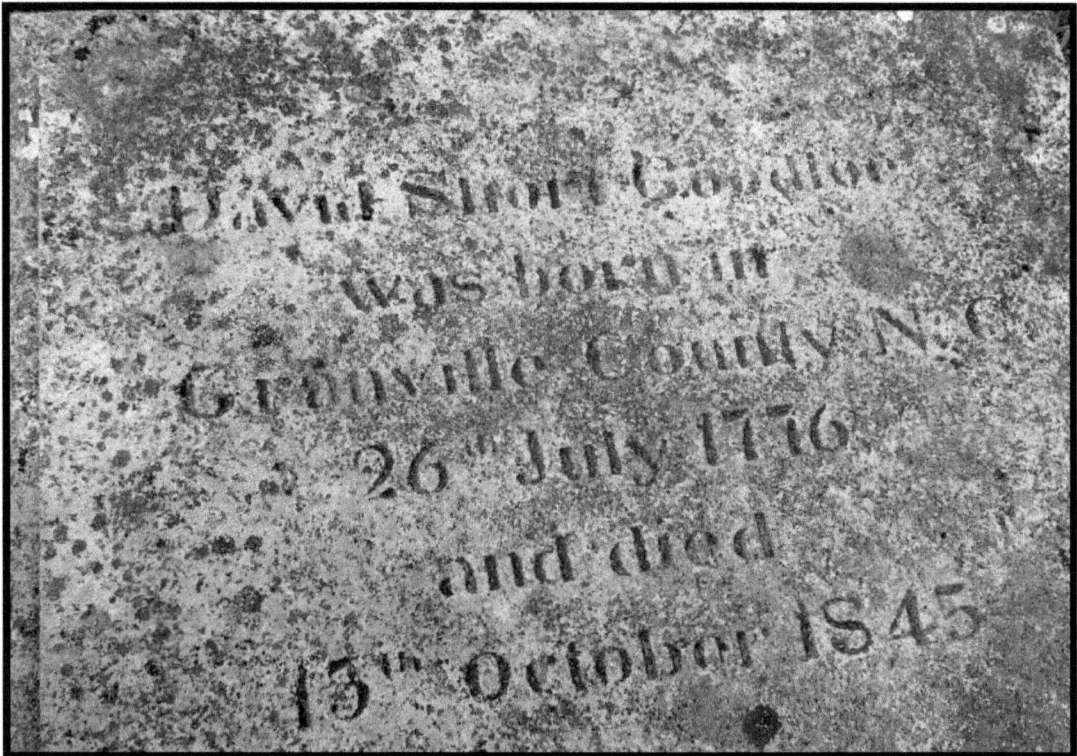

David Short Goodloe first married Mary Louisa Hill on May 1, 1801. Mary was born in 1781, and she died September 16, 1831, at Tuscumbia in Colbert County, Alabama, at 50 years of age. David Short Goodloe and Mary Louisa Hill Goodloe had the following children:

1) William Hill Goodloe was born on August 3, 1804, and he died in 1834.

2) Sarah Louise Goodloe was born in Granville County, North Carolina, on December 4, 1807, and she died on May 24, 1826, at 18 years of age.

3) David Short Goodloe, Jr. was born in Granville County, North Carolina, on March 25, 1810. He died August 15, 1859 in Monroe, Virginia, at 49 years of age. David's occupation was listed as planter/minister.

4) Albert Gallatin Goodloe was born in Granville County, North Carolina, on April 13, 1812. He died January 1, 1887, at Tuscumbia in Colbert County, Alabama, at 74 years of age. His body was interred near Tuscumbia in Colbert County, Alabama.

5) Robert Atlas Goodloe was born in Granville County, North Carolina, on December 7, 1814. He died March 8, 1882, at Lane Springs in Franklin County, Alabama, at 67 years of age. He married Mary Lane in Morgan County, Alabama, on December 24, 1835. She was born in Wake County, North Carolina, on August 16, 1817. Mary was the daughter of Isaac Lane and Mary Hunter "Polly" Pride. She died October 23, 1874, at Barton Station in Franklin County, Alabama, at 57 years of age. A. T. Goodloe referred to him as "my guardian" in the Family Bible death record."

6) John Calvin Goodloe was born in North Carolina, on May 21, 1817. He died February 25, 1895, at Tuscumbia in Colbert County, Alabama, at 77 years of age. He married Harriet Ann Rebecca Turner at Huntsville, Madison County, Alabama, on November 1, 1838. She was born in Huntsville in Madison County, Alabama, on November 21, 1821. Harriet was the daughter of Sugars Turner and Rebecca DeLoney. She died November 12, 1900, at 78 years of age.

7) Paul Hill Goodloe was born, November 22, 1820. He died in 1898 at Memphis in Shelby County, Tennessee, at 77 years of age. Paul's occupation was listed as a professor. Paul was their seventh child and he was the only one born in Franklin County, Alabama. Their other six children were born in North Carolina.

After the death of Mary Hill Goodloe on September 16, 1831, David married Elizabeth Pride. Elizabeth Pride Goodloe was born in February 1785, and she died at Pride Landing in Franklin County, Alabama, on November 29, 1845. Elizabeth was buried in Pride Cemetery at Hawk Pride in present-day

Colbert County, Alabama (Find a Grave Memorial Number 76879877). Elizabeth's father was Major Edward Mitchell Pride (1755 1839). Elizabeth Pride Goodloe's siblings were:

1) Ruth Emma Pride Carloss (1783-1824);
2) Mary Hunter Pride Lane (1788-1863);
3) Nathaniel J. Pride (1795-1875);
4) Edward Mitchell Pride, Jr. (1797-1811);
5) Halcott J. Pride (1803-1889).

According to an article submitted by R. Reams Goodloe Sr. to the Heritage of Colbert County, Alabama Book, "David Short Goodloe was the first Goodloe known to have come to the Tuscumbia area of Franklin County, now Colbert County, Alabama. He was the great great grandson of the immigrant, George Goodloe. David moved to Tuscumbia from Granville County, North Carolina, about 1820 with his wife the former Mary Hill and six children. His seventh child, Paul Hill Goodloe was born in 1820 in the Tuscumbia area. After Mary's death in 1831 in Franklin County, Alabama, David married Elizabeth Pride. David was a good businessman, farmer, and financier. He was Methodist. He was on the Board of Directors of the company that built the Tuscumbia and Decatur Railroad. He sold his businesses in 1837 and built a new home known as "Myrtle Hall" on a large plantation between Cherokee and the Tennessee River very near where Natchez Trace now crosses."

Robert A. Goodloe

Robert Atlas Goodloe was born on December 7, 1814, in Granville County, North Carolina, and he died on March 8, 1882, at Cherokee in Colbert County, Alabama. His parents were David Short Goodloe and Mary Louisa Hill Goodloe. He married Mary Lane Goodloe. Robert was buried in the Lane Cemetery in Colbert County, Alabama (Find a Grave Memorial Number 125235229).

Mary Lane Goodloe was born on August 16, 1817, in Wake County, North Carolina. She died on October 23, 1874, in Colbert County, Alabama. Her parents were Isaac Lane (1787-1862) and Mary Hunter Pride Lane (1788-1863). Robert and Mary Lane Goodloe had two children, Susan Turner Goodloe Rutland (1851-1896) and Little Paul Goodloe (1852-1853). She is buried in the Lane Cemetery in Colbert County, Alabama (Find a Grave Memorial Number 125235945).

According to the 1850 Franklin County, Alabama Slave Census, Robert A. Goodloe owned 78 black slaves. As found in the 1850 Franklin County, Alabama Agricultural Census, Robert A. Goodloe owned 600 acres of improved land and 1000 acres of unimproved land. His farm was valued at $1500 with the value of implements and machinery being $200. Robert owned some $4,000 worth of livestock.

The 1860 United States Census of the Western Division of Franklin County, Alabama states that Robert Atlas Goodloe was a white 45 year old male born in North Carolina. Also listed household identification number 151 is Mary Goodloe a 42 year old female from North Carolina, Isaac L. Goodloe a 23 year

old male born in Alabama, Sallie L. Goodloe an 18 year old female born in Alabama, Mary Goodloe a 16 year old female born in Alabama, Robert A. Goodloe a 14 year old male born in Alabama, Jas M. Goodloe a 12 year old male born in Alabama, and Susan T. Goodloe a nine year old female born in Alabama.

According to the 1860 Franklin County, Alabama Slave Census, Robert A. Goodloe owned 156 black slaves that he used on his cotton plantation. He was also listed in the 1866 Alabama State Census as a resident of Franklin County, Alabama.

John Calvin Goodloe

Colonel John Calvin Goodloe was born on May 21, 1817, and he died at 77 years old on February 25, 1895, at Cherokee in Colbert County, Alabama. He was the husband of Harrietta A. Goodloe; his parents were David Short Goodloe and Mary Louisa Hill Goodloe. John and Harrietta had a son that they also named David Short Goodloe (1846-1866) who is buried at Oakwood Cemetery in Tuscumbia, Colbert County, Alabama (Find a Grave Memorial Number 75281052).

Colonel John Calvin Goodloe

Harriett A. Goodloe was born on March 21, 1826, and died on November 12, 1900; she was the wife of John Calvin Goodloe. She had one son, David S. Goodloe. John Calvin Goodloe was buried in the Oakwood Cemetery at Tuscumbia in Colbert County, Alabama (Find a Grave Memorial Number 75281088).

According to the 1850 Franklin County, Alabama Census, John C. Goodloe was a 32 year old white male who was born in North Carolina. He is listed with his wife Harriett A. Goodloe who was 39 and born in North Carolina; Kemp Goodloe a 11 year old male born in Alabama; Mary Goodloe a nine year old female born in Alabama; William Goodloe a six year old male born in Alabama; David Goodloe a four year old male born in Alabama; and, Calvin Goodloe a two year old male born in Alabama.

The 1850 Franklin County, Alabama Slave Census says that John C. Goodloe owned 101 black slaves while another source says he owned 75 slaves. In the 1850 Franklin County, Alabama Agricultural Census, John C. Goodloe owned 850 acres of improved land and 1400 acres of unimproved land. The cash value of his farm was given as $30,000 with his implements and machinery estimated at $3000; he also had $6,520 worth of livestock.

According to the 1860 Western Division, Franklin, Alabama, United States Census, John C. Goodloe was 40 year old white male born in North Carolina. Also listed is his wife Harriett T Goodloe a 36 year old born in Alabama; James Camp Goodloe a 21 year old male born in Alabama; Mary H. Goodloe an 18 year old female born in Alabama; Wm. H. Goodloe a 16 year old male born in Alabama; David L. Goodloe a 14 year old male born in Alabama; John C. Goodloe a 12 year old male born in Alabama; Robert P. Goodloe a 10 year old male born in Alabama; Rebecca A. Goodloe an eight year old female born in Alabama; Paul T. Goodloe a six year old male born in Alabama; Edward L. Goodloe a four year old male born in Alabama; and, Geo Cracraft a 22 year old male born in Virginia.

In 1860 Franklin County, Alabama Slave Census, John C. Goodloe is listed as owning 100 black slaves. John Calvin Goodloe is also listed on page 14 of the 1866 Alabama State Census of Franklin County, Alabama, with Certificate Number 44317.

From the 1850 cash valve of John Calvin Goodloe at $39,520, his cash value after the Civil War dropped to $4,500. According to the 1870 Franklin County, Alabama Agricultural Census, John C. Goodloe's real estate value was $1500, and his personal estate value was only $3000. Many cotton plantation owners in North Alabama lost their fortune and slaves after the Civil War; however, some were able to hold on to large tracts of land which would eventually provide wealth to their future family generations.

Colonel John Calvin Goodloe House, Tuscumbia, Alabama
Alex Bush on August 30, 1935, Library of Congress.

Albert Gallatin Goodloe

Albert Gallatin Goodloe, the son of David Short and Mary Hill Goodloe, was born in North Carolina, on April 13, 1812. On April 23, 1833, Albert married Susan Mattison in Franlkin County, Alabama; she was born on July 31, 1803. They had five children while living in Franklin County: William Paul Goodloe, Calvin Goodloe, Charles Goodloe, Emma Goodloe, and Joseph M. Goodloe.

On December 8, 1834, Albert G. Goodloe purchased lot number 182 in the Town of Coldwater or Tuscumbia, Alabama. The lot was originally owned by James Jackson with certificate number 7405 (Cowart, 1985).

The 1840 Franklin County, Alabama Census lists Albert G. Goodloe on page number 243. According to the 1850 Franklin County, Alabama Census, House Number 489, Albert Goodloe is listed as a 38 year old white male born in North Carolina. Also given is Jesse Allen a 35 year old male born in Tennessee, Mary Allen a 24 year old female born in Tennessee, and Samuel Allen a six year old male born in Tennessee.

In the 1850 Franklin County, Alabama Agricultural Census, Albert Goodloe owned 200 acres of improved land and 440 acres of unimproved land. The cash value of his farm was $2,500 with his implements and machinery valued at $400. Albert's livestock was valued at $1,210.

On page 28 of the 1855 Franklin County, Alabama State Census, Albert G. Goodloe is listed as living in the county. He and his wife must have gone west after the census was taken.

In 1855 as did a lot of other plantation owners in Franklin County, Alabama, Albert and Susan moved west to seek wealth in more productive cotton country. They settled in Bexar County, Texas, near Cibolo Creek where they purchased 1500 acres of land. In 1856, Susan Goodloe registered a cattle brand in Bexar County, Texas, stating that she and her husband lived on Cibolo Creek. Susan inherited the estate of her brother Smith Mattison and used the money to buy more property in the eastern portion of Bexar County. In 1857, Albert G. Goodloe paid taxes on 1,500 acres in the Maria Jose Rodriguez survey in Bexar County.

During the Civil War, William Paul Goodloe and Calvin Goodloe were in the Confederate States of America, Fourth Texas Infantry as soldiers in the Mustang Greys of Bexar County, Texas. They were sent to Richmond, Virginia, where their regiment was officially organized on September 30, 1861. In October 1861, the Fourth Infantry was placed under the command of Texan John Bell Hood.

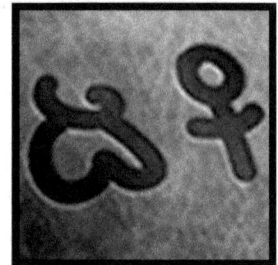

In the 1866 Alabama State Census, Albert Goodloe is listed as living in Franklin County, Alabama, on page 85 with certificate number 47933. Apparently, Albert and Susan must have returned to Alabama shortly after the Civil War ended.

In 1870, Charles Goodloe was given power of attorney to sell Albert G. and Susan Goodloe's Texas property. Some believe that it was about the same time that Albert Gallatin and Susan Goodloe returned to present-day Colbert County, Alabama. In 1870, Charles sold the 1,500 acre Goodloe plantation in Bexar County, Texas, afterwhich he and his brothers moved to San Antonio, Texas.

Susan M. Goodloe died on November 6, 1886, and she was buried in the Rutland Cemetery at Cherokee in Colbert County, Alabama. The inscription on her tombstone identified Susan as the "Wife of A.G. Goodloe." Albert Gallatin Goodloe died at the residence of his daughter Mrs. H. C. Barton near Barton, Alabama, on January 1, 1887.

Hailey, James T.

According to the 1850 Franklin County, Alabama, United States Census, James T. Hailey was a 46 year old white male born in North Carolina. He was listed with Rebecca Hailey a 34 year old female born in North Carolina, Leonidus B. Hailey a 16 year old male born in North Carolina, William A. Hailey a 14 year old male born in North Carolina, Josephine Hailey a 12 year old female born in North Carolina, Mark R. Hailey a five year old male born in North Carolina, and Granberry Hailey a two year old male born in North Carolina.

According to the 1850 Franklin County, Alabama Agricultural Census, James T. Hailey owned 450 acres of improved land and 170 acres of unimproved land. The cash value of his farm was $7,000 with his implements and machinery valued at $250. James' livestock was valued at $2,200. In 1850, James T. Hailey owned some 54 black slaves.

According to the 1860 Franklin County, Alabama, United States Census, James T. Hailey is a 55 year old white male born in North Carolina. Living in his household is Rebecca Hailey a 44 year old female born in Virginia, L. B. Hailey a 25 year old male born in North Carolina, Wm. Hailey a 23 year old male born in North Carolina, Josaphine Hailey a 19 year old female born in Alabama, Mark B. Hailey a 14 year old male born in Alabama, and Wm. J. Askews a 23 year old male born in Alabama. According to the 1860 Franklin County, Alabama, Slave Schedule, James T. Hailey owned 75 black slaves.

Harris, Benjamin

There were two "Benjamin Harris" cotton planters and slave owners in Franklin County, Alabama. One Benjamin Harris was born May 12, 1786, and the other Benjamin Harris was born September 9, 1788. There was a Benjamin Harris in the 1820, 1830, and 1840 censuses of Franklin County, but it could be either one of the two.

Benjamin Harris-1

Benjamin Harris was born in Grainger County, Tennessee, on May 12, 1786, and he died on June 28, 1858, at Russellville in Franklin County, Alabama. His father Peter Harris was born on March 1, 1750, in Virginia and died on April 6, 1832, in Grainger County, Tennessee. His mother Honour Harris was born in 1753 and died on November 25, 1835, in Grainger County, Tennessee. Peter and Honour Harris had 14 children: Samuel, Thomas, Sarah, Mary Caroline, Peter, James G., Nehemiah, William, John, Benjamin, Jesse, Isaac, Elizabeth, and Keziah. John and Benjamin were twins.

Benjamin first married Lucinda who died in 1825, and they had three girls: Harriet, Mary, and Lucy. Benjamin Harris' second wife was Nancy Brigham who was born on March 11, 1796, at Sudbury, Massachusetts, and died on June 14, 1878, at Russellville in Franklin County, Alabama. Nancy's father was Joseph Brigham who was born on September 26, 1764, and died January 17, 1842 at Sudbury, Massachusetts. Her mother was Rebecca Haynes who was born on July 29, 1770, and died on January 12, 1853, at Sudbury, Massachusetts.

Benjamin and Nancy had two children: John C. Harris who was born in 1836; and, Rebecca Brigham Harris Sargent who was born on January 17, 1842, in Franklin County, Alabama. Rebecca married Harvey Gholson Sargent on April 7, 1868, at Russellville in Franklin County, Alabama. According to the 1850 census, the Sargent family owned 23 black slaves. Rebecca died June 11, 1914, at Pocahontas, Alabama with burial in the Knights of Pythias Cemetery in Russellville. Rebecca Harris Sargent was a graduate of Ward Seminary in Nashville and was the author of several short stories relating to the Confederacy (Find a Grave Memorial Number 58712692).

Beginning on September 13, 1809, through August 29, 1856, Benjamin Harris entered some 4,730 acres of land in Lawrence, Lauderdale, Limestone, Franklin, and present-day Colbert Counties of Alabama. From September 14, 1818, through February 22, 1830, Benjamin Harris entered some 560 in Lawrence County. From March 30, 1818, through July 27, 1831, he entered some 240 acres in Lauderdale County. The Old Land Records of Lauderdale County by Margaret Cowart says that Benjamin Harris is from Tennessee.

From September 13, 1809, through February 10, 1818, Benjamin Harris entered some 449 acres in Limestone County. From November 7, 1818, through August 29, 1856, Benjamin entered some 1,895 in Franklin County. From October 5, 1836, through April 11, 1838, he entered some 1,140 acres of land in present-day Colbert County, Alabama (Cowart, 1984, 1985, 1986, 1991, and 1996).

Benjamin Harris testified in support of Samuel Meredith's application for bounty land for serving in the War of 1812. Benjamin stated that he served in the same unit of the Tennessee Militia as Samuel Meredith.

According to the 1820 census of Lawrence County, Alabama, Benjamin Harris owned 26 black slaves. In 1822, Benjamin Harris was the deputy surveyor of the southern district of Alabama; he was a friend of Andrew Jackson.

In the 1830 census of Lawrence County, Alabama, Benjamin Harris had five people living in his household, one white male between 40 and 50 years old, one white male between 20 and 30 years old, one white male under five years old, one white female between 20 and 30 years old, and one white female between five and ten years old.

By 1840, Benjamin Harris lived some six miles east of Russellville in Franklin County, Alabama. According to the 1850 Franklin County, Alabama, United States Census, Benjamin Harris was a 62 year old white male born in Tennessee. In his household number 623 was Nancy Harris a 33 year old female born in Massachusetts, Mary H. Harris a 22 year old female born in Alabama, Lucy W. Harris a 20 year old female born in Alabama, John C. Harris a 15 year old male born in Alabama, Rebecca Harris an eight year old female born in Alabama, and E. H. Crocker a 26 year old male born in Massachusetts. Nancy had been married to Daniel H. Crocker (1797-1825), and E. H. Crocker was her stepson.

The 1850 Franklin County, Alabama Slave Schedule indicates that Benjamin Harris owned 80 black slaves. In the 1850 Franklin County, Alabama Agricultural Census, Benjamin Harris owned 1,000 acres of improved land and 2,540 acres unimproved land. The cash value of his farm was $21,000 including $1,080 worth of implements and machinery. Benjamin's livestock was valued at $3120.

The 1855 Franklin County, Alabama State Census lists Benjamin Harris and Nancy Harris. In the 1860 United States Census of the Eastern Subdivision of Franklin County, Alabama, with household identification number 50, Nancy Harris is a 64 year old white female who was born in Massachusetts. Also listed is John C. Harris a 24 year old male born in Alabama, Rebecca Harris an 18 year old female born in Alabama, and James G. Harris a 78 year old male born in Virginia. By 1860, Benjamin Harris is probably deceased.

Page number 20 of the 1870 Franklin County, Alabama, United States Census of household identification number 136 gives Nancy Harris as a 74 year old white female born between 1795 and 1796 in Massachusetts. Also listed is John Harris a 34 year old male born in Alabama, Gilbert Harris a 14 year old male born in Alabama, Jemima Harris a 11 year old female born in Alabama, Catharine Harris a 24 year old female born in Alabama, Luella Harris a nine year old female born in Alabama, Brice Harris a six year old male born in Alabama, Percy Harris a one year old male born in Alabama.

Benjamin Harris-2

The other Benjamin Harris of Franklin County, Alabama, was born on September 9, 1788, in Goochland County, Virginia. Benjamin Harris married Minerva Tazewell Jones Harris who was born on August 17, 1801, in North Carolina, and died on November 1, 1859, in Panola County, Texas.

According to the 1850 census, it appears that Benjamin Harris and Minerva Tazewell Jones Harris had three children:

1) Benjamin Harris, Junior was born about1828.
2) Sarah J. Harris was born circa 1832.
3) Minerva Amanda (Mannie) Harris Kelley was born May 23, 1835, and she married David Campbell Kelley on January 4, 1854. Mannie became a missionary to China on March 19, 1854. Mannie died May 15, 1867, and was buried in the Cedar Grove Cemetery at Lebanon in Wilson County, Tennessee (Find a Grave Memorial Number 8062460).

Benjamin Harris died on July 29, 1847, in Franklin (Colbert) County, Alabama. He was buried in the Cross Family Cemetery at Cherokee in present-day Colbert County, Alabama. The inscription on his tombstone reads: "IN MEMORY OF BENJAMIN HARRIS, Born in Goochland County, VA., Sept. the 9th, 1788, Departed this life in Franklin County, Alabama, July the 29th, 1847,

Aged 58 years 10 months & 20 days, An Honest Man The Noblest Work of God" (Find a Grave Memorial Number 102044873).

According to the 1850 Franklin County, Alabama, United States Census, house number 354, Manerva J. Harris is a 50 year old white female born in Virginia and widow of Benjamin Harris of Franklin County, Alabama. Also listed in the household is Benjamin Harris a 22 year old male born in Virginia, Sarah J. Harris an 18 year old female born in Virginia, Manerva A. Harris a 15 year old female born in Virginia, and Phobe Harris a 100 year old female born in Virginia. Phobe Harris is probably the mother of Benjamin Harris and lived in the household of her daughter-in-law.

According to the 1850 Franklin County, Alabama, Slave Census, Minerva Harris owned 24 black slaves. The 1850 Franklin County, Alabama Agricultural Census says that Minerva Harris owned 380 acres of improved land and 260 acres of unimproved land. The cash value of her farm was $8000 with implements and machinery valued at $40. In addition, her livestock was valued at $770.

According to the 1860 census (enumerated in July 1860) of Beat 1, Panola, Texas, Post Office Bethany, Family Number 166, Minerva Harris was a

58 year old white female born in North Carolina. Also living in her home in 1860, Ben Harriss was 32, Sallie Harriss was 26, Sallie Betty was 9, Mary Betty was 8, Matilda Betty was 3, Benjamin Betty was 2, and J. F. Craddock was 25.

Since Minerva Harris was listed in the 1860 census, she probably died in 1860 but her tombstone gives the year of death as November 1, 1859; therefore, the date of death may be off by one year. Minerva's cause of death is listed as bronchitis; she is buried in the Grand Bluff Cemetery in Panola County, Texas (Find a Grave Memorial Number 79659343).

Hobgood, Elijah

Elijah Hobgood was born circa 1756. Elijah was the son of John Hobgood (-1783) and Frances Morgan (1728-c. 1810) of Halifax County, North Carolina. John and Frances had 11 children born in Halifax County, North Carolina: Phereba 1750, Lemuel 1754, Elijah 1756, Micajah 1758, Samuel 1760, Frances 1762, John 1764, Elizabeth 1766, Ruthemah 1768, William 1770, and Penelope 1772. After the death of John Hobgood in 1783, the Hobgood plantation and slaves in North Carolina were divided among the children of John and Frances.

In 1790 census of Halifax County, North Carolina, Elijah Hobgood was listed with his brother Lemuel Hobgood. Ten years later in 1800, Elijah was living in Halifax County, North Carolina, with his brothers Lemuel and Micajah. In 1810, Elijah Hobgood was living in Halifax County, North Carolina near his brother Micajah Hobgood. About 1818, Elijah and his sons Elijah Jr and John migrated to Madison County, Alabama. According to the 1830 Madison County, Alabama, United States Census, Elijah Hobgood and his son Elijah Hobgood Jr. were living in Madison County. Elijah Hobgood, Sr. died after 1830 in Alabama.

Both Elijah Hobgood, Jr. and his brother John H. Hobgood migrated from Madison County to Franklin (Colbert) County, Alabama. In 1840, Elijah, Jr. and John are found in the 1840 Franklin County, Alabama, United States Census, and are listed as owners of black slaves.

John Hobgood

John Hobgood was the son of Elijah Hobgood, Sr. The tombstone of John Hobgood indicates that he was born on October 10, 1800, in Halifax County, North Carolina; he married Martha Ann Alsobrook who was born on May 20, 1810. John and Martha had the following children:

1) John Hobgood Jr., who according to census records, was born November 25, 1836, and died July 12, 1855.
2) William H. Hobgood was, born about 1838 in Tuscumbia, Alabama, and he died after 1880 in Colbert County, Alabama. William married Virginia Williams about 1869 in Colbert County, Alabama. Virginia Williams Hobgood (1839-1891) is buried in LaGrange Cemetery, Leighton, Alabama.
3) Sarah Anne Hobgood Hicks was born in 1844 in Tuscumbia, and she died in 1894 in Colbert County, Alabama. Sarah married David Waters Hicks about 1860 in Colbert County.
4) Robert Hobgood was born in Tuscumbia, Alabama, in May 1845, and died after 1910 in Alabama. Robert married Willie Anna Hobgood January 31, 1872 in Colbert County, Alabama. Willie Anna Hobgood Hobgood, born about 1847 in Louisiana and died November 17, 1915, is buried in Confederate Memorial Park Cemetery at Mountain Creek in Chilton County, Alabama.
5) Charlotte Hobgood was born on April 24, 1846, in Tuscumbia, Alabama and died November 1, 1926 at LaGrange. She never married and is buried in Oakwood Cemetery at Tuscumbia, Alabama.

According to the 1840 Franklin County, Alabama Census, John Hobgood household had four white inhabitants and he owned 29 black slaves. By the time of the 1850 Franklin County, Alabama Slaves Census, John Hobgood owned 55 black slaves.

According to the 1850 Franklin County, Alabama Census, United States Census, House Number 741, John Hobgood is a 50 year old white male born in North Carolina. Also listed in the household is Martha Hobgood a 40 year old female born in North Carolina, John Hobgood a 14 year old male born in Alabama, William N. Hobgood a 12 year old male born in Alabama, Robert

Hobgood a nine year old male born in Alabama, Sarah Hobgood a seven year old female born in Alabama, and Charlotte Hobgood a five year old female born in Alabama.

According to the 1850 Franklin County, Alabama, Agricultural Census, John Hobgood owned 800 acres of improved land and 200 acres of unimproved land. His estate was valued at $10,000 with $1,000 worth of farm equipment. John also owned $3,000 worth of livestock.

According to page 209B of the 1860 Franklin County, Alabama, Slave Schedule, John Hobgood was deceased and his heirs including William and three others were given ownership of John's 95 black slaves. John Hobgood died a year before the census on February 13, 1859.

John's wife Martha Ann Alsobrook Hobgood died on February 27, 1885. They were buried in Hobgood Cemetery near the southeast corner of Muscle Shoals in present-day Colbert County, Alabama, in the southeast ¼ of Section 7 in Township 4 South, Range 10West.

The inscription on John's tombstone is, "In Memory of John Hobgood, born in Halifax Co. Va., Oct 10 AD 1800, Migrated to Alabama AD 1818, Died Feb 13, 1859, Sleep on dear father for thou art blest, God called him home to take thy rest." The inscription for Martha reads, "In Memory of Martha A. Wife of John Hobgood, born May 20, 1810, died Feb 27, 1885, Aged 71 yrs. 9 mos. 7 days" (Find a Grave Memorial Number 102633589).

John Hobgood, Jr. is also buried in the Hobgood Cemetery; his tombstone inscription reads, "Sacred to the memory of John Hobgood Jr., Son of John and Martha A Hobgood, born Nov. 25, 1846, died July 12, 1855. He was a student of LaGrange College at the time of his death." Sister Ann Marah Hicks 1868-1884 tombstone inscription reads, "Yea upon the harp will I praise thee of God My God." If John was actually born in 1846, he would have been only nine years old at the time of his death; however, census records indicate he was born in 1836.

Sarah Hobgood Hicks is buried in the Hobgood Cemetery; her tombstone reads, "Mother Sarah Hobgood Hicks, 1844-1894, A devoted wife and Loving Mother." Her husband David Water Hicks (August 31, 1830-1919) is buried Oakwood Cemetery, Tuscumbia. Sarah and David Water Hicks' son David Bernard Hicks is also buried in Oakwook Cemetery. His tombstone inscription reads, "David Benard, son of D. W. and S. A. Hicks, born Aug 19, 1865, died Nov. 18, 1868, Kindred sprits called the darling, Home to thy Saviors breast, In the land of the blissfull rest."

Elijah Hobgood, Jr.

According to the 1840 Franklin County, Alabama Census, Elijah Hobgood household had nine white inhabitants. The census also states that Elijah owned 33 black slaves.

According to House Number 742 of the 1850 Franklin County, Alabama, United States Census, Elijah Hobgood is a 54 year old white male born in North Carolina. Also listed is Lusinda Hobgood a 42 year old female born in Alabama, John L Hobgood a 20 year old male born in Alabama, James Hobgood a 17 year old male born in Alabama, Elizabeth Hobgood a 13 year old female born in Alabama, Alice Hobgood a 11 year old female born in Alabama, Frances Hobgood a nine year old female born in Alabama, Samuel Hobgood a seven year old male born in Alabama, and Madora Hamilton a six year old female born in Alabama.

According to the 1850 Franklin County, Alabama, Agricultural Census, Elijah Hobgood owned 800 acres of improved land and 300 acres of unimproved land. His estate was worth $15,000 with $1000 worth of farm equipment. Elijah owned $2,000 worth of livestock. According to the 1850 Franklin County, Alabama Slaves Census, Elijah owned 43 black slaves.

Hogan, John

John Hogan (1783-1860) was born to Lemuel Hogan and Mary Smith of North Carolina. John was the grandson of General James A. Hogan and Ruth, the widow of Thomas Norfleet. John Hogan first married Elizabeth Hoskins on April 24, 1811, and they had a son John Hoskins Hogan.

Around 1818, John Hogan moved to Alabama and entered 78 acres in Township 1 South and Range 10 West in Lauderdale County, Alabama, on March 6, 1818. He also entered 160 acres in Township 5 South and Range 7 West in Lawrence County, Alabama, on September 11, 1818. On November 3, 1818, John Hogan entered 80 acres in Township 4 South and Range 10 West in Franklin (Colbert) County, Alabama; he entered another 80 acres adjacent to his property on June 22, 1831. In addition, his brothers James and Smith Hogan entered land in the same area in 1831(Cowart, 1985, 1991 and 1996).

By 1820, John Hogan moved to Franklin County, Alabama, and settled in Tuscumbia. He owned three lots in Coldwater or Tuscumbia; lot 219 was entered on June 12, 1820, and lots 320 and 321 were entered on October 26, 1820 (Cowart, 1985). John had three brothers who also lived in Franklin County, Alabama near Tuscumbia. The brothers are listed in 1820 with the number of their slaves: Smith Hogan owned 46 black slaves; Arthur Hogan owned 63 black slaves; and, James Hogan owned 27 black slaves.

According to the 1820 census of Franklin County, Alabama, John Hogan' household had one white male over 21 years old, three white males under 21 years old, three white females over 21 years old. In the 1820 census, John Hogan is listed as owning 48 black slaves.

On October 11, 1822, John Hogan of Franklin County, Alabama, had a slave named John that escaped. John Hogan said that the slave had attempted to escape before and that the slave's back was considerably scarred by a whipping he had received the day before he ran away.

According to the marriage records of Franklin County, Alabama, John Hogan married the second time to Thermusthus Waters Gist by Reverend J. C. Hicks on November 12, 1833; she was the widow of Levi J. Gist. John's daughter Louisa B. Hogan was married to Colonel Samuel Meredith by Reverend Bester on November 13, 1833. In 1846, John's son John Hoskins Hogan married Thermuthis' daughter Sarah Gist.

On December 16, 1836, John Hogan was listed as a trustee for the The Franklin Female Institute of Tuscumbia along with Peter Walker, John Bradley, Jacob Haigh, Chas. Cooper, Isaac Winston, Burt Harrington, C. T. Barton, M. Tarver, A. S. Christian, G. W. Carroll, and N. J. Huston.

According to the 1850 Franklin County, Alabama, Slave Schedule, John Hogan owned 126 black slaves and listed next to him was his son John H. Hogan. According to the 1850 Franklin County, Alabama, Agricultural Census, John Hogan owned 1,000 acres of improved land and 200 acres of unimproved land with a cash value of $22,000. He also owned $1,000 worth of farming equipment and $5,000 worth of livestock.

About 1864, a Register of Freedmen listed some of the freed slaves of that belonged to John Hogan of Tuscumbia in Franklin County, Alabama. The freed slaves were: Martha Hogan age 9; Laura Hogan age 7; William Hogan age 7; Judith Hogan age 50; Louisa Hogan age 20; Isabella Hogan age 4; Jane Hogan age 5months; and, Rebecca Hogan age 25.

John Hoskins Hogan

John Hoskins Hogan was the son of John Hogan and Elizabeth Hoskins. In October 1846, John Hoskins Hogan married Sarah Gist the daughter of Levi Gist and Thermuthis Waters Gist Hogan. In the 1820 census, Thermuthis' first husband Levi Gist owned 29 black slaves. In other words, John Hoskins Hogan married his dad's step daughter or his stepmother's daughter. According to the 1850 Franklin County, Alabama, Slave Schedule, John Hoskins Hogan owned 40 black slaves.

Hutson/Houston, Nathan J.

Nathan or Nathaniel Hutson/Houston was born in Virginia about 1808. He married Rebecca Bell who was born about 1816 in North Carolina. By 1838, they moved to Alabama and lived in Franklin County. Based on census records, Nathan and Rebecca had seven children:

1) Mary H. Andrews was born on October 15, 1837, and died on February 25, 1917. She was buried in the Alamo Masonic Cemetery at San Antonio in Bexar County, Texas (Find a Grave Memorial Number 15768459).

2) Nellie Huston was born about 1838.
3) Annie E. Smith was born in 1842 and married George Harvey Smith. She died in Manhattan, New York, New York, on October 26, 1908. Annie was listed on her tombstone as 66 years old, and she was buried in the famous national historic landmark Green Wood Cemetery in Brooklyn, New York (Find a Grave Memorial Number 40330166).
4) James W. Huston was listed as 38 years old in the 1880 census of Colbert County, Alabama. At that time, James was married to Suezne who was listed as 31 years old.
5) P. Gratton Huston was born in May 1847, in Alabama, and he married Emma Carlock on November 24, 1870. Gratton died before December 15, 1931, in Wharton County, Texas.
6) Robert B. Huston was born about 1850.
7) A. B. Huston was born about 1855.

On December 16, 1836, Nathan J. Huston is listed as a trustee of the Franklin Female Institute of Tuscumbia. Other trustees include Peter Walker, John Hogun, John Bradley, Jacob Haigh, Chas. Cooper, Isaac Winston, Burt Harrington, C. T. Barton, M. Tarver, A. S. Christian, and G. W. Carroll.

According to the 1850 Franklin County, Alabama, Slave Census, Nathan J. Huston owned 38 black slaves. In the1850 Franklin County, Alabama Agricultural Census, N. J. Huston owned 600 acres of improved land and 409 acres of unimproved land with a cash value of $20,000. His farm equipment was valued at $700 and his livestock at $3000. The 1860 Franklin County, Alabama Slave Census listed Nathan J. Huston as owner of 73 black slaves.

According to the Eastern Subdivision of the 1860 Franklin County, Alabama, United States Census, Nathan J. Houston was a 52 year old white male born in Virginia. He is listed with Rebecca Houston a 44 year old female born in North Carolina, Nellie Houston a 22 year old female born in Alabama, Annie Houston a 19 year old female born in Alabama, James W. Houston a 17 year old male born in Alabama, Gratten Houston a 13 year old male born in Alabama, Robert B Houston a 10 year old male born in Alabama, and A. B. Houston a five year old male born in Alabama.

The 1870 Franklin County, Alabama, United States Census identifies Nathan Huston as a 62 year old white male born in Virginia. Also listed is Rebecca Huston a 54 year old female born in North Carolina, Annie Smith a 24 year old female born in Alabama, Lee Smith a four year old male born in New York, and Sarah Spence a 35 year old female born in Maryland. Based on earlier census records, Annie Huston Smith should have been about 29 years old in the 1870 census records. It is very likely that Lee Smith is the son of Annie Huston Smith.

Jackson, George M.-Moorefields Plantation

George Moore Jackson was born on February 17, 1829, at the Forks of Cypress which was built by his father James Jackson in 1820. The huge plantation home was on a flat ridge which overlooked the beautiful bottom lands

of the fertile valley that lay between Big and Little Cypress Creeks in Lauderdale County, Alabama. Supposedly, the son of Chickamauga Chief Doublehead was also named Doublehead and resided on the land that he sold to James Jackson.

George Moore Jackson was the youngest son of ten children of James Jackson and Sarah "Sallie" Moore McCulloch. James Jackson was born October 25, 1782, in Ireland, and James died on August 17, 1840. Sarah Moore (July 10, 1790-December 24, 1879) was the daughter of George Moore and Mary Walters; Sarah was born in Halifax County, North Carolina.

George Moore Jackson's siblings and half sibling include:
1) Elizabeth McCulloch Kirkman (1809-1871);
2) Mary Steele Jackson Kirkman (1811-March 13, 1833);
3) Martha Jackson Mitchell (1812- August 15, 1879);
4) Ellen Kirkman Jackson Hunt (1814-1897);

5) Andrew Jackson(1816–1838);
6) Sarah Moore Jackson(1819-April 15, 1879);
7) James Jackson (1822-August 14, 1878);
8) William Moore Jackson (1824-December 21, 1899);
9) Jane Jackson (1831-August 1839).

George Moore Jackson married Sarah Cabell Perkins on October 4, 1853; she was born on May 23, 1834. Sarah was the daughter of William O'Neal Perkins (1791-1840) and Pocahontas Rebecca Bolling Meredith (1806-1838). George and Sarah had the following children:

1) Alexander Jackson (July 4, 1854-1940);
2) Elizabeth Jackson (1856-1861);
3) Jane Jackson, born April 10, 1858, married George Washington Polk of Tennessee and died in 1947;
4) Martha Jackson (1860-1862);
5) Rufus Polk Jackson (1861-August 24, 1861);
6) Kate Brekenridge was born November 24, 1863;
7) Richard Harrison Jackson (1866–1971) who died at 105 years old became a United States Navy commander of the Pacific battlefleet and four star Admiral.

George Moore and Sarah Jackson moved to Franklin County where they built Moorefield's Plantation between Tuscumbia and Leighton. Their home was near Tuscumbia in present-day Colbert County, Alabama, and was named "Moorefields." During the civil war, the Moorefields plantation house was used as a hospital, but burned down after the war.

According to the 1860 Eastern Subdivision, Franklin, Alabama, United States Census, George Moore Jackson was a 31 year old white male born in Alabama. Household members included Sarah E. Jackson who was 25 years old, Alex Jackson was five years old, Elizabeth Jackson was four years old, Jane Jackson was two years old, and Martha Jackson was four months old.

According to the 1860 Franklin County, Alabama, Largest Slave Owners, George Moore Jackson owned 93 black slaves. In 1860 George Jackson's real estate value was $31,000.00 and his personal estate value was $75,000.00.

Shortly after the Civil War, George Moore Jackson estate value had dropped drastically. According to the 1870 census, George Jackson's real estate value was $10,000.00 and his personal estate was $1,000.00.

According to the 1870 Colbert County, Alabama, United States Census, George Moore Jackson was a 41 year old white male that lived in Township 3 South and Range 10 West with the post office being Tuscumbia. Included in his household was Alex Jackson who was 15 years old, Janie Jackson was 12 years old, Rufus Jackson was nine years old, Kate Jackson was six years old, Harrisson Jackson was four years old, Rosa Lawlep was 26 years old, Thomas Shott was 75 years old, Francis Shott was 30 years old, John Shott was five years old, James Jackson was 48 years old, Elizabeth Jackson was 38 years old, William Jackson was 17 years old, Elenord Jackson was 11years old, Kirkman Jackson was nine years old, Charles Jackson was five years old, Robert Jackson was three years old, Lizzie Jackson was six months old, and Jane Jackson was 52 years old.

According to the 1880 United States Census of South Florence in Colbert County, Alabama, George Moore Jackson was a 57 year old white male widower who was born in Alabama. His father's birthplace was listed as Ireland, and his mother's birth place was listed as North Carolina. His occupation was listed as a farmer. Family members living in his household included R. T. Jackson age 18, Katie B. Jackson age 16, R. H. Jackson age 14, and Jane Jackson age 22.

George Moore Jackson and his wife Sarah Cabell Perkins are buried in a double grave at the Jackson Cemetery in Lauderdale County, Alabama. George died in 1883 in Colbert County and is buried in the Jackson Cemetery in Lauderdale County, Alabama (Find a Grave Memorial Number 31708735). Sarah died in March 16, 1868 and was buried at Forks of Cypress Cemetery in Lauderdale County, Alabama (Find a Grave Memorial Number 31712072).

Jackson, William Moore-Glencoe Plantation

William Moore Jackson was born on June 19, 1824, in Lauderdale County, Alabama, to James Jackson, Sr. (1782-1840) and Sarah Moore Jackson (1790- 1879). On June 16, 1846, in Franklin County, Alabama, William Moore Jackson married Thermuthis Waters McKiernan (1809-September 5, 1902), the daughter of Major Bernard McKiernan and Mary Anthony Waters McKiernan of Colbert County, Alabama. Based on census and other records, William and Thermuthis had the following children:

1) Sarah Moore Jackson (1847-1910);
2) James Jackson (July 20, 1848-March 1, 1937);
3) Lurano Jackson born (1849);
4) Susannah McKiernan Jackson (December 1, 1849-January 2, 1930);
5) Mary McKiernan Jackson (1851-October 1914);
6) Martha Jackson (February 26, 1853-September 1853);
7) Thomas Hunt Jackson (September 25, 1854-December 27, 1925);
8) Barnard M. Jackson (1856-December 28, 1901);
9) Ellen Hunt Jackson (1858-January 24, 1941);
10) Temustic M. Jackson (February 2, 1859-1866);
11) Elizabeth McCulloch Jackson (1861-August 8, 1947);
12) Jane Jennie Jackson (February 1862-May 11, 1950

William Moore Jackson named his plantation Glencoe after the name of his father's favorite racing horse that was named Glencoe. William Moore Jackson's sons James, Thomas H., and Bernard M. Jackson all became attorneys-at-law.

According to the 1850 Franklin County, Alabama, United States Census, House Number 763, William Moore Jackson is a 26 year old white male born in Tennessee. Also listed in the household is Thimathey Jackson a 22 year old female born in Alabama, Sarah Jackson a two year old female, Jamey Jackson a two year old male, and Lurano Jackson a one year old female.

According to the 1850 Franklin County, Alabama, Slave Census, William Jackson owned 34 black slaves. In the 1850 Franklin County, Alabama, Agricultural Census, William Jackson owned 500 of improved land and 900 acres of unimproved land worth $15,000. In addition, he owned $1500 worth of farm equipment and $2,500 worth of livestock.

The 1860 Eastern Subdivision, Franklin County, Alabama, United States Census lists William Moore Jackson as a 36 year old white male born in Alabama. Also listed in 1860 is Thermather W. Jackson a 32 yearold female, Sarah Jackson a 13 year old female, James Jackson a 12 year old male, Susannah M. Jackson a ten year old female, Mary Jackson a eight year old female, Thomas H. Jackson a five year old male, Barnard M. Jackson a four year old male, Ellen Jackson a two year old female, and Temustic M. Jackson a one year old female. All of the family was listed as being born in Alabama.

By the 1860 Franklin County, Alabama, Slave Schedule, William Moore Jackson owned 60 black slaves. His real estate value was $110,000.00 and his personal estate value was $140,000.00. By the 1870 census, William Moore Jackson had lost his fortune; his real estate value was only $15,000 with a personal value of $1,000, but he was still listed as a planter.

According to the 1870 Colbert County, Alabama, City of Tuscumbia, United States Census, William Moore Jackson is a 45 year old white male born in Alabama. Also listed in 1870 is Thermuthis Jackson a 40 year old female, Sarah Jackson a 22 year old female, James Jackson a 21 year old male, Susanah Jackson a 19 year old female, Thomas Jackson a 15 year old male, Bernard Jackson a 13 year old male, Ellen Jackson a 12 year old female, Elizabeth Jackson a nine year old female, Jane Jackson an eight year old female, Ann York a 21 year old female, William York a four year old male, and Annie York a female baby. All residents of the household were born in Alabama.

The following is found in the "History of Alabama," Volume 3, by Thomas M. Owen and Marie Bankhead Owen, 1921, "William Moore Jackson, planter and public official… son of James and Sarah Moore McCollough Jackson, of "The Forks" Florence; brother of James Jackson Jr. He was educated by private tutors; entered the University of North Carolina; studied law at the Transylvania University, KY; but engaged more extensively in cotton planting than in the practice of his profession. He acquired large tracts of land both in Alabama and Arkansas and during the latter part of the War of Secession, he caused to be burned three hundred bales of cotton, in Arkansas, to prevent it falling into the Federal hands. In 1857, he represented Colbert County in the legislature; in the senate, 1859-65, when the U.S. Military forces took charge of the administration of affairs in Alabama. Later he was a notary public in Lauderdale. He was a Democrat, a member of the convention that seceded from the Union and voted for secession. His plantation home was alternately headquarters for Confederate and Federal officers. A division of Gen. Hood's army was encamped on his plantation, at one time, while Generals Stephen D. Lee, Frank Cheatham and A.T. Stewart were guests at his house. Married: June 16, 1846, to Thermis Waters, daughter of Bernard and Marianne (Waters) McKiernan, of Hagerstown, MD. Children: 1. Sarah M., married O.H. Bynum; 2. Mary M. married Edward Winston; 3. James married Althea Wardlaw; 4. Thomas Hunt, married Rebecca McKay; 5. Bernard M.; 6. Susannah M. married John Harris. Last residence Florence."

Also found in the Northern Alabama Historical and Biographical is the following, "JACKSON, William Moore, was born in Lauderdale County, this State, June 19, 1824. His parents were James and Sarah (Moore) Jackson, the former a native of Ireland, and the latter of the State of North Carolina. Mrs. Jackson was a greatgranddaughter of the celebrated James Moore, who, in his lifetime, filled the offices of governor, at different times, of the colonies of both North and South Carolina. James Jackson came to this county from Nashville, Tenn., in 1810, and here followed planting and stock breeding the rest of his life, dying in 1840, at the age of 58 years. He was a Whig in politics, represented this county several terms in the Legislature, and the district two or three times in the State Senate, of which he was twice president. He was one of the pioneers of Lauderdale. In fact, he was one of the company of five that composed the very first settlers of the county. The subject of this sketch was educated at the University of North Carolina, and subsequently studied law at Transylvania University, Lexington. Ky. Since 1848 up to the present time, he has been interested in cotton planting, both in Alabama and Arkansas. He has made his home in Florence since 1875. He was the representative to the Legislature from Franklin County, session of 1857; was in the Senate from 1859 to 1S65: and was a member until the time of the military government. He has always taken an active interest in politics, is a good Democrat, and has represented his party many times as delegate to the various State and Congressional Conventions. He is at present living in virtual retirement, though discharging the duties of Notary Public. He was married in Franklin County (now Colbert) in 1840, to Miss Thirmnthies McKiernan, daughter of Maj. Bernard McKiernan, an extensive planter of Colbert. Mr. Jackson's sons, James, Thomas H. and B. M. are all attorneys at law" (DeLand and Smith, 1888).

According to home.earthlink.net, William Moore Jackson, "Devoted much of his life to public service, eight years of which were given to his state, Alabama, as a member of the Legislature. He was an original secessionist-one of the convention that voted Alabama out of the Union. Confederate Senator from 1861 to 1865. His furnishing uniforms for the "Franklin Rifles" company, at his own expense; the burning of three hundred bales of cotton to avoid it falling into the hands of the federals; and, whenever the opportunity presented itself, to encourage the support of the Confederate Cause. His plantation estate on the Tennessee River a few miles above Tuscumbia, named in honor of his father's famous race horse Glencoe, was used alternately by the Federals and Confederates for headquarters."

William Moore Jackson died December 21, 1899, at Florence in Lauderdale County, Alabama. He is buried in the Jackson Cemetery in Lauderdale County, Alabama (Find a Grave Memorial Number 31712154). His wife Thermuthis Waters McKiernan Jackson died on September 5, 1902, at Tuscumbia in Colbert County, Alabama, at the age of 93 years old and was buried in Florence, Alabama.

Johnson, Jacob Vanpool

Jacob Vanpool Johnson was born in 1786 to Henry Johnson (1738-1815) and Rachel Holeman of Rowan, North Carolina. Henry Johnson married Rachel Holeman in March 1763 in Lancaster, Pennsylvania. Henry was born in Ireland in 1738 and died in 1815 at Springfield in Robertson County, Tennessee. Rachel was born about 1744 and died March 10, 1815, at Springfield in Robertson County, Tennessee. Henry and Rachel Holeman Johnson had the following children:

1) William Johnson was born July 2, 1764, and died July 13, 1864, in Newton County, Mississippi.
2) Thomas Johnson was born on July 4, 1766, and died in 1826 in Robertson County, Tennessee.
3) Henry Johnson was born on October 2, 1768, and died on September 12, 1856, in Robertson County, Tennessee.
4) Elizabeth Johnson Matthews was born on November 30, 1770, in North Carolina, and died on July 14, 1847, in Robertson County, Tennessee.
5) Isaac Johnson was born around 1775 and died in November 1838, in Overton County, Tennessee.
6) Joseph Johnson died in Robertson County, Tennessee.
7) Jacob Vanpool Johnson died in Franklin County, Alabama, in 1863.
8) Rebecca Johnson Crockett was born in North Carolina, and died in Tennessee.
9) Mary "Polly" Johnson Frey was born in 1801 in North Carolina, and died in 1857 in Robertson County, Tennessee.

In 1840, Jacob Vanpool Johnson married Sally Jarman in Humphreys County, Tennessee. Shortly after Jacob and Sally married, they migrated to Franklin County, Alabama. Jacob became a medical doctor.

On January 1, 1849, Jacob V. Johnson entered 160 acres in Township 5 South and Range 15 West in Franklin County, Alabama. Between June 13, 1839 and August 6, 1849, Jacob V. Johnson entered 593 acres in Township 4 South and Range 15 West in Franklin County, Alabama (Cowart, 1985). The land Jacob entered was near the Mississippi state line and had recently been a part of the Chickasaw Nation.

According to the 1850 Franklin County, Alabama, Slave Schedule, Jacob Johnson owned 34 black slaves. Also in 1850 Franklin County, Alabama, Agricultural Census, Jacob owned 450 acres of improved land and 1,311 acres of unimproved land valued at $25,000. His farm equipment was valued at $1,050 with his livestock worth $22,000.

According to the 1850 Franklin County, Alabama, United States Census, household identification number 137, Jacob V. Johnson was a 65 year old white male born in South Carolina. Also listed in his household was Sarah Johnson a 55 year old female born in South Carolina, and Nancy Jarmon a 16 year old female born in Alabama.

According to the 1860 Western Division, Franklin, Alabama, United States Census, household identification number 309, Jacob V. Johnson was a 74 year old white male born in North Carolina. Also listed is Sarah Johnson a 64 year old female born in North Carolina, Andrew P. Parker a 40 year old male born in Alabama, and Rachael Parker a 25 year old female born in Alabama.

Jacob died in 1863 at Allsboro in Franklin County, Alabama. Allsboro is an unincorporated community located in the far western area of Franklin County. The community is about nine miles southwest of the Town of Cherokee, Alabama, near the eastern Mississippi state border.

On April 15, 1864, the will of Dr. Jacob V. Johnson was probated in the probate court of Franklin County, Alabama. The case references Mrs. Sarah Johnson, the widow of Dr. Johnson.

Lane, Isaac-Lane Springs Plantation

Isaac Lane was born on February 12, 1787, in Wake County, North Carolina, and he was the eldest son of Joseph and Pherebee Lane. His father was Joseph Lane who was born on April 6, 1761 in Wake, North Carolina. His mother was Phererre (Pherebee) Hunter who was born on January 25, 1765, in Wake, North Carolina.

On January 11, 1810, Isaac Lane married Mary Hunter Pride (June 14, 1788-October 18, 1862); she was born on June 14, 1788, in Raleigh, North Carolina. Mary's parents were Edward Pride who was born on November 30, 1755, in Chesterfield, Virginia, and died February 7, 1839, at Tuscumbia in Chesterfield County, Virginia. Edward was the son of William Pride and Elizabeth Baugh. Edward married Sarah "Sally" High on October 9, 1781. Sarah High was the daughter of John High, Jr. and Ruth Mitchell. Sarah was born July 28, 1759, in Prince George County, Virginia (later became Dinwiddie County), and she died on October 25, 1821, at Decatur in Morgan County, Alabama.

Isaac and Polly Pride Lane had the following children:
1) Wylie Pope Lane (1810-1837);
2) Sarah Pride Lane Gillespie (1812-1835);
3) Isaac Hunter Lane (1815-1831);
4) Mary Lane Goodloe (1817-1847); Mary Lane Goodloe was the oldest living child and she died at 30 years of age (Find a Grave Memorial Number 125235945).
5) Joseph Lane (1829);
6) Edward Pride Lane (1831-1852).

112

In 1817, Colonel Isaac Lane, Mary (Polly) Pride Lane, their family, and Isaac's parents moved from Wake County, North Carolina, to the area west of Decatur in Morgan County, Alabama, and settled near Trinity. At the time of their move, the Lanes came as a family unit in a wagon train along Indian trails and roads.

From February 23, 1818, through November 16, 1841, Isaac Lane entered some 3,360 acres in Lawrence, Limestone, and Morgan Counties of North Alabama. Over 2,500 acres of the land that Isaac entered were in Morgan County with most of the property in Township 5 South and Range 5 West (Cowart, 1981, 1984, and 1991).

In June 1820, Isaac Lane was a member of the Decatur Land Company that received patents to build the Town of Decatur; therefore, Lane became one of the original founders of Decatur in Morgan County, Alabama.

In the 1830 Morgan County, Alabama, United States Census, Isaac Lane is shown with four children and 36 black slaves. In

Isaac Lane lived in George Colbert's house while his was being built at Lane Springs

1832, Isaac Lane was on the board of directors of the newly created Decatur Bank. In 1834, Colonel Isaac Lane served as a state representative from Morgan County in the Alabama Legislature.

With the removal of the Chickasaw Indians immenient, Isaac Lane, as did many other planters, began looking west to new cotton lands. In the early 1830s, Isaac Lane made contact with Chickasaw Chief George Colbert and negotiated for vast tracts of Chickasaw Nation lands that would be open after their removal. Lane moved to George Town and lived in the home built for George Colbert at Colbert's Ferry at the Natchez Trace crossing of the Tennesse River until his mansion at Lane Springs Plantation could be completed.

From July 27, 1831, through January 1, 1849, Isaac Lane entered some 6,030 acres of land in Franklin (Colbert) County, Alabama. The majority of the property was located in Townships 2 and 3 South and Range 14 West in present-day Colbert County, Alabama (Cowart, 1985 and 1986).

Around 1837, Colonel Isaac and Polly Lane moved to Franklin County and began building their house just west of Natchez Trace. The Lane home and plantation was adjacent to the David Short Goodloe plantation. The Lane Springs Plantation home was a two-storied salt box type house that was built on a hill above Lane Springs. The Lane home was located just a few miles south of the Tennessee River at Colbert's Ferry, west of Natchez Trace, and some six miles north of the Town of Cherokee in Franklin County, Alabama.

By 1850, Isaac Lane became one of the wealthiest cotton planters and largest landholders in North Alabama. According to the 1850 Franklin County, Alabama, Agricultural Census, Colonel Isaac Lane owned 1,400 acres of improved land and 65,000 acres of unimproved land with a value of $50,000. His farm equipment was worth $1,000 and he owned $5,585 worth of livestock. Much of his livestock consisted of many fine racing horses.

According to "Riverton" by Freda S. Daily (2014), on July 7, 1850, Isaac Lane along with James Robb, Robert Brinkley, and John Calvin Goodloe, Sr. whose brother Robert Goodloe was Issac's son-in-law formed the Chickasaw Land Company. Lane entered and bought large property holdings from the early settlers of the area including the lands that were owned by Henry D. Smith. Isaac Lane viewed the area near the mouth of Bear Creek on the Tennessee River as an ideal site for a huge export city for his cotton plantation.

Remains of Isaac Lane home

Not only did Isaac Lane see the potential of the town near the mouth of Bear Creek, but so did the Chickasaw Indians. Very early in their settlement of the area, the Chickasaws had recognized the great importance of the land at the mouth of Ocohappo-Bear Creek in their language.

Scotsman James Logan Colbert married three Chickasaw women, and he had settled near the mouth of Bear Creek to raise his mixed-blood Chickasaw family. Colbert had six half Scots and half Chickasaw sons: William, George, Levi, Samuel, Joseph, and James. Samuel and Joseph died fairly young, but the other four half blood Chickasaw sons became important leaders of the Chickasaw Nation.

Isaac Lane's Chickasaw Land Company surveyed one acre blocks for the Town of Point Smith on the Tennessee River that was named in honor of Henry Smith. The first United States post office at Point Smith was established on December 28, 1846, and Oliver E. Spencer was the first postmaster. The name of the town and post office was officially changed from Point Smith to Chickasaw on May 26, 1851 (Daily, 2014). The name of the town was changed to honor Chickasaw Chief George Colbert and the Chickasaw Indians that had inhabitated the area for hundreds of years.

Issac Lane was interested in developing the town into a great cotton exporting port and industrial city of the Tennessee Valley based on the presence of iron ore. With the iron minerals readily available and the labor of his 150 black slaves, Issac Lane was determined to make his Lane Springs Plantation the crown jewel of northwest Alabama, but rumors of the Civil War put his grandiose plans on hold.

In 1851, Isaac Lane hired William Frye an Austrian artist from Huntsville to paint a twelve by nine foot Lane Family portrait at Lane Springs in Franklin (Colbert) County, Alabama. The frame of the painting was gold leafed. Henry Clay's saddle was a deep rich tan on two blankets of dark red and blue. Noah's coat was tan over black pants and jacket. The Lane Family portrait hung in the parlor of the Lane Springs Plantation Mansion.

Noah (servant), Isaac Lane, Henry Clay (horse), Polly Lane, Venus (dog)

According to the 1850 Slave Schedule of Franklin County, Alabama, Colonel Isaac Lane owned 106 black slaves. As found in the 1860 United States Census Slave Schedules for Franklin County, Alabama, Isaac Lane owned 124 black slaves. Colonel Isaac Lane's will in 1858 indicate that he owned about 150 black slaves. The 1860 census records his estate value at $250,000. Prior to his death in 1862, Isaac Lane owned vast tracts of land in Alabama, Mississippi, Louisiana, Arkansas, and Texas.

On January 19, 1862, Isaac died at the Lane Springs Plantation in Franklin County, Alabama. Isaac and Mary (Polly) Hunter Pride Lane are buried in the Lane Cemetery in present-day Colbert County, Alabama (Find a Grave Memorial Number 40788681).

Colonel Isaac Lane's obituary by Isaac Milner reads, "Died of an attack of paralysis on the 19th of January 1862 at his late residence in Franklin County, Alabama. Colonel Isaac Lane in the 75th year of his age. The deceased was born in Wake County, North Carolina in 1787. Moved to Morgan County, Alabama, in 1818 and to Franklin County, Alabama, in 1837. Colonel Lane was a man of sound practical mind and indomitable energy. Providence crowned his efforts with abundant success, and gave him a large share of this world's goods. By these things he often became 'eyes to the blind, feet to the lame, and a father to the poor.' At his home the itinerant often found a pleasant home, the prophet's room was set apart with 'bed and table, stool and candlestick' and everything to contribute to his comfort; and in more than one instance, when the preacher lost his horse has this generous donor supplied their lack. But these things are not sufficient to purchase salvation. This he felt and acknowledged. He came to the Savior like the poet-In my hand no price I bring, simply to the cross I cling. He came a poor sinner, with the publican's prayer, trusting in him who says, he that cometh unto me, I will in no-wise cast out. May the God of all grace comfort his disconsolate widow."

In 1867 after the Civil War, Colbert County was created from northern Franklin County; the new county was named in honor of the Chickasaw Chief George Colbert of Georgetown and his family. Due to the death of Issac Lane and during the immediate post Civil War period, the Lane Springs Plantation began a steady decline into state of deterioration because of the loss of family leadership and loss of free black slave labor.

About 1887, the Town of Point Smith just west of the Lane Springs Plantation at the mouth of Bear Creek, which was originally visualized by Issac Lane to be a great metropolitian city, had another name change. The town name was changed again from Chickasaw to Riverton. Today, most of the original townsite along the river and dream city of Issac Lane has been flooded by the backwaters of Pickwick Dam, but the small rural community area is still known as Riverton.

Colonel Issac Lane's daughter Mary Lane Goodloe, wife of Robert Atlas Goodloe, was the sole survivor of Isaac and Polly Lane. Mary and her children inherited and received the entire Lane estate, but she could not stop the once glorious plantation from falling into ruin.

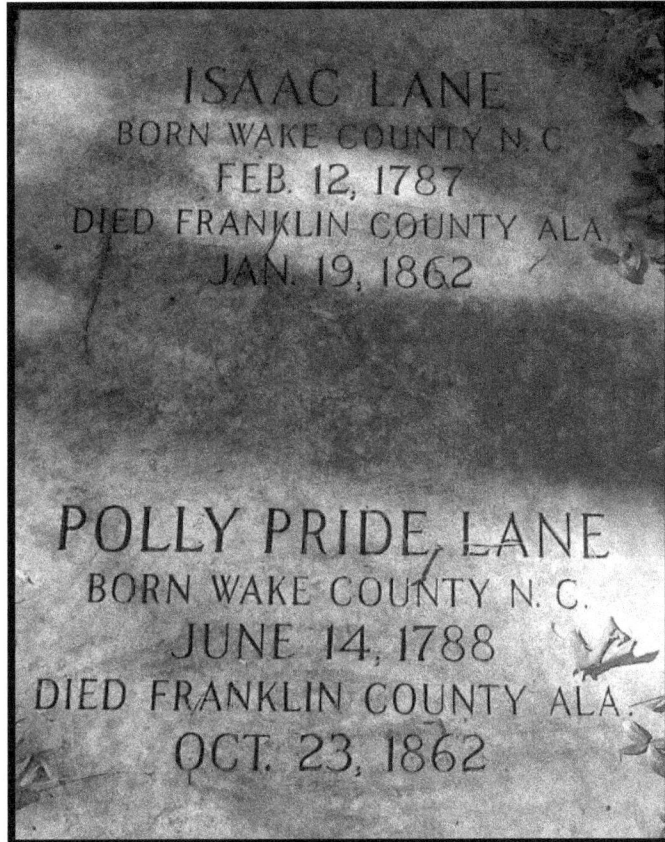

Isaac Lane is buried in the Lane Springs Plantation Cemetery located in the southeast ¼ of the northwest ¼ of Section 2 of Township 3 South and Range 14 West in present-day Colbert County, Alabama, on an original portion of the Lane Springs Plantation. The cemetery was separated into a portion for the black families and the white families of the plantation. Internments in the Lane Springs Plantation Cemetery include:

1) Ike Lane, born January 7, 1875, and died February 7, 1948.
2) Laura J. Lane, born 1897 and died 1965.
3) Nellie Lane, died July 31, 1923, aged 107 years.
4) Annie Lane, died January 17, 1915, aged 44 years.
5) Isaac H. Lane, son of Colonel Isaac and Polly Lane, born in Wake County, North Carolina, born May 30, 1815, died April 1, 1831.
6) Joseph Lane, son of Colonel Isaac and Polly Lane, born July 1, 1829, died July 10, 1829.

7) Sarah Pride Lane Gillespie, wife of William Gillespie and daughter of Colonel Isaac and Polly Lane, born in Wake County, North Carolina, born November 13, 1812, died in Morgan County, Alabama, March 27, 1853.
8) Mary E. Lane, daughter of William F. and Sarah Pride Lane, born November 14, 1834, died August 11, 1836.
9) Isaac Lane born in Wake County, North Carolina, February 12, 1787, died in Franklin County, Alabama, January 19, 1862.
10) Polly Pride Lane born in Wake County, North Carolina, June 14, 1788, died in Franklin County, Alabama, October 23, 1863.
11) Edward P. Lane, son of Edward P. and Mary Lane, born February 24, 1853, died April 3, 1857.
12) Edward Pride Lane, born November 3, 1831, married Mary Agnes Hunter, November 15, 1851, died December 28, 1852.
13) Wylie Pope Lane, son of Isaac and Polly Lane, born in Wake County, North Carolina, October 29, 1810, died in Franklin County, Alabama, June 3, 1837.
14) Infant Goodloe, daughter of J. C. and H. A. Goodloe, born and died April 10, 1843.
15) Little Paul Goodloe, son of Robert A. and Mary Goodloe, born July 19, 1852, died October 20, 1853.
16) Sarah B. Preston, born August 29, 1804, died August 22, 1842.
17) W. H. Preston, died March 10, 1867, aged 67 years.
18) Jesse H. Davis, born March 1, 1799, died April 12, 1849.
19) Nancy A. Walker, died July 9, 1852, aged 88 years.

Malone, John Thomas

In the spring of 1818, some of the Malone family traveled by ox carts from North Carolina, to Franklin County, Alabama. Initially, the Malones settled five to six miles east of Russellville, Alabama, near the Gaines Trace at Tharp Springs. A few months later part of the family moved on to the western part of Franklin County and settled near the eastern boundary of the Chickasaw Nation. This Indian boundary had been established by the Turkey Town Treaty of September 16 and 18, 1816, and followed Cane Creek from the Tennessee River south through Frankfort. .

It appears that six children of John Thomas Malone came to Franklin County, Alabama, shortly after it opened up for settlement. Some of the children traveled with one sister Amy Malone Hester. The possible brothers with Amy were John Pumphrey Malone, James Richard Malone, Goodloe Warren Malone, David Malone, and Robert Blackwell Malone. Their father, John Thomas Malone, was born about 1762, and their mother, Nancy Ann Blackwell Malone, was born about 1766. John Malone and Nancy Ann Blackwell were married on July 25, 1786.

Amy Malone Hester, the older sister of the Malone brothers, was born on March 17, 1789, in Granville County, North Carolina. Amy married William "Buck"Hester who was born January 27, 1780. Amy died on January 23, 1840, at Frankfort in Franklin County, Alabama (Find a Grave Memorial Number 30394006).

James Richard Malone was born on August 13, 1797, in Franklin County, North Carolina. James died August 13, 1879, in Franklin County, Alabama (Find a Grave Memorial Number 29667177).

In November 1818, James Richard, David, and Robert Blackwell Malone entered land in Franklin County, Alabama. On November 10, 1818, James Richard Malone entered 160 acres in Township 6 South and Range 12 West. On November 28, 1818, David Malone entered 80 acres in Township 6 South and Range 12 West. On November 2, 1818, Robert Blackwell Malone entered 320 acres in Township 3 South and Range 10 West.

On June 9, 1820, Robert Malone bought lot number 114 in the Town of Coldwater which is the present-day Town of Tuscumbia in Colbert County, Alabama. On June 6, 1820, Goodloe Warren Malone bought lot 131 at York Bluff in Franklin County which is present-day Sheffield in Colbert County, Alabama. Between November 2, 1818, and December 10, 1830, Robert Malone entered 940 acres in Franklin County, Alabama (Cowart, 1985). On February 11, 1818, John P. Malone entered 80 acres in Township 4 South and Range 5 West (Cowart, 1984).

Goodloe Warren Malone

Goodloe Warren Malone was born on April 17, 1798, in Caswell County, North Carolina. He died on February 18, 1871, in Colbert County, Alabama. Goodloe W. Malone married Mary L. Bate from North Carolina.

Goodloe Warren Malone probably came to Franklin County, Alabama, after his sister and brothers came in the spring of 1818, but for sure, he was in Franklin County by 1820. After the Chickasaw Indians were removed from the portion of the county west of Cane Creek, Goodloe Warren Malone purchased some of his land from Pamela Reynolds; she was the daughter Chickasaw Chief George Colbert. Pamela was the Chickasaw Indian wife of Francis M. Reynolds, a white man who was the son of the Chickasaw Agent Benjamin Reynolds. Pamela owned land in Townships 2, 3, 4 South and Ranges 13, 15 West in Franklin County, Alabama.

In the 1840 Franklin County, Alabama Census, G. W. Malone is listed on page 240. Goodloe Warren Malone Jr., the infant son of Goodloe Warren Malone and Mary L. Bate Malone, was born on December 21, 1844, and died on March 2, 1845. He was buried in the Malone Cemetery at Frankfort in Colbert County, Alabama. Based on census records, Goodloe and Mary had other children besides Goodloe, Jr. including Mary, Anna, Lucy B., and Sarah J.

According to the 1850 Franklin County, Alabama, United States Census, house number 349, Goodloe W. Malone was a 52 year old white male born in North Carolina. Also listed in his household was Mary L. Malone a 30 year old female born in North Carolina, Mary Malone a seven year old female born in Alabama, Anna Malone a five year old female born in Alabama, Lucy B. Malone a three year old female born in Alabama, Sarah J. Malone a two year old female born in Alabama, David G. Burton a 28 year old male born in Alabama, and Ulis G. Burton a 19 year old male born in Alabama.

According to the 1850 Franklin County, Alabama, Slave Schedule, Goodloe Warren Malone owned 116 black slaves. Also in the 1850 Franklin County, Alabama, Agricultural Census, Goodloe W. Malone owned 100 acres of improved land and 1,112 acres of unimproved land with a cash value of his farm being $25,500. The value of his implements and machinery was $1000 and his livestock was valued at $5,045.

The 1855 Franklin County, Alabama, State Census lists G. W. Malone on page 43 with image number 931. After his brother Robert's death, Goodloe W. Malone served as a guardian of his nephew John Lewis Malone, who was the heir of Robert Blackwell Malone.

According to the 1860 Western Division of Franklin County, Alabama, United States Census, household number 150, Goodloe Malone is a 62 year old white male born in North Carolina. Also living in his household is Thos Malone a 28 year old male born in Tennessee, Anna Malone a 14 year old female born in Alabama, and Lucy Malone a 13 year old female born in Alabama.

However, in the 1860 Franklin County, Alabama, Slave Schedule, Goodloe W. Malone is listed with only 80 black slaves. Some of his slaves may have been sent to Mississippi since Goodloe Malone's account book lists about 70 names and ages of black slaves in Mississippi.

In the 1866 Franklin County, Alabama, State Census, Goodloe Warren Malone is listed on page 11and image number 949. In October 1869, Goodloe W. Malone's daughter Lucie Blackwell Malone (b. 1847) and Joseph N. Thompson of Barton Station, Alabama, were married. The marriage connected the Malone and Thompson families.

Goodloe Warren Malone died on February 18, 1871, in Colbert County, Alabama. Goodloe is buried in the Malone Cemetery at Frankfort in Colbert County, Alabama (Find a Grave Memorial Number 102207694).

Malone, John Lewis

John Lewis Malone, the nephew of Goodloe Warren Malone, was born in 1827. John's parents were Robert Blackwell Malone, who was born about 1802, and Eliza Minerva Cockrill (1806-1835). Robert Blackwell Malone and Eliza Cockrill Malone had the following children:

1) Goodloe Warren Malone
2) Armistead Barton Malone
3) Amanda Barton Malone
4) Eliza Cockrill Malone
5) John Lewis Malone (1827-1908)
6) Robert Blackwell Malone Jr.(March 20, 1831-1866)
7) Mary Jane Malone

The wife of John Lewis Malone was Mary Jane Barton Malone (1830-1910); they were married on December 21, 1848. Based on census records, John and Mary Jane Malone had the following children:

1) G. M. Malone (November 23, 1850-May 14, 1873)
2) Armstead Malone
3) Amanda Malone
4) John L. Malone Jr. (1857-1932)
5) M. J. Malone.

According to the 1850 Franklin County, Alabama, United States Census, house number 563, John Lewis Malone was a 23 year old white male born in Alabama. Also listed in the household was Mary J. Malone a 24 year old female born in Alabama, and Robert B. Malone a 19 year old male born in Alabama. Robert B. Malone was probably the younger brother of John Lewis Malone.

According to the 1850 Franklin County, Alabama, Slave Census, John Lewis Malone owned 87 black slaves. The 1850 Franklin County, Alabama, Agricultural Census, states that John L. Malone owned 700 acres of improved land and 200 acres of unimproved land with the cash value of his farm being $18,000. His farm implements and machinery were valued at $400, and his livestock was worth $3,000.

On page 28 of the 1855 Franklin County, Alabama State Census, John L Malone is listed in Franklin County, Alabama. John is also listed on page 19 of the 1866 Franklin County, Alabama State Census.

According to the 1860, Western Division, Franklin County, Alabama, United States Census, household number 105, John L. Malone was a 33 year old white male born in Alabama. Also listed in his household is Mary J. Malone a 30 year old female, G. M. Malone a 10 year old male, Armstead Malone a seven year old male, Amanda Malone a five year old female, Jno L. Malone a three year old male, and M. J. Malone a one year old female. All the family members were born in Alabama.

John L. Malone died in 1908, and he was buried in the Oakwood Cemetery at Tuscumbia in Colbert County, Alabama (Find a Grave Memorial Number 68194244). John Lewis Malone's wife Mary Jane Barton Malone died in 1910, and she was buried in the Oakwood Cemetery at Tuscumbia in Colbert County, Alabama (Find a Grave Memorial Number 68194270).

McKiernan, Bernard-Spring Hill Plantation

Major Bernard McKiernan owned the Spring Hill Plantation on the River Road in the vicinity of present-day Ford City in Colbert County, Alabama. McKiernan Creek in Colbert County is named in honor of the plantation owner of the land in the creek's drainage. The Old River Road crosses McKiernan Creek about one mile west of the present-day crossroads of the River Road and County Line Road at Ford City in Colbert County, Alabama. The creek ran through the large 3,100 acre plantation of the slave owning Bernard McKiernan. Bernard owned land all the way to the Tennessee River including McKiernan's Island in the middle of the river.

Bernard McKiernan married Mariana C. or Mary Anthony Waters who was born in Maryland on March 9, 1792. Their children included: 1) Lawrence Bernard McKiernan, his tombstone in the Spring Hill Plantation Cemetery reads, "Sacred to the memory of McKiernan, Lawrence Bernard, 22 Nov 1825, 17 Feb 1832, son of B. & M. C. McKiernan; In memory of." 2) Charles B. McKiernan, 3) Thermuthis Waters McKiernan (1809-September 5, 1902) and in 1846 she married William Moore Jackson, 4) Susanna McKiernan married General Hugh Dunlap from Franklin, Tennessee, and 5) Judge Bernard F. McKiernan of Memphis, Tennessee, died July 11, 1866.

Prior to Indian removal, black slaves would sometimes escape into Indian Territory. Into the middle and late 1830's, the western part of Franklin County and east of Morgan County was Chickasaw and Cherokee Indian Territory in North Alabama. After the removal of Indian nations from east of the Mississippi River, runaway slaves usually tried to go northward to slave free territory. Many times the run away slave would work in the north earning enough money to pay for the freedom, escape, or release of his family.

The following is a shortend version of a 1978 article entiled "A Slave Family's Struggle for Freedom" by Dr. Kenneth Johnson, a history professor at the University of North Alabama. "Bernard McKiernan owned about 100 black slaves, and he would rent his slaves out to other farmers for a small fee. The former slave Peter Still of the adjacent Gist Plantation eventually earned his personal freedom, but the rest of his family was slaves of Bernard McKiernan. While in the north, Peter made enough money to pay a white man by the name of

Seth Concklin to get a boat and come back to Colbert County, Alabama, to steal his family and bring them north. While on a weekend permission to leave the Spring Hill Plantation, Peter's family who were slaves of Bernard McKiernan attempted an escaped to the north with help from the Underground Railroad that assisted black slaves to get free of bondage. With the aid of the white abolitionist, four members of Peter's family belonging to Bernard McKiernan escaped in a row boat and paddled down the Tennessee River heading for freedom in the north. The slave family was apprehended in Indiana and brought back to the Spring Hill Plantation in Colbert County, Alabama. Seth Concklin was taken prisoner and placed in chains. While traveling back down the Ohio River to stand trial, Concklin tried to escape by jumping to another boat, but he fell in the water and immediately drowned. Former slave Peter Still refused to give up freeing his family. In August 1851, Bernard McKiernan said he would take $5,000 for the freedom of Peter's family. After nearly two long years of unending solicitation in October 1854, Peter Still finally raised the $5,000 to buy his family's freedom. John Simpson, a local Florence merchant, handled the details for Peter, and in January 1855, Peter and his family were reunited in Philadelphia."

Like many other wealthy slave holding plantation owners in northwest Alabama, Bernard McKiernan owned stock in the Tuscumbia, Courtland, and Decatur Railroad which was incorporated on January 13, 1832. The original railroad was called the Tuscumbia Railway that was chartered on January 16, 1830. The first section of railway was about two miles in length and went from downtown Tuscumbia to Tuscumbia Landing at the mouth of Spring or Cold Water Creek on the Tennessee River. The rail line was used to transport cotton from the Town of Tuscumbia to the Tennessee River where it could be loaded on keelboats headed to New Orleans and other profitable markets. Later, the extension to Decatur allowed the North Alabama cotton planters to transport their cotton around the dangerous Elk River Shoals, Big Muscle Shoals, and Little Muscle Shoals to Tuscumbia Landing. Downstream from Tuscumbia Landing, the river was navigable enough to transport cotton to New Orleans.

The Spring Hill Plantation of Bernard McKiernan extended to the middle of the Tennessee River and included islands in the river. During the Civil War, McKiernan's Island was an important skirmish site between the Confederate and Union forces which was described by Norman Farrell of General Phillip Dale Roddy's Cavalry. Farrell was a rebel soldier who wrote about the Civil War fight that occurred in May 1864 near McKiernan's Island. The rebel forces became pinned down behind the cut out bank of a smaller island by the Union forces until dark.

After sunset, some sixty Confederate cavalry soldiers including Norman Farrell made their escape by swimming their horses to McKiernan's Island in the middle of the Tennessee River. During their escape, Farrell's group crossed the dry bed of the western end of the abandoned Big Muscle Shoals Canal which was completed in the 1830's, but had been not used a great deal because the lower Little Muscle Shoals and the upper Elk River Shoals were still impassable. The Confederate forces made their way beyond the dry bed of Big Muscle Shoals Canal where there were a series of smaller islands which were located just east of the mouth of Shoals Creek; these islands were used to ford the river during low water levels. Shoals Creek enters the Tennessee River from the north and is directly across the river from the mouth of McKiernan Creek on the south side of the river in present-day Colbert County. After facing overwhelming odds and being fired on repeatedly, Normar Farrell and the Confederates made it to the south side of the Tennessee River to safety. Norman Farrell is buried at Mt. Olivet Cemetery in Nashville, Tennessee.

According to the 1850 Franklin County, Alabama, Slave Schedule, Benard McKiernan owned 92 black slaves. According to the 1850 Franklin County, Alabama, Agricultural Census, Benard McKiernan owned 1,900 acres of improved land and 1,200 acres of unimproved land worth $50,000. He had $800 worth of farm implements and machinery with $4,400 worth of livestock. One of the slaves of Bernard McKiernan named William Handy was a shoemaker, charged with the duty of making and repairing shoes for the slaves on the Spring Hill Plantation.

On Friday, March 19, 1858, the following obituary of Major Benard McKiernan was printed on page three of the Moulton Democrat of Lawrence County, Alabama. "DIED---At his residence in this county, on Wednesday, after a severe illness, Major Bernard McKiernan, an old and highly respected citizen."

On June 24, 1881, the North Alabamian printed the following on page three. "Mrs. Bernard McKiernan who spends most of her time with her son Maj.

Charles McKiernan, is visiting relatives here. Although eighty-eight years old, she is as cheerful and entertaining as she was many years ago, when she dispensed the most liberal and cordial hospitality to a host of friends. She was always fond of the society of young people by whom she was greatly beloved. Although suffering from a fall received several years since, she is in fair health which we hope she may enjoy for a long time yet."

On Friday, February 13, 1885, the North Alabamian printed the following on page two. "A remarkable woman, Mrs. Mary A. McKiernan, died on Friday last, at the residence of her son, Maj. C. B. McKiernan, not far from Florence, Tuscumbia and Leighton, in Colbert County, Ala. Mrs. McKiernan was born in Maryland, March 9, 1792, and her maiden name was Mary Anthony Waters, a sister of Dr. John Waters, an esteemed and wealthy citizen of Nashville many years ago. She came to this city in early life and lived in the family of Dr. Felix Robertson, who married her sister, and was married at his residence in 1814 to Bernard McKiernan.

Several years after their marriage, they removed to Alabama when the county was inhabited by the Indians. Her husband opened a cotton plantation in what is now Colbert County, and was a successful planter. He was afterwards a commission merchant in New Orleans, living there in the winter, and spending his summers on his plantation. After the death of her husband she lived with her son, Maj. Charles B. McKiernan. She was the mother of eight children, one of whom was Judge McKiernan of Memphis, who died there many years ago. Two of her sons were buried in the clothes bought for their wedding garments, their deaths occurring before their marriage; two years apart, however. One of her daughters was a noted belle in her days, and was married to Gen. Hugh Dunlap, of Louisiana. Another daughter was married to W. M. Jackson, of Florence. Mrs. George W. Donigan, of this city, is a granddaughter of the deceased. All her relatives were highly respectable people.

The memory of the deceased was wonderful. Ninety-three years of age, a physical wreck, yet with a mind as vigorous and clear, and her memory as retentive, both as to past and present events, as it was seventy years ago. Scarcely such another case is on record. Only one month before her death that evidence was taken to prove the death of an old citizen of her county, who died sixty years ago. She gave the history of the family, the names of the children, to whom they were married, when the old man died and where buried, with as much minuteness as though it had occurred at a recent date. She signed her name plainly to the deposition, and the attorney said it was the most remarkable case he had ever witnessed.

Her burial took place on Sunday last, at 11 0'clock in the presence of numerous relatives and friends and a number of old servants, all of whom were devotedly attached to the good old woman. She passed away to the spirit land calmly, peacefully, quietly. She rests from her labors and her works will follow her. A very large circle of relatives and friends in Alabama, Tennessee and other States will mourn the departure of this aged saint."

On Saturday, February 14, 1885, the Florence Gazette on page three printed the following. "On last Friday evening, that sweet-souled lady, Mrs. Mary C. [sic] McKiernan sank to her unending rest, 'as dies a wave along the shore,' at the ripe old age of 92 [sic], at the residence of her son Maj. Chas. B. McKiernan, of Colbert county. She was a native of Maryland, but had lived for a lengthy period in the past, in this State, and had been for some 60 years a consistent member of the Methodist church. Her loving daughter, Mrs. William M. Jackson, was with her, beside her dying bed."

Charles B. McKiernan

Charles B. McKiernan, the son of Bernard and Mary A. McKiernan, was born March 15, 1815, in Nashville, Tennessee. In 1848, Charles married Rebecca Baxter of Clarkesville, Tennessee. Charles and Rebecca's children include Charles B. McKiernan, Jr., and Mrs. George Donnegan of Nashville, Tennessee.

Old black folk tales of Charles McKiernan are not all glorious; it is said that Charles punished one of his black slaves by putting a saddle on the man and riding him until he died. Another story indicates that Charles McKiernan also made some of his black slaves eat watermelons rind and all because he thought they had stolen some of his melons. These are just two short stories as told by the descendants of some of black slaves; however, records of these stories were not found in written historical documents. In addition, the author did not find a record indicating that Charles McKiernan actually owned slaves. Also, Charles did not return to live at the Spring Hill Plantation site in Colbert County,

Alabama, until after the Civil War in 1865 after slavery had been abolished; therefore, these black folk stories may have been falsely attributed to him.

According to the 1870 United States Census of South Florence Post Office in Colbert County, Alabama, Charles McKiernan is listed as the head of the household which contains four blacks and one mulatto boy as follows: Charles McKiernan,, age 54, male, white, farmer, born in Tennessee; Rebecca, age 40, female, white, keeping house, born in Tennessee; Charles, age 21, male, white, clerk, born in Alabama; Mary, age14, female, white, at home, born in Alabama; Mary Jacobsen, age 53, female, white, from Sweeden; Parmelia Bailey, age 40, female, white, born in Alabama; Levi A., age 20, male, white, farm laborer, born in Alabama; John, age 17, male, white, Alabama; Josephine Patrek, age 22, female, black, cook, born in Alabama; Stephen, age 2, male, black, born in Alabama; Harriet McKendan, age 18, female, black, milk maid, born in Alabama; Laura, age 2, female, black, born in Alabama; Sambo, age 5/12, male, mulatto, born in Alabama. According to the 1870 census of Colbert County, some 30 black and mulatto folks with the last name McKiernan are listed as living in the area of South Florence Post Office.

On Saturday, July 25, 1890, the death of Major Charles B. McKiernan was reported on page three of the Florence Times, "An Old Citizen Gone. Major Charles B. McKiernan, an old and well known citizen of Colbert, died at his home, Spring Hill, in that county, on the 18th instant, at the advanced age of 75 years. Maj. McKiernan was one of the most brilliant men intellectually in Alabama and possessed a versatility of talent that made him a most pleasant companion. He was a lawyer by profession, but for many years he had lived upon his plantation, where he greatly enjoyed the company of his friends and the association of his books. He was a brother of Mrs. Wm. M. Jackson of Florence, and had many friends here, who will regret to hear of his death. THE TIMES in its next issue will give a more extended sketch of his life."

On Saturday, August 1, 1890, the life and death of Major Charles McKiernan was reported on page one of the Florence Times, "Charles B. McKiernan was born at Nashville, Tenn., March, 15th, 1813. While he was still an infant his father, Bernard McKiernan, moved from Nashville to reside on his Spring Hill Plantation in Colbert County, Ala., where the subject of this sketch was reared to manhood. He was educated at Georgetown, D. C. Returning from college, he was sent by his father to Madison Parish, La. to read law with his brother-in-law, Gen. Hugh Dunlap. After a thorough course of reading with that able lawyer, he entered upon the practice, which he pursued with marked success for several years, when the Mexican War was declared in 1846. He immediately raised a company of which he was elected captain, and which was assigned to duty in the Fifth Regiment of Louisiana volunteers commanded by the notable Bailie Peyton. After that brief campaign, which was so glorious to American Arms, he resumed his law practice at Richmond, La. [sic] but continued in it only a few years when large business interests called him into another field of endeavors. In 1850, he moved to Montgomery County, near Clarkesville, Tenn., and entered the firm of Jackson, McKiernan & Co. in the manufacture of iron. This firm did a large and very lucrative business, but it collapsed as a result of the outburst of the civil war [sic]. For the past twenty five years, he has resided at the old family homestead in Colbert County, Ala., where by strict attention to farming he has maintained his family in comfort and dispensed a generous hospitality. In 1848 he married Miss Rebecca Baxter, of Clarkesville, Tenn., whom he leaves surviving him, also a son, Charles B. McKiernan, Jr., of Colbert county, Ala., a daughter, Mrs. Geo. Donnegan of Nashville, Tenn., and a sister, Mrs. Wm. M. Jackson of Florence, Ala. When he went to the bar, S. S. Prentiss, Sharkey, Joe Holt, Chilton, Bailie Payton [sic] and a host of other legal celebrities were in the heyday of their success and fame. He was thrown into intimate association with them all. The old regime was at the height of its pride and power. Had he written his reminiscences of life in the Southwest fifty years ago, it would be a rarely interesting volume. As it was, in telling of those days and scenes he could hold the unflagging attention of his hearers for hours, so perfect was his command of language, so winning even to fascination were his manner and method of narration. Of ready and acute perceptions, a forcible writer, a most impressive public speaker, he must inevitably have risen to high distinction, had he remained for any length of time at the bar. But perhaps he has raised for himself a more valuable, a more enduring monument. He has enshrined himself in the hearts and memories not only of those with whom he was bound by the sacred bonds of kinship, but also of those with whom he was connected by the less intimate ties of friendship. And very many were his friends; few if any, were his enemies. When a young man he was quick and violent in resenting what he fancied to be an insult or a wrong, yet so kind and forgiving was he that the sun never went down leaving him in wrath and enmity against any of God's creatures. Generous to his own hurt, impulsive at times to imprudence, gifted as he was intellectually, he was as free from guile as a little child. Himself untainted by selfishness, deceit, chicanery or falsehood, he could not easily believe them to exist in others. To the writer, it was frequently a beautiful manifestation of this trait his simple faith in his kind, born of his own purity to see him cajoled and imposed upon, in minor concerns, himself wholly unconscious of the fraud. A good man, a brave man has fallen one who was faithful and true in every relation of life one who leaves behind him in all the wide range of his acquaintance, no one who does not feel that the world is better for his having lived in it. He sleeps tenderly guarded by the watchful love of those who were so near and dear to him those to whom he was so near and dear, he will awake in the Resurrection Morn."

Major Charles B. McKiernan was buried in the Spring Hill Plantation Cemetery. The cemetery is located just a few yards north of the Old River Road about one mile west of Ford City in Colbert County, Alabama, and is on the property that once made up Spring Hill Plantation that was owned by the McKiernan family. This cemetery is on the hill northwest of the River Road Bridge crossing McKiernan Creek or Donnegan Slough and is surrounded by numerous red cedar trees that encircle the graves. The old cemetery is on a small knoll near an old barn and on the property of Dr. Heaton.

The inscription on Charles McKiernan's tombstone reads: "McKiernan, Charles Bernard, 15 Mar 1815, 18 Jul 1890, b Nashville, TN; d Colbert Co AL; Rest until thou art called." Another tombstone in the cemetery reads, "Watters, Sarah, 23 May 1770, 3 Feb 1844, b Anne Arundel Co MD; d Franklin Co AL." Sarah may be the grandmother of Charles B. McKiernan, and the mother of Mary A. Waters McKiernan, wife of Bernard McKiernan.

Mhoon, James George-Mhoontown Plantation

According to Ancestry.com, James George Mhoon was born on April 22, 1792, in Bertie County, North Carolina. James Mhoon's parents were John Mhoon and Mary Spivey. His father John Mhoon was born in 1760, and he died March 4, 1816. His mother Mary Spivey Mhoon was born in 1758, and she died on October 16, 1838, in Tuscumbia, Alabama.

James George Mhoon married Lucinda (Lucy) W. Granberry Fraser on January 16, 1824, in Northampton, North Carolina. Lucinda W. Granberry Mhoon was born on May 31, 1798. James and Lucy had the following children:

James George Mhoon

1) John Joseph Mhoon was born about 1820 in North Carolina.
2) James E. Mhoon was born on April 6, 1821, and died in 1868.
3) John W. M. Fraser was born in 1821, and died in 1841.
4) William Junius Mhoon was born in Bertie, North Carolina, on December 6, 1826, and died in 1878.
5) Elizabeth Mary Mhoon Brinkley was born in Bertie, North Carolina, on October 11, 1828, and died in 1890.

James Mhoon's siblings include: James George Mhoon (1792-1853); John Mhoon was born in 1795 in North Carolina; William Spivey Mhoon was born in Bertie County, North Carolina on December 25, 1801, and died on December 26, 1844, in Franklin County, Alabama.

According to the 1830 Bertie County, North Carolina, United States census, James G. Mhoon owned 53 black slaves. By the middle 1830's, James G. Mhoon had moved with his family and slaves to his Mhoontown Plantation in Franklin County, Alabama. From September 12, 1837, through December 8, 1840, he had entered approximately 1,440 acres of land; most of his land entrys were adjacent to Chickasaw Chief George Colbert's property.

According to the 1850 Franklin County, Alabama, Slave Census, James G. Mhoon owned 100 black slaves, and Lucinda Mhoon owned 65 slaves. In other records Lucinda goes by Lucy; Lucinda was the wife of James G. Mhoon; therefore, they owned 165 black slaves.

According to the 1850 Franklin County, Alabama, United States Census, James Mhoon is listed as a 58 year old white male born in North Carolina. Also listed in the household is Lucy Mhoon 52 years old, William J. Mhoon 23 years old, and Elizabeth Mhoon 22 years old.

According to the 1860 Franklin County, Alabama Largest Slave Holders, Lucinda A. Mhoon and three others owned 77 black slaves. James G. Mhoon died in 1853, and the owners of his slaves were his heirs.

James George Mhoon died on January 15, 1853, at Mhoontown in Franklin County, Alabama. James is buried in the Mhoontown Cemetery at Cherokee in Colbert County, Alabama (Find a Grave Memorial Number 15114429). Lucinda W. Granberry Mhoon died on August 10, 1862; her parents were William Granberry (____ 1808) and Letitia Bishop Cotten

(1775-1849). She was buried in the Mhoontown Cemetery at Cherokee in Colbert County, Alabama (Find a Grave Memorial Number 15114393).

The following is an April 26, 1997, article titled Mhoontown Cemetery Holds Special Fascination For Cherokee Area Residents by Gene Vandiver a Times-Daily Writer. "Cemeteries dot the countryside around Cherokee, like freckles of the face of a small boy. Pride Cemetery, Smith Cemetery, Malone Cemetery and Lane Cemetery all tell just a little of the history surrounding the area, but Mhoontown Cemetery holds a special fascination for many of the residents. Perhaps it's the tombs-the six great marble and granite slabs which remind all who see them the people buried underneath were something special. The 12 foot monuments are the dominant feature of the cemetery, leaping into view as soon as the final turn in the road to the gravesite is made. Perhaps it's the setting- the tall ancient fir trees which issue almost humanlike groans when the wind blows or the haunting isolation of the well-manicured cemetery and church grounds. At any rate, for many years the citizens of Cherokee and the surrounding area have told their children tales of the burial place that is older than the state itself. Probably many a child has lain awake after his grandmother told him of the Mhoon ghosts walking about at midnight, or of the gold that supposedly was buried with the owners under the weathered tombs. Or maybe the child wondered how the robbers got to the top of George Mhoon's tomb to steal the fortune that was reportedly hidden in the huge urn there. But while citizens of the area told their children these stories, they themselves wondered just who the Mhoons were and what made them come to the country that was then so wild and unsettled.

Mrs. Rita Dailey, author of "A History of the Rose Trail" said in a recent interview that very little is known about the family. "The Mhoons were the older members of the Pride family, a well-known Colbert County family." explained Mrs. Dailey. "They came to the region in the early 1800's and then left for California during the gold rush. Mrs. Dailey said the Mhoons came from North Carolina, and that they were apparently a fairly wealthy family. A check of the 1790 U.S. Census reveals that John Mhoon head of the family was a resident of Bertie County, North Carolina, had five sons and three daughters, and was the owner of four slaves. The Mhoons arrived in North Alabama about 1801, and remained until the excitement of California Gold Rush caught the remaining family members in its grip. The last surviving Mhoon daughter-in-law died in childbirth, leaving no one to carry on the family name in what had by then become Franklin County, Alabama. That county was split into smaller counties in 1867, so Mhoontown is now located in Colbert County. The inscriptions on the tomb tell something of the family's history during their Alabama years. For instance, near the circle of tombs, adjacent to Mary Mhoon's grave, is a small stone slab which reads: "Enclosed are the remains of John, infant son." which indicates another child was born to Mary Mhoon, family matriarch, soon after arriving in Alabama. Another inscription tells of how the family or at least part of the family, went back to North Carolina to fetch Lucy Mhoon's mother when her second husband died. The mother's grave is near the other tombs. The plot the family chose as their gravesite is isolated even now. The cemetery is located about five miles north of Cherokee, about a quarter-mile from the Tennessee River. Mrs. Dailey explained how the large and ornate tombs got to their site. "The marble for the tombs came from Italy," explained the North Alabama historian. "The tombs were made by a firm in St. Louis, and then shipped down the Mississippi around and up the Ohio River, and down the Tennessee. Then they were hauled over by oxcart." Since it took such a long time for the tombs to arrive the dead were often buried and the tombs ordered with the funeral held after they arrived. Mrs. Dailey told of how one North Alabama family sent out engraved invitations to the services. The Mhoons left, but their influence on the immediate area remained. The spot they chose as a cemetery became the spot for a church and the people continued to come to worship, to wonder at the old tombs, and to bury their dead in the cemetery. Naturally, many stories grew from the number of people speculation about the old burial spot. Mrs. Maggie Smith,

84, a lifelong resident of Cherokee, explained how at least one of the notions, the one concerning the ghosts roaming at midnight came to be dispelled. According to Mrs. Smith, one of her relatives, the Reverend Jeff Smith, was pastor at the Mhoontown Methodist Church. The Reverend Smith had become a minister at 14, and continued his ministry until he died at 105. Some of the people in the church had reported seeing lights in the old cemetery at night, and he decided to show them there was nothing to fear. He stayed awake all one night in the church, observing the lights and in the morning happily reported to his flock what they had been seeing was not the lights of the Mhoon Family congregation around the old tombs, but plain old foxfire (a phosphorescent substance which glows in the dark.) Of course, some of the legends still exist, and rightly so, because they are as much a part of the cemetery as the huge tombs themselves. And the tombs along with the legends comprise a central part of Northern Alabama's history."

The following are found in the Mhoontown Cemetery:

1) Mhoon, John - Infant son of Lucinda I. and William S. Mhoon. Born in Raleigh, North Carolina Oct 11, 1831; died Tuscumbia, Alabama Jan. 25, 1837.
2) Mhoon, William S.-This monument is erected to the memory of William S. Mhoon, Born in Bertie Co., North Carolina Dec 25, 1801, died in Franklin Co., AL .Dec, 26 1841. Age 43 years.
3) Mhoon, William Spivey-Was the son of John Mhoon and Mary his wife, John was born in Marine Co., NC, Nov 12, 1761, and died March 4, 1816. He was the son of Josiah Mhoon and Mourning his wife.
4) Mhoon, Mary-was born in Bertie CO., NC, Oct 5, 1758, died in Tuscumbia, AL, Oct 16, 1838. She was the daughter of Mose Spivey and Jemima, his wife. Moses S. was born Oct 19, 1729, and died Aug 2, 1771, and was the son of Joshua Spivey and Alie his wife. Jemima the mother was born Nov 4, 1734, and was the daughter of Jonathan Stanley and Margaret his wife. Mary was married to James Bate June 20, 1776, who died June 3, 1787. Married to John Mhoon Feb 8, 1790, who was born Nov. 12, 1761, and died March 4, 1816. "In death and for many years before she enjoyed most perfect assurance of immortal life."

5) Mhoon, Mary daughter Jas. E. and Mary A. Mhoon-born Oct 5, 1858-Died Nov 11, 1861.
6) Mhoon, James E. son of J.G. and A. Mhoon b. April 6, 1821, d. Feb. 16, 1868, 46 years, 10 months, 10 days.
7) Mhoon, James George erected to the Memory of. b. in Bertie Co., NC April 22, 1792, d. in Franklin Co., AL Jan 15, 1853.
8) Mhoon, Lucinda W.-May 31, 1798-Aug 10, 1862, Wife of James G. Mhoon.

Morgan, John

According to Ancestry.com, John S. Morgan was born in 1804 in Ohio. He and his wife Sarah had four children; John Morgan, Jr., Mary C., Clara W., and Samuel Peters Morgan.

The June 1, 1840, Franklin County, Alabama, United States Census gives John Morgan's residence as Franklin, Alabama. Also living in the John S. Morgan household is one free white male under five; one free white male from five through nine; one free white male from 30 through 39; one free white female from 10 through 14; one free white female from 20 through 29; two male slaves under 10; one male slave from 24 through 35; two female slaves under 10; 1 female slave from 24 through 35. Two persons employed in agriculture; one person employed in manufacture and trade. Three free white persons under 20; two free white persons from 20 through 49; five total free white persons; six total slaves. Total all persons-free white, free colored, slaves 11.

From September 27, 1848, through March 21, 1859, John S. and his wife Sarah Morgan entered some 1,160 acres in Township 5 South and Ranges 12, 13 West in present-day Colbert County, Alabama (Cowart, 1985). The land they entered was about six miles south of the Tennessee River and about four miles east of Cane Creek in Colbert County.

According to the January 28, 1850, Franklin County, Alabama, United States Census, John S. Morgan, wife Sarah, and their four children were living at home on their farm in District 5 of Franklin County, Alabama, on this date. John Morgan (John S Morgan) was listed as a 46 year old male born in Ohio. Also living in the household number 934 was Sarah Morgan age 42, John Morgan, Jr.

age 18, Mary Commins age 18, Clara W Morgan age 16, and Samuel Peters Morgan age 10. The 1850 Federal Census also states daughter Mary A. Morgan (1832-1910), birth of son John, Jr. Morgan (1832-), birth of daughter Clara W. Morgan (1834-), Alabama, and birth of son Samuel Peters Morgan (1840-1935).

According to the 1850, District 5, Franklin County, Alabama, Federal Census, Slave Schedules, John S. Morgan owned 10 black slaves with six males ages 40, 19, 17, seven, one, and six; and, four female ages 42, 14, 12, and nine years old. According to the census on January 28, 1850, John S. Morgan's real estate value on this date was $8,000.00.

According to the July 20, 1860, Franklin County, Alabama, United States Census, John S. and wife Sarah and their just married son, Samuel P. and his wife Abyssinia 'Abbie' Brown Morgan were living at home on their farm in Eastern Subdivision in Franklin County, Alabama, which was their residence on this date. John S Morgan is listed as a 52 year old male born in Ohio with a Tuscumbia post office. Also listed in household number 243 was Sarah Morgan age 52, Samuel P. Morgan age 20, Abbie Morgan age 18, Charles Woodest age 31, and Ann Woodest age 22.

John was identified as a farmer by trade on this date July 20, 1860, with a real estate value of $3200 and a personal value of the estate being $6250. According to the 1860 Franklin County, Alabama, Slave Schedule, by his agent, R. S. McReaynolds, John S. Morgan owned 90 black slaves. John Morgan was listed as one of the largest slave holders in Franklin County, Alabama in 1860.

John Morgan was 62 years old when he died of typhoid fever in December 1869 in Colbert County, Alabama. John was listed as a tailor at his death. His son Samuel Morgan was 29 years old when he died in January 1870 of pneumonia. Samuel was listed as a carpenter at his death. After the Civil War, John S. Morgan as well as numerous other slave holders lost most all their planter wealth and resorted to other trades.

Oats, Samuel Kinnard-Newport Plantation

Samuel Kinnard Oats was born on January 14, 1796, in Fairfield County, South Carolina; he was the son of Samuel Oates and Fanney Cannon. Fanney was born on June 20, 1762, in North Carolina, and died on April 1, 1841, in Franklin County, Alabama (Find a Grave Memorial Number 106894636).

Samuel K. Oates family consisted of twelve children. Some of the children were: 1) Mariah F. Oates, born February 12, 1821, died May 8, 1846; 2) Martha E. Oates, born June 15, 1823, died Jan 1, 1856; 3) Polly J. Oates, born May 8, 1844, died July 22, 1854; 4) Frances Amelia Oates; and, 5) S. K. Oates, Jr.

Samuel Kinnard Oats lived for a while in Limestone County, Alabama. By 1830, Samuel moved to Lawrence County, Alabama. From November 25, 1829, through November 19, 1833, Samuel Kinnard Oats entered about 1,180 acres in Townships 4, 5 South and Ranges 6, 7 West in Lawrence County, Alabama (Cowart, 1991).

According to the 1830 Lawrence County, Alabama, United States Census, Samuel Oats household had two white males under five years old, one white male between five and ten years old, one white male 10 to 15 years old, one white male 30 to 40 years old, two white females five to ten years old, and one white female 20 to 30 years old.

On April 25, 1830, Samuel Kinnard Oats made his first land entry in present-day Colbert County, Alabama. He entered 39.85 acres in the southeast ¼ of the northeast ¼ of Section 23 in Township 4 South and Range 12 West in Colbert County. On October 5, 1836, his next entry in Colbert County was 160 acres in Section 25 of Township 2 South and Range 14 West. Between January 18, 1840, and July 2, 1849, Samuel Kinnard Oats made his final land entries in Colbert County consisting of 1,070 acres in Township 4 South and Range 13 West (Cowart, 1985). The total acres he entered between 1830 and 1849 were 1,270 acres.

Samuel Kinnard Oats bought the entire Section 28 in Township 3 South and Range 13 West where he established his Newport Plantation. On October 6, 1840, this Section 28 was set aside for Kilpatrick Carter, son-in-law of Levi

Colbert near the Town of Cherokee (Cowart, 1985). In the Chickasaw Treaty of 1832, the land was granted to Kilpatrick Carter, a white man who had married Phalishta "Pat" Malacha Colbert, a daughter of half blood Chickasaw Chief Levi Colbert. Kilpatrick and Pat Colbert Carter lived on the Natchez Trace at Buzzard Roost Spring in Colbert County, Alabama. According to the 1820 census of Franklin County, Kilpatrick Carter owned 45 black slaves.

According to the 1850 Franklin County, Alabama, Agricultural Census, Samuel K. Oats owned 600 acres of improved land and 1207 acres of unimproved land worth $20,000. He also had $1,000 worth of farm equipment and machinery with $3,710 worth of livestock. According to the 1850 Franklin County, Alabama, Slave Schedule, Samuel Kinnard Oats owned 96 black slaves to work the 1,807 acres of land on his Newport Plantation.

Samuel Kinnard Oats died on June 22, 1854, at Memphis in Shelby County, Tennessee. Samuel was buried in the Newport or Oats Plantation Cemetery in Colbert County, Alabama (Find a Grave Memorial Number 106894152).

The Newport Plantation or Oats Plantation Cemetery is north of Barton in the south ½ of the northeast ¼ of the southeast ¼ of Section 28 in Township 3 South and Range 13 West on a hill above Mulberry Creek in Colbert County, Alabama. Originally, the cemetery was the burial site for the Newport or Oats Plantation, but cemetery is presently on Tennessee Valley Authority property near Pickwick Lake.

David Cannon Oats

After his death, the land and slaves of Samuel Kinnard Oats was passed to his son David Cannon Oats. According to the 1860 Franklin County, Alabama, Slave Schedule, David C. Oats of the Oats Plantation owned 123 black slaves. In the 1860, David Oats owned $100,000 in personal property and $20,000 worth of real estate. By 1865, the Oats Plantation consisted of 2,546 acres of land.

According to a portion of the following article titled "The Oaks or Newport Plantation, Colbert County, Alabama History," contributed by Lewis C. Gibbs Jr. in May 2004. "Another of his sons was mentioned as a merchant in

Cherokee, Al. at this time, S. K. Oates, Jr. After his mother died in 1840, he established a cemetery on this property. She was buried in the cemetery and four of his children were buried there also. His mother being the first, and a Mrs. Linsey was the last. Sometime in the 1880 or 1890, my wife's great grandmother, great grandfather, and one of their daughters were buried in this cemetery. Mr. A. W. Jackson told me about helping dig the grave for Mrs. Linsey in the 1920's.

Mr. D. C. Oates first child was born in 1862. In 1854, D.C. Oates was appointed the first post master of Cherokee, which was located on the Newport Road at this time. Later the Post Office was moved to the Town of Cherokee, Alabama.

After the Civil War was over, D.C. sold the plantation to his mother. The deed is dated November 25, 1865 and called for 2,546 acres. This included the Cheatham ferry track. Where the ferry landing was located on the west side of the river and consisted of 120 acres. S. K. Oates operated the ferry before his death. After this, his son D. C. acquired the ferry rights and operated it until 1867 when he sold the rights to Columbus Smith.

The date his mother bought the plantation back, she gave him power of attorney. He could rent, lease or hire people to work for him. In other words, to manage at his own will. Amelia Oates died in 1874 and is buried in the Oates Cemetery. This is probably where the Ragen family (Lewis Gibbs wife's family) came in as a renter of the land. It is on record where he borrowed money from Columbus Smith to finance his crop.

Slavery was over and they had to make other arrangements to work the land. The price of 120 slaves at an average of $500 per slave was a big loss to any plantation owner.

Mr. D. C. Oates continued to operate the plantation until the late 1870's but ran into financial trouble, according to the mortgage records in the Colbert County Courthouse. The records of a foreclosure on the place could not be found, but in 1878, Section 28 was sold to R. E. Parker and her husband A. J. Parker and remained in their possession for the next several years. When we were young this was known as the Parker Place.

The 120 acres at the ferry landing to the north was lost because of the taxes and sold by the sheriff of the county in Alabama, to a Mr. Whittmore. D. C. Oates sued Mr. Whittmore trying to reclaim it, but the court ruled in favor of Mr. Whittmore. He in turn sold it to Columbus Smith, who had acquired a lot of land by foreclosure of loans.

D. C. Oates was also in debt to Mr. Smith. He conveyed to Smith his part of Henry Thompson and John Smith's crops in 1877.

In 1886, R. E. and A. J. Parker conveyed Section 28 to Columbus Smith on a trust deed and also a 60 saw magnolia cotton gin and condenser, a 12 HP steam engine, and a gristmill. This is what we call a lease purchase contract today. The Parkers defaulted on the loan in 1892, and Section 28 was sold to Columbus Smith for $4,200.

Columbus Smith never lived on this land. He died in 1900. His son, C. L. Smith and daughter Bessie Smith Reeder and son-in-law J. T. Reeder were executors of his estate in 1918. The land was divided and J. T. and Bessie Reeder became owners of most of the land that he (Columbus Smith) owned in Colbert County. J. T. Reeder managed the land until his death in 1923. Another manager was appointed in 1932. The court ordered Section 28 sold for debts. In 1936 TVA bought 30.6 acres along Mulberry Creek including the cemetery. It seems that Section 28 was farmed by a number of different tenants while the land was under Columbus Smith and his descendants-the Wallaces, the Ragans, the Skipworths, and others.

Mr. John S. Wallace, who is buried in the cemetery, was an associate of Columbus Smith. His name appears on several documents as a witness. It is believed that he ran a store on the south side of the river at Newport for Mr. Smith.

This land is now owned by Carter Reid. There were several owners after Reeder and Smith sold it. Mr. Luke Thomason and Mr. Charlie Chambers were two that I remember owning it."

The Newport or Oats Plantation, like many others, fell into financial difficulties after the Civil War. The abolishments of slavery caused a lack in the availability of farm workers to plant and harvest the cotton crops; therefore, many former plantations had to depend on tenant farmers to work the cotton lands which were more costly and not near as productive as the labor of black slaves. Eventually, after the war was over many of the large pre-Civil War plantations were divided and sold to small farmers or businesses, such as the Oats Plantation.

Newport or Oats Plantation Cemetery

Most of the markers in the cemetery were concrete slabs covering the graves with most of the tombstone names related to the Oats family. The following is some of the tombstones in the cemetery:

1) S. K. Oates, born Jan 14, 1796, son of Samuel Oates/Fanney Cannon, died June 22, 1854.
2) Fanney Cannon, born June 29, 1762, mother of S. K. Oates, died April 1, 1841.
3) James Oates, born Sept. 16, 1789, brother of S. K. Oates, died July 10, 1846.
4) James C. Oates, born April 17, 1839, son of James Oates, died May 29, 1844.
5) Mariah F. Oates, born February 12, 1821, daughter of S. K. Oates, died May 8, 1846.
6) Polly J. Oates, born May 8, 1844, daughter of S. K. Oates, died July 22, 1854.
7) Martha E. Oates, born June 15, 1823, daughter of S. K. Oates, died

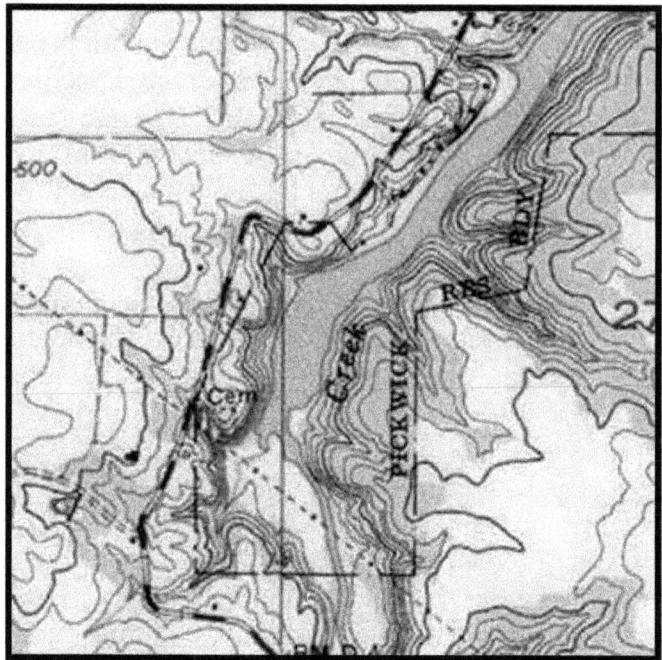

Topographic Map showing Oats Cemetery

146

Jan 1, 1856.
8) Narcis Catharine Ragan, born August ?, 1856, died May 8, 1876.
9) Dr. Benjamin Adams, born Jan 6, 1829, husband of Frances Amelia Oates (daughter of S. K. Oates), died Dec. 21, 1873.
10) Mrs. J. L. Cullicn, born May 18, 1818, died Jan 12, 1879.
11) John S. Wallace.

Patterson, James A.

James A. Patterson was born in Trumble County, Ohio, on March 17, 1813. On June 29, 1837, James A. Patterson married Nancy C. Martin in Morgan County, Alabama. Based on the census records, James and Nancy had the following children: James A. Patterson, Jr., Lan Patterson, Idelia Patterson Crawford, Danny Patterson, Susan Patterson, Martin Patterson, Annie Eliza Patterson (1849-1929), Asel Patterson, and Worley Patterson,

Since James Patterson entered land as early as September 1818, there were two James Pattersons in the Turkey Town cessions of northwest Alabama. The older James may have been the father of the James A. Patterson born on March 17, 1813. From September 11, 1818, through September 18, 1818, the elder James Patterson entered 601 acres in Townships 6, 7 South and Ranges 7, 8, 9 West in Lawrence County, Alabama. From July 17, 1818, through November 4, 1832, James Patterson entered 482 acres in Townships 6, 7, 8 South and Ranges 3, 4, 5 West in Morgan County, Alabama.

According to the 1840 Morgan County, Alabama, United States Census, James A. Patterson household had one white male between 15 and 20; one white male between 20 and 30; one white female between zero and five; one white female between 20 and 30; one male slave; two female slave; and a total of three black slaves.

In November 1833, James Patterson entered 40 acres in Township 6 South and Range 12 West in Franklin County, Alabama, but his family was listed in the 1840 Morgan County census. If this is the same James A. Patterson, he and his family were living in Franklin County, Alabama, by 1850.

According to the 1850 Franklin County, Alabama, United States Census, James A. Patterson was listed as a 37 year old white male born in Ohio. Also living in his household number 799 was Nancy Patterson a 33 year old female born in Georgia, Lan Patterson a 11 year old female born in Alabama, Idelia Patterson a nine year old female born in Alabama, Danny Patterson an eight year old male born in Alabama, Susan Patterson a seven year old female born in Alabama, Martin Patterson a five year old male born in Alabama, Ann Patterson a three year old female born in Alabama, and Asel Patterson an infant male born in Alabama.

According to the 1850 Franklin County, Alabama, Slave Schedule, James A. Patterson owned 12 black slaves. However, by the 1860 Franklin County, Alabama, Largest Slaveholders, James A. Patterson owned 103 black slaves.

According to the 1860 Eastern Subdivision, Franklin County, Alabama, United States Census, James A. Patterson is listed as a 49 year old white male born in Ohio. Also listed in the household is James A. Patterson a 19 year old male born in Alabama, Ida Patterson a 19 year old female born in Alabama, Susee Patterson a five year old female born in Alabama, Martin Patterson a 13 year old male born in Alabama, Ann E. Patterson a 12 year old female born in Alabama, Asel Patterson a ten year old male born in Alabama, Worley Patterson an eight year old male born in Alabama, Malenea J. Patterson a 49 year old female born in Ohio, Sally Lightfoot a 24 year old female born in Alabama, John F. Lightfoot a 20 year old male born in Alabama, Lucy Lightfoot a 12 year old female born in Alabama, Minecus Lightfoot a 11 year old male born in Alabama, and Henry Lightfoot a ten year old male born in Alabama.

According to the 1870 Colbert County, Alabama, United States Census, James Patterson is a 57 year old male born in Ohio with a Tuscumbia, Alabama post office. Household members include Martin Patterson age 22, Susan G. Patterson age 20, Asel A. Patterson age 18, Ann E. Patterson age 17, Worley Patterson age 16, and Kelley Kenley age 55.

According to the 1880 Colbert County, Alabama, United States Census, James Patterson is a 63 white male widower farmer born in Ohio. His father's and mother's birthplace was listed as Ohio. Other household members include Asel Patterson age 28, Annie Patterson age 26, Idela Crawford age 37, and Nannie Lou

Crawford age seven. Idela Patterson Crawford is the daughter of James Patterson. Nannie Lou is probably the daughter of Idela and granddaughter of James Patterson.

James A. Patterson died on August 2, 1892. Inscription on his tombstone reads, "Born in Trumble Co., Ohio." James is supposedly buried in the Oakwood Cemetery at Tuscumbia in Colbert County, Alabama, Plot 674 (Find a Grave Memorial Number 96203729). This information was recorded from a survey in 1934 by Dr. Roland Harper.

Pearsall, Edward

Edward Pearsall was born November 16, 1785, at Grove Hill near Kenansville in Duplin County, North Carolina. His father was Jeremiah Pearsall and his mother was Hannah Johnston. Edward Pearsall married Parthenia Shearon; she was born on March 12, 1800, in North Carolina. Parthenia married Edward in 1816, and she died on December 12, 1892.

Based on census records, the children of Edward and Parthenia are:

1) Nathan Pearsall born about 1832.
2) Laticia or Letitia Pearsall Rather born about 1834 and died about 1893.
3) Anna Pearsall born about 1837.
4) Thomasella Pearsall born about 1839. All the Pearsall children were born in Alabama.

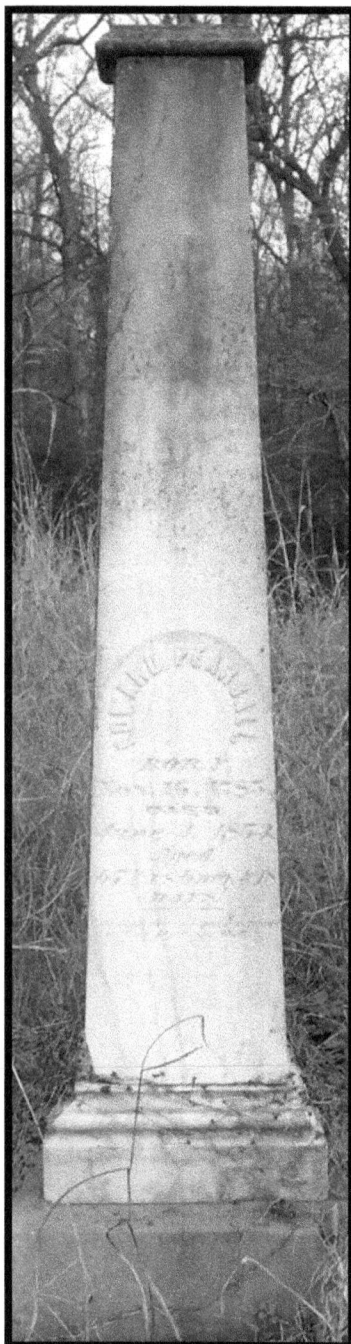

On November 2, 1818, Edward Pearsall entered 320 acres in the east ½ of Section 30 of Township 3 South and Range 10 West in present-day Colbert County, Alabama. He also entered 160 acres in the southeast ¼ of Section 32 of Township 3 South and Range 10 West. On November 27, 1829, Edward Pearsall entered 160 acres under the River Improvement Act in the southeast ¼ of Section 19 of Township 3 South and Range 10 West in present-day Colbert County, Alabama.

According to the 1830 Franklin County, Alabama, United States Census, the Edward Pearsall household had one white male between 0 and 5, two white males between 5 and 10, two white males between 40 and 50, one white females between 0 and 5, two white females between 5 and 10, one white female between 30 and 40, 11 male slaves, 16 females slaves, and a total of 27 black slaves.

According to the 1840 Franklin County, Alabama, United States Census, the Edward Pearsall household had one white male between 5 and 10, one white male between 10 and 15, one white male between 15 and 20, one white male between 50 and 60, two white females between 0 and 5, one white female between 5 and 10, one white female between 40 and 50, 25 male slaves, 22 female slaves, and a total of 47 slaves.

According to the 1850 Franklin County, Alabama, United States Census, Edward Pearsall was a 66 year old white male born in North Carolina. Living in house number 746 with Edward Pearsall was Perthenia Pearsall a 51 year old female born in, Nathan Pearsall an 18 year old male born in Alabama, Laticia Pearsall a 15 year old female born in Alabama, Anna Pearsall a 13 year old female born in Alabama, and Thomasella Pearsall an 11 year old female born in Alabama.

According to the 1850 Franklin County, Alabama, Agricultural Census, Edward Pearsall owned 550 of improved land and 550 acres of unimproved land worth $22,000. His farm equipment and machinery was worth $500, and his livestock was worth $3000. According to the 1850 Franklin County, Alabama, Slave Schedule, Edward Pearsall owned 62 black slaves.

Edward Pearsall died on June 3, 1853, at an age of 67 years, six months, and 18 days. He is buried in the Pearsall Cemetery in Colbert County, Alabama (Find a Grave Memorial Number 44906436).

John Walter Rand's son was Dr. John Walter Rand who had a brother-in-law, Moore Burns, who wrote a Civil War era journal. Burns' entry for Sunday, January 13, 1861, mentions that his widowed mother-in-law, Parthenia Shearon Pearsall, was ill with rheumatism, and that Dr John Walter Rand came to see her with his father. At age 76, John Walter Rand Sr.was able to go with his son to visit widow ladies during the dead of winter.

Peden, Warren Washington

Warren Washington Peden lived in Franklin (Colbert) County, Alabama, near the junction of the County Line Road and Second Street. Warren lived near the Peeden Cemetery on Bainbridge Loop which was originally a route of Doublehead's Trace. Later, the Indian trail became a portion of Byler's Old Turnpike that ran from the Town of Bainbridge located on the Tennessee River at Campbell's Ferry just west of the mouth of McKiernan Creek. The road ran toward the east to an old stagecoach stop before turning south separating the counties of Lawrence and Franklin; later, the route became known as the County Line Road. Today, Bainbridge Loop is an original portion of Doublehead's Trace and Byler Road from the nearby Town of Bainbridge.

Warren Washington Peden married Sarah Green Mills on August 16, 1823, in Sumner County, Tennessee. Sarah was born on November 19, 1808, in Sumner County, Tennessee, and died in Franklin County, Alabama. Supposedly, she was poisoned by slaves in 1861 (some records indicated she died in March 1853). Sarah Green Mills Peden is buried in the Peden Cemetery in present-day Colbert County, Alabama.

Warren Washington Peeden was listed in the 1830 census of Franklin County, Alabama. According to the Old Land Records of Colbert County, Alabama, by Margaret Matthews Cowart, Warren Peeden entered 80 acres on March 6, 1830, and another 80 acres on March 15, 1830, in Section 9 of Township 3 South and Range 10 West. He also entered two tracts of land in Sections 20 and 21 on December 16, 1839. On November 12, 1853, Warren entered 78.37 acres in Section 31 of Township 5 South and Range 10 West. His brothers Elisha and Calvin also entered land in 1830 in Franklin County, Alabama (Cowart, 1985).

According to the 1840 census of Franklin County, Warren W. Peeden owned 21 black slaves. By the 1850 Franklin County, Alabama Slave Census, Warren Washington Peeden owned 31 black slaves; however, he is not listed in the slave census of 1860.

According to the 1850 Franklin County, Alabama Agricultural Census, Warren Peeden owned 680 acres of improved land and 707 acres of unimproved land which had a cash value of $28,000. The value of implements and machinery was $250.00, and his livestock was valued at $4,000.

According to the 1850 Franklin County, Alabama, United States Census, Warren Peden was a 50 year old white male born in North Carolina. Also listed in his house number 772 is Sarah Peden a 42 year old female born in North Carolina; John Peden a 20 year old male born in North Carolina; Ann Peden a 16 year old female born in North Carolina, Sarah Peden a three year old female born in North Carolina, and Sarah Kemper a 16 year old female born in North Carolina. John Peden ended up in Arkansas. In the 1855 Alabama State Census, Warren W. Peden was listed as a resident of Franklin County, Alabama.

In the 1860 Franklin County, Alabama, United States Census, Warren W. Peeden is listed as a 60 year old white male born in North Carolina. Also listed in his household is Sarah L. Peeden a 47 year old female born in Maryland; Mary Madison Peeden a 20 year old female born in New York; and Frances Peeden a 12 year old female born in Alabama. In 1860, Warren Peden was listed as a 60 year old farmer with a real estate value of $26,000.00 and a personal estate value of $60,000.00.

John Amos Peden

Warren W. Peeden was born in Johnson County, North Carolina, in 1800 to John Amos Peden and Ann Ritor Howell. John Amos Peden was married to four different women; his wives listed below were:

1) Elizabeth Ann Baker;
2) Elizabeth Ann Genny Archer;
3) Ann Ritor Howell was born about 1770 in Johnston County, North Carolina;
4) Polly Edwards was born in 1769 in Johnston County, North Carolina.

John Amos Peeden's father was James Peeden who was born around 1740 in Northampton County, North Carolina. James died in died in 1790 in Johnston County, North Carolina, at 50 years old. John Amos Peeden's mother was Patience who was born about 1745 in Northampton County, North Carolina; she died in 1800 in Johnston County, North Carolina, at 55 years old. John Amos Peden's father was James Peden; James and Patience married about 1767.

According to Ancestry.com, John Amos Peden was listed in the Muster Rolls of 1812 as a member of the Johnston County Regiment, Johnston County, North Carolina. His military record is listed as Reference Number Peden 06 (DNA Group 4), Person ID I19511 Peden1, Family ID F6053 Group Sheet.

The children of John Amos Peeden and his four wives are:
1) Elisha Peden was born on September 20, 1794, in Johnston County, North Carolina. Elisha died on February 1, 1878, at Campbellsville in Giles County, Tennessee, at age of 83 years.

2) Warren Washington Peden was born about 1800 in Johnston County, North Carolina. Warren W. Peden died after 1860.

3) Calvin Peden was born on December 28, 1802, in Johnston County, North Carolina. Calvin died on March 29, 1856, in Lauderdale County, Alabama, at the age of 53 years.

4) Howell Peden was born March 12, 1807, in North Carolina. Howell died on January 9, 1881, in Clay County, Mississippi, at the age of 73 years.

5) Levi Peden was born about 1809 in North Carolina. Levi died after 1880 in Clay County, Mississippi, at the age of 72 years.

6) Bryant Howell Peden was born May 22, 1810, in Johnston County, North Carolina. Bryant died on March 29, 1895, at Pulaski in Giles County, Tennessee, at the age of Age 84 years.

7) Nancy Caroline Peden was born on November 9, 1813, in North Carolina. Nancy died in 1892 in Conecuh County, Alabama, at the age of 78 years.

8) Ransom Peden was born in 1818 and died in September 1866 in Franklin County, Alabama. Ransom is buried in the Peden Cemetery near Bainbridge Loop in Colbert County, Alabama. Ransom Peden ran the Bainbridge Ferry about 1840, and he also served as the overseer of his brother Warren Peden's black slaves. According to the 1840 Franklin County census, Ransom was living next to his brother Warren and owned three black slaves. Ransom Peeden married Amanda Wisener Fairchild in 1838 in Franklin County, Alabama. Amanda was born in 1820 in Tennessee, and she died in 1880 in Colbert County, Alabama.

9) Thomas Henry Peeden owned a saloon near Lock 6. Thomas and his bartender had to go to Huntsville as witnesses for the trial of Frank James who had robbed the Lock 6 paymaster. The stolen money was to pay the workers on the Muscle Shoals Canal. Frank had gone to the saloon prior to the robbery to get a drink, but Thomas said he could not identify him because Frank was wearing a hat in his saloon.

Pride, Edward M.-Pride Station

Major Edward Mitchell Pride was born on November 30, 1755, in Chesterfield County, Virginia. Edward married Sarah "Sally" High on October 9, 1781; she was the daughter of John High, Jr. and Ruth Mitchell. Sarah was born on July 28, 1759, in Prince George County, Virginia, which later became Dinwiddie County. Sarah died on October 25, 1821, at Decatur in Morgan County, Alabama. The children of Edward Pride and Sarah High are:

1) Ruth Emma Pride was born on January 10, 1783, at Halifax in Wake County, North Carolina. She married Archelaus Carloss who was born in North Carolina.
2) Elizabeth Pride was, born on February 20, 1785, and she married David Short Goodloe who was born on July 26, 1776, in Granville County, North Carolina. Elizabeth died October 15, 1845, in Colbert County, Alabama.
3) Mary Pride was born on June 14, 1788, in Wake County, North Carolina. She moved to Morgan County about 1817, and then to Colbert County about 1837. Mary (Polly) Pride died on October 18, 1862, at the Lane Springs Plantation in Colbert County, Alabama. She married Issac Lane on January 11, 1810, in Wake County, North Carolina. Isaac was born on Feburary 12, 1787, in Wake County, North Carolina, and he died January 19, 1862, at his Lane Springs Plantation in Colbert County, Alabama.
4) John Fletcher Pride was born on August 26, 1791. John died on June 15, 1891.
5) Nathaniel Jones Pride was born on May 6, 1795. Nathaniel died on October 23, 1875.
6) Edward Mitchell Pride, Jr. was born on November 6, 1797. Edward died about 1816.
7) William H. Pride was born on May 31, 1801.
8) Halcote J. Pride was born on October 11, 1803. Halcote and died on May 27, 1889.
9) Thomas E. Pride was born on May 16, 1805, at Raleigh in Wake County, North Carolina, and he died on October 18, 1859. Thomas married Caroline Allen who was born in Ponotoc, Mississippi.

Edward Mitchell Pride was the son of William Pride and Elizabeth Baugh. William and Elizabeth had the following childen:
1) Thomas Pride born about 1751 and died about 1779;
2) William Pride born in 1753 and died about 1779;
3) Edward Mitchell Pride (11/30/1755-2/7/1839);
4) Martha Pride born in 1757;
5) John Pride died on 2/8/1796;
6) Elizabeth Pride;
7) Peter Pride died about 1804.

Edward M. Pride became a Methodist preacher early in life and rode a circuit through Virginia and North Carolina. When Paul Revere made his famous ride, Edward Pride notified him that he would not only be a bearer of arms, but would he be the bearer of the message of Paul the Apostle. Edward Pride volunteered in General Davidson's Brigade and ministered to the spiritual needs of this brigade throughout the war. In 1797, he left his North Carolina home, crossed the Blue Ridge Mountains, and finally settled near Decatur, Alabama. Later, he followed his sons to Franklin County, now Colbert, and established a home where he spent the remainder of his days.

Major Edward Mitchell Pride died on February 7, 1839, and is buried in the Pride Cemetery in Colbert County, Alabama (Find a Grave Memorial Number 76853452). There is a Daughters of the American Revolution (D.A.R.) Marker over the grave of Edward Pride. Pride Cemetery is located five miles west of Tuscumbia, Alabama off United States Highway 72 West, at the foot of Hawk Pride Mountain.

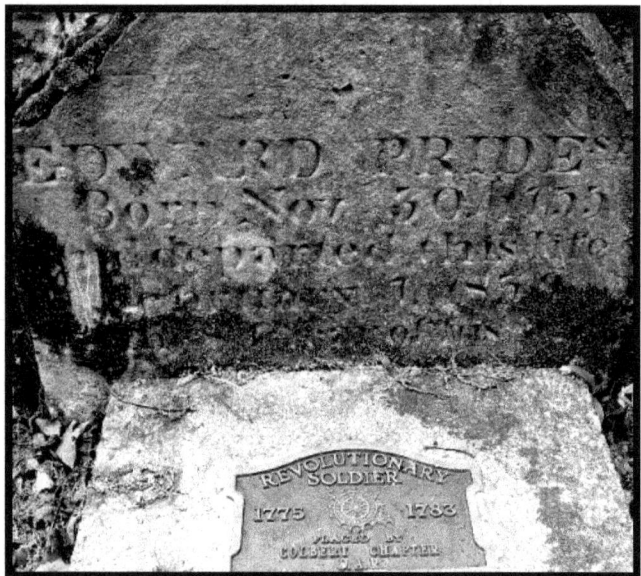

John Fletcher Pride

John Fletcher Pride was born on August 26, 1791, at Raleigh in Wake County, North Carolina. In 1831, he married Susannah Smith Barrett in Limestone County, Alabama; she was the daughter of James Barrett and Temperance Peterson. Susannah was born September 22, 1804, at Weldon in Halifax County, North Carolina, and she died on July 22, 1885, at Pride Station in Colbert County, Alabama.

From October 2, 1837, through June 25, 1855, John Fletcher Pride entered 575 acres in Township 4 South and Range 12 West in Colbert County, Alabama. On January 7, 1841, he entered 160.57 acres in Section 26 of Township 4 South and Range 13 West in Colbert County, Alabama. On January 21, 1851, John entered 320 acres in Sections 10 and 11 of Township 5 South and Range 13 West in Colbert County, Alabama (Cowart, 1985).

According to the 1850 Franklin County, Alabama, United States Census, John Pride is a 58 year old white male. Also listed in his house number 955 is Susan age 45, James age 18, Joseph P. Pride age 15, Fletcher age 13, George age 11, Susan age nine, and William age five.

According to the 1860 Franklin County, Alabama, United States Census, John F. Pride is listed as a 69 year old white male. Also living in house number 725 is Susan Pride age 52, John F. Pride age 22, George Pride age 21, Jaquiline age 18, and Melville Pride age 14.

In the 1880 Franklin County, Alabama, United States Census, John F. Pride is listed as a 90 year old white male farmer born in North Carolina. Also listed in the household is his wife Susan Smith Pride age 78.

157

According to the 1860 Franklin County, Slave Schedule, John Fletcher Pride owned 82 black slaves, and his son Joseph P. Pride owned 55 black slaves. Therefore, John and his 25 year old son Joseph owned 137 black slaves.

On June 20, 1891, the obituary of Captain John Fletcher Pride was published in the Florence Times. "Capt. J. F. Pride Dead. Capt. J. F. Pride, the oldest man probably in the Tennessee valley, died suddenly at his home at Pride's station on Monday night last at 8:30 o'clock. He had been in his usual health throughout the day and had eaten a hearty supper, when, with little or no premonition of the end, he suddenly passed away.

Captain Pride was in the 100th year of his age, and if he had lived until August he would have rounded out an even century! It was an ardent desire of his that he should live to fill the period of an even hundred years of existence, and in all likelihood he would have done so but for an accident which befell him from a fall several months ago, when he was, for one his age, seriously hurt.

Capt. Pride was born in Wake County, North Carolina, and moved to Tuscumbia in 1818, about the time of the founding of Florence. He leaves four children to mourn his loss, and has gone to his grave full of years and with the respent of a large circle of relatives and friends."

John Fletcher Pride died on June 15, 1891, at Pride Station in Colbert County, Alabama. John and his wife Susan Barrett Pride are buried in the Oakwood Cemetery at Tuscumbia in Colbert County, Alabama (Find a Grave Memorial Number 39953501).

Nathaniel Jones Pride

Nathaniel Jones Pride was born on May 6, 1795, at Raleigh in Wake County, North Carolina. He married Susanna Jane Martin on April 26, 1827, at Decatur in Morgan County, Alabama. She was the daughter of Dabney Amos Martin and Elizabeth Walker. Susanna was born on May 12, 1809, at Decatur in Morgan County, Alabama, and died on May 5, 1854, at Cherokee in Colbert County, Alabama. Nathaniel also married Martha Mosley. About 1830, Nathaniel J. Pride came to the area near Cherokee, Alabama, and settled at what is now known as Pride Station in Colbert County, Alabama.

From March 4, 1830, through January 30, 1834, Nathaniel Jones Pride entered 320 acres in Township 4 South and Range 12 West in Colbert County, Alabama. From March 10, 1848, through March 1, 1853, Nathaniel entered 800 acres in Township 3 South and Range 14 West in Colbert County, Alabama; he entered a total of 1,120 acres (Cowart, 1985).

According to the 1850 Franklin County, Alabama, United States Census, Nathaniel J. Pride is 54 year old white male born in North Carolina. Also listed in his house number 303 is Susan Pride age 42, William H. Pride age 26, Sarah Pride age 21, Mary Pride age 19, Goodloe Pride age 15, Charles Pride age 10, Susan Pride age seven, Ruth Pride age six, Ann Pride age 5, and Lucy Pride age two.

According to the 1850 Franklin County, Alabama, Agricultural Census, Nathaniel Pride owned 500 acres of improved land and 1,090 acres of unimproved land worth $1000. He owned $500 worth of farm equipment and $2,200 worth of livestock. In 1860 Franklin County, Alabama, Slave Census, Nathaniel Pride owned 31 black slaves.

Nathaniel Jones Pride died on October 23, 1875, at Cherokee in Colbert County, Alabama (Find a Grave Memorial Number 76853344). He is buried in Pride Cemetery at Hawk Pride in Colbert County, Alabama.

Goodloe Pride

Goodloe Pride was born October 20, 1834, in Colbert County, Alabama, and died May 18, 1918, in Colbert County, Alabama. He was the son of Nathaniel Jones Pride and Susanna Jane Martin. He married Margaret Francis Rutland, daughter of John Watson Rutland and Margaret Ann Barton. Margaret was born on January 24, 1842, and died on May 17, 1901, in Colbert County, Alabama. She was buried in the Rutland Cemetery at Cherokee in Colbert County, Alabama. Goodloe Pride was buried in Rutland Cemetery at Cherokee in Colbert County, Alabama.

Goodloe Pride was a Second Lieutenant during the Civil War. The following is from the book "Early Settlers of Alabama," by Colonel James Edmonds Saunders, which was originally published in 1899. "The Sixteenth was organized in Courtland, Lawrence County, Alabama; August 8, 1861, COMPANY A…Second Lieut. Goodloe Pride, too, was of good stock, and was, like Dixon, gentlemanly, brave and efficient. They had been reared together, and were warm friends. The day after Dixon was wounded; Pride (who had become first lieutenant) was seriously wounded by the explosion of a shell. The clothes were nearly torn from his body and he bled from his ears. He is still living."

Halcote (Hawk) J. Pride

Halcote (Hawk) J. Pride, the son of Major Edward M. Pride and Sarah High, was born on October 11, 1803, at Raleigh in Wake County, North Carolina. Halcote married Eliza F. Murphy who was born in 1824 in Morgan County,

Alabama. Eliza died on March 7, 1879, and is buried in the Pride Family Cemetery at Pride Station in Colbert County, Alabama.

From March 4, 1830, through April 12, 1855, Halcote J. Pride entered 800 acres in Township 4 South and Range 12 West in Colbert County, Alabama (Cowart, 1985).

According to the 1850 Franklin County, Alabama, Agricultural Census, H. J. Pride owned 560 acres of improved land and 900 acres of unimproved land worth $7000. He had $500 worth of farm equipment and machinery with $3000 worth of livestock.

According to the 1860 Franklin County, Alabama, United States Census, Halcote J. Pride is a 55 year old white male. Living in his house numbered 719 is Eliza F. Pride age 36, George W. Pride age 8, Sarah Kimbell age 65, Harris A. Green age 23, Thomas E. Pride age 21, and Anne Swell age five.

According to the 1860 Franklin County, Slave Schedule, H. J. Pride owned 71 black slaves.

Halcote (Hawk) J. Pride died on May 27, 1889, at Pride Station in Colbert County, Aalbama. He is buried in the Pride Cemetery at Hawk Pride Mountain in Colbert County, Alabama, which bears his name (Find a Grave Memorial Number 52939694).

William Pride

William Pride was born on May 31, 1801; he was the son of Major Edward M. Pride and Sarah High. From February 19, 1855, William Pride entered 655 acres in Townships 4, 5 South and Ranges 12, 13 West in present-day Colbert County, Alabama. According to the 1860 Franklin County, Alabama, Slave Census, William owned 27 black slaves.

Rand, John Walter

John Walter Rand was born on October 20, 1786, in Isle of Wight County, Virginia. John's parents were Walter Rand (June 15, 1761-1812) and Mary Ann Parker Rand (April 14, 1765-1841) who were of Scots Irish ancestry. Some of John W. Rand's siblings include Parker Rand (1793-1876), Nathaniel Greene Rand (1796-1883), Harrison Burchett Rand (1798-1861), and Molsey Rand Moore (1801-1831).

In February 1789, John, the eldest of six boys and two girls, traveled with his parents to Wake County, North Carolina. The family settled at the Falls of Swift Creek near Garner in Wake County, North Carolina. The land they settled on was property inherited from the assassinated Senator John Rand; John's uncle who was his namesake. While living in Wake County, Walter Rand became a very wealthy miller and cotton planter. Following in footsteps of his father, John Walter Rand became a planter and miller as was his grandfather and his uncle Senator John Rand.

On June 19, 1805, John was nineteen years old when he married Martha 'Patsey' Curtis (1790-1845). Martha was only fifteen year old when she married John in Wake County, North Carolina. Martha was the second of four daughters born to John Curtis and Mary Shaw Curtis.

John Walter Rand and Martha Curtis Rand had eleven children:

1) Louisa Rand was born on June 25, 1807, and she died on March 9, 1884. Louisa married William F. Mullens of Kentucky, and they had five children. Louisa is buried in Madison Cemetery in Madison County, Alabama (Find a Grave Memorial Number 8432838).

2) Evelina Mary Rand was born in 1808; Evelina died when she was only three years old in 1811 in Wake County, North Carolina.

3) Pemantha Cemetha Rand was born in 1812, and she died in 1874; Pemantha married Robert Allison Lampkin.

4) Anthaline Parker Rand was born in 1814, and she died at the age of five years old in 1819 died in Wake County, North Carolina.

5) Jackson Curtis Rand was born in 1816, and he died in 1858. Jackson married Cornelia Miller, and they had ten children.

6) Martha Curtis Rand was born in 1818, and she died in 1840. Martha was the wife of Reece Cook, of Vicksburg, Mississippi.

7) Dr. John Walter Rand was born in 1820, and he died in 1888. John was a medical doctor and served with the Confederate States of America.

8) William Harrison 'Hal' Rand was born in 1822, and he died in 1909. William moved to Texas before the Civil War.

9) Molsey Ann Rand was born in 1824, and she died in 1862 near the beginning of the Civil War. Molsey married Colonel Fletcher Curtis

Vinson who served with the Confederate States of America during the Civil War.

10) Captain Parker Nathaniel Greene Rand was born in 1829, and he died in 1909. Parker was born at LaGrange in Franklin County, Alabama, and served with the Confederate States of America during the Civil War. Parker married Martha A. Smith, and they had seven children.

11) Mary Anthaline Rand was born in 1831, and she died in Texas in 1852. Mary married Dr. William Stephenson.

In the War of 1812, John Walter Rand served in the North Carolina Detached Militia with Wiley Womack in Sixth Company of the Fifth Regiment and Second Brigade. After the War of 1812, John with his brothers-in-law bought sold property from 1817 to early 1820. The land they purchased and traded laid on both sides Marlow's Creek near Orr's Mill Branch, and the north side of Swift Creek in North Carolina.

In 1826, John W. Rand and his wife Martha Curtis Rand moved their family from Wake County, North Carolina, to the area near LaGrange in Franklin County, Alabama. John and Martha Curtis Rand brought all their belongings and black slaves to continue their cotton planting activities on new fertile lands. They traveled over some mountainous terrain in a wagon train of some fifteen wagons which carried the Rand family and his wife's sisters and husbands.

Martha Curtis Rand's sisters who came with her to Franklin County, Alabama were:

1) Burchet Curtis King was born in 1785. Burchet was married to Hartwell Richard King; she died in 1873.

2) Mary Elizabeth Curtis Vinson was born in 1793. Mary was married to Drury Vinson; she died in 1877.

3) Anne Curtis Matt was born in1788. Anne was married to Aldridge Myatt; she died in 1840.

The four Curtis sisters and their families were some of the founding families around LaGrange, Cottontown, and Leighton in present-day Colbert County, Alabama. These families have numerous descendants that live in the counties of northwest Alabama. Once arriving in the Leighton area, John and

Martha Rand purchased two farms. One of the farms was originally in Lawrence County, and the other farm was originally in Franklin County, Alabama; today, both areas are in present-day Colbert County, Alabama, which was formed from both counties after the Civil War.

According to family tradition, John Rand was a descendant of builders and millers. The family's oral history is that John loaded his millwheel onto one of his wagons and transported the millstone from North Carolina to Alabama. He probably crossed the Muscle Shoals of the Tennessee River at Campbell's Ferry at the Town of Bainbridge. The road leading from Bainbridge to Leighton and White Oak near LaGrange Mountain was Byler's Old Turnpike. The Byler Road was authorized by the Alabama legislature on December 16, 1819, at Huntsville, Alabama, and was the first state road in Alabama.

One of the first things John did upon his arrival in the area of LaGrange was to set up his mill on Town Creek close to Cotton Town in Lawrence County. His mill was near the property his brother-in-law Hartwell Richard King and the present King Cemetery. While John was getting his mill ready for work, his richer brothers-in-law were busy buying up farming property.

John Rand's mill was located in what was then Lawrence County, Alabama. The county lines between Franklin and Lawrence originally followed the Byler Road or County Line Road which had earlier been one of the routes of Doublehead's Trace. The county line between Franklin and Lawrence passed through the center of Leighton and White Oak. The Franklin County portion west of the Byler Road was annexed into Colbert in 1867, and the Lawrence County portion west of Town Creek and east of the Byler Road was annexed into Colbert County in the 1897.

Like other cotton planters during the slave plantation times, John and Martha Rand had a mountain home on LaGrange Mountain; they also had a valley home near the settlement of Leighton. Mosquitoes which caused malaria and yellow fever were the reason planters maintained mountain and valley homes. During the warm wet months, they would live in the mountain home and during cold weather they lived in the valley home. During the 1800's, many cotton planters in the Tennessee Valley had the two home living arrangement.

From September 17, 1818, through December 1, 1846, John Rand entered 525 acres in Township 4 South and Ranges 9, 10 West which at the time was in Lawrence County, Alabama, but now in present-day Colbert County, Alabama (Cowart, 1985). Two of John Walter Rand's brothers-in-law Hartwell Richard King and Drury Vinson also entered land in the same area in September 1818. It appears that they had someone to enter the land for them, or they made an earlier trip to the area and entered the land themselves then brought their families later.

In the mid 1840s, Martha Patsey Curtis Rand took ill with consumption. During her illness, John hired an artist to paint his wife's picture. Martha Patsey Curtis Rand died on Christmas Day, December 25, 1845 (Find a Grave Memorial Number (100876831). John had lost his beloved wife of forty years, but he would survive for another nineteen years.

According to the 1850 Franklin County, Alabama, Slave Census, John Walter Rand is listed as a 64 year old planter with 40 black slaves. In 1850, his estate was worth $15,000. In the August 1860 Franklin County, Alabama, Slave Schedule, John Walter Rand owned 28 black slaves. His estate was worth $40,000 to $45,000.

John lived long enough to see Alabama secede from the Union. By the time of his death in 1863, John had been very successful in accumulating wealth of at least $45,000 and a large amount of land, but at the end of the Civil War, his estate and fortune were greatly diminished.

John Walter Rand died at the age of seventy six years on June 20, 1863, in present-day Colbert County, Alabama. John Rand was burial at Rand Cemetery in Colbert County, Alabama (Find a Grave Memorial number 100876800).

When the Civil War broke out, John Walter Rand, Jr. and Parker Nathaniel Greene Rand served with Alabama regiments of the Confederacy; however, John Sr. did not live to see them return from the war. Most of his children remained in Alabama where they married and raised children. His now quite infamous son, William "Hal" Harrison Rand, left Alabama with his family in the 1850s and died in Texas where he settled before the War.

Parker Nathaniel Greene Rand

Parker Nathaniel Greene Rand was born at LaGrange on October 18, 1829. He was reared on his father's plantation and attended the common schools during his youth. In 1845, he entered LaGrange College and graduated in 1849 with the degree of Bachelor of Arts. After his graduation, he was engaged with his father in farming and became one of the leading planters of Colbert County, Alabama.

In February 1855, Parker married Martha A. Smith, daughter of John Smith, of Lawrence County, Alabama. They had the following children: 1) Pattie; 2) Parker Jr., merchant at Leighton; 3) Dr. Edgar Rand of Leighton; 4) Henry A.; 5) Martha B., wife of Henry P. Kumpe; 6) Hal, wholesale grocery house in Memphis; 7) John B.; and 8) Mary S., graduate of the Huntsville Female College.

After marriage, Parker and Martha lived three and a half miles southwest of Leighton, and nine and a half miles southeast of Tuscumbia. In the spring of 1863, he raised a company of soldiers and was elected captain. His company entered a battalion under Major Williams of the Confederate Army. His company remained a part of the battalion until its major was killed, after which it was merged into Company H of the Eleventh Alabama, commanded by Colonel James Burtwell, a graduate of West Point.

Parker Rand remained with this regiment until the close of the war. He was mostly engaged as a scout and participated at the Battle of Tishomingo Creek and at the fall of Selma. In April of 1865, Parker surrendered his company at Wheeler's Station or Pond Springs in Lawrence County, Alabama.

After the war, Parker returned home and resumed farming. Having lost most of his fortune, he went to work with energy and succeeded in replenishing his wealth. Parker Rand was elected magistrate in Colbert County, an office he held for more than forty years.

Parker Nathaniel Greene Rand died on August 17, 1909 (Find a Grave Memorial Number 96203753). He was buried in plot 681 in the Oakwood Cemetery at Tuscumbia in Colbert County, Alabama.

Ragland, Samuel

Samuel John Ragland was the son of Edward Mercer and Ursula Ragland. Edward Mercer Ragland was born about 1771 in Louisa County, Virginia, and he died in 1813 in Smith County, Tennessee. Samuel's mother was Ursula Dudley Brown who was born in 1768 in Hanover County, Virginia.

Edward Mercer Ragland and Ursula Dudley Brown were married in 1791 in Hanover County, Virginia; they had the following children:

1) John Dudley Ragland was born in 1793 in Hanover County, Virginia, and died in 1852 in Franklin County, Alabama.
2) Nathaniel A. F. Ragland was born in 1798 in Hanover County, Virginia, and died in 1854 in Franklin County, Alabama.
3) William A. Ragland was born in 1797 in Hanover County, Virginia, and died in 1854 in Franklin County, Alabama.
4) George Orville Ragland was born in 1800 in Hanover County, Virginia, and died in 1859 in Franklin County, Alabama.
5) Fenelon Ragland was born in 1801 in Hanover County, Virginia, and died in Louisiana before 1850.
6) Samuel John Ragland was born about 1804 in Smith County, Tennessee.

It appears that the Edward and Ursula Ragland family moved from Louisa County, Virginia, to Hanover County, Virginia, and then to Smith County, Tennessee. Edward died in Smith County, but his wife and children moved to Franklin County, Alabama.

Samuel John Ragland's siblings came with him to Franklin County, Alabama, along with his mother. According to the Franklin County, Alabama, United States Census, Samuel John Ragland and his family were listed as residents of the county in the census of 1830, 1840, and 1850.

In the 1850 Franklin County, Alabama, United States Census, Samuel Ragland was a 44 year old white male born in Tennessee. Also listed in his house number 789 was the following people: Elizabeth Ragland, a 30 year old female born in Tennessee; James Ragland, a 17 year old male born in Tennessee; Fenlow

Ragland, a 15 year old male born in Tennessee; Beverly Ragland, a 13 year old male born in Tennessee; Samuel Ragland, a 12 year old male born in Tennessee; John Ragland, a 10 year old male born in Tennessee; Keefer Ragland, a five year old male born in Tennessee; Nat Ragland, a one year old male born in Tennessee; Ursula Ragland, an 82 year old female born in Virginia; John Ragland, a 57 year old male born in Virginia; William A. Ragland, a 52 year old male born in Virginia; and Nathaniel Ragland, a 47 year old male born in Virginia.

Based on the 1850 census, Elizabeth Ragland was probably the wife of John Samuel Ragland. Ursula Ragland was Samuel John Ragland's mother. John, William, and Nathaniel Ragland listed in Samuel John Ragland's household were his brothers.

According to the 1850 Franklin County, Alabama, Agricultural Census, Samuel John Ragland owned 180 acres of improved land and 55 acres of unimproved land with a cash value of his farm at $5,000. Samuel's implements and machinery was valued at $500, and his livestock was valued at $2500. According to the 1850 Franklin County, Alabama, Slave Schedule, Samuel John Ragland owned 53 black slaves.

Ragland Kinfolks

Samuel John Ragland's grandparents were John Ragland (1749-February 14, 1785) and Anne Beverly Dudley (1749-February 14, 1795); John and Anne had the following children:

1) Nathaniel Ragland born before 1764.
2) Sally Ragland born on April 14, 1764, in Louisa County, Virginia, and died in 1852.
3) Edward Mercer Ragland was born about 1771 in Louisa County, Virginia, and died in 1813.
4) Sergeant Major Samuel Ragland was born in 1773 in Louisa County, Virginia, and died 1852.
5) Beverly Dudley Ragland was born in 1760 in Louisa County, Virginia, and died on July 11, 1803.
6) Seaman, a plantation owner, left his estate to Samuel.

Nathaniel and Sergeant Major Samuel Ragland, brothers of Edward Mercer Ragland, were plantation owners in Madison County, Alabama. In 1835, Sergeant Major Samuel Ragland of Madison County, Alabama, was listed as owner of a famous mare named Polly Balloo; the mare was bred by Dancy's Old Timoleon owned by Colonel David Dancy.

Between 1818 and 1833, Nathaniel Ragland, born in Virginia, entered some 450 acres of land in Madison County, Alabama. According to the 1830 Madison County census, Nathaniel Ragland owned 96 black slaves. Nathaniel probably had a son named Samuel that was born about 1802.

In 1833, Samuel (son of the older Nathaniel) entered 320 acres next to his father in Madison County, Alabama. On June 12, 1837, Samuel Ragland entered 240 acres in Section 22 of Township 4 South and Range 3 West in Limestone County, Alabama. On December 23, 1837, Samuel Ragland owner of a plantation in Madison County, Alabama, placed an ad in the Huntsville Advocate offering a $250 reward for the return of one of his runaway slaves named Isham who was a great blacksmith. He said Isham has a scar upon his breast and under the lip from the bite of a dog. According to the 1850 Limestone County, Alabama, Slave Census, Samuel Ragland owned 54 black slaves.

Ricks, Abraham-The Oaks Plantation

Abraham Ricks was born on October 16, 1791, in Halifax County, North Carolina; he married his first cousin Charlotte Bryan Forte. Charlotte was born on December 29, 1795, in Halifax County, North Carolina, and she died on March 19, 1874, at Tuscumbia in Colbert County, Alabama (Find a Grave Memorial Number 40816560).

The following was written by Frank Richey for "The Alabama Restoration Journal" in April 2011. "Charlotte Ricks was a special lady. She was described as an unusually lovable character, and an angel of mercy. Her obituary which appeared in the March 26, 1874 issue of the North Alabamian newspaper (whose editor was Captain A. H. Keller, father of Helen Keller), and was one of the longest obituaries ever printed by the paper. The article spoke extensively for her love for and ability to grow flowers. The obituary went on to say, "She was truly a ministering angel to her family and friends. Possessing a mind unusually bright, a clear judgment, and a heart that knew not evil. Every virtue found a home in her heart, and made her loved and lovely.

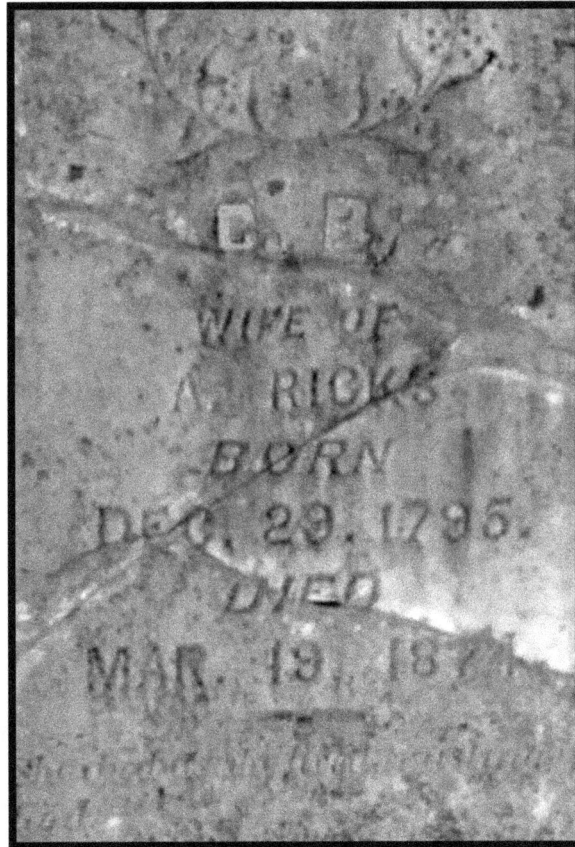

The obituary extolled her virtues in many areas, including hospitality, stating, 'For two generations her name has been the synonym of hospitality in this community. And where has such hospitality ever been excelled?' Charlotte Rick's concern for others extended to the slaves on the plantation. Her granddaughter said, 'Many of our servants were taught to read and write, and my grandmother would teach the little house Negroes the Catechism on Sundays after she had sent them home for their mothers to bathe and dress them.' It was probably in these Bible classes that a young George Ricks developed a love for the Word of God and determined to become a gospel preacher. Later, as a man, George Ricks would become a leader in the black community, loved and respected by both races. It was probably at the feet of Charlotte Ricks that George learned to read and write."

Abraham and Charlotte Ricks had the following children:

1) William Fort Ricks was born on April 10, 1818, in Halifax County, North Carolina, and died on January 25, 1902 (Find a Grave Memorial Number 40816673). He is buried in the LaGrange Cemetery in Colbert County, Alabama.

2) Richard Henry Ricks was born on March 28, 1820, in Halifax County, North Carolina, and died on February 24, 1858 (Find a Grave Memorial Number 40816633). He is buried at LaGrange in Colbert County, Alabama.

3) Abraham Ricks, Jr. was born on December 18, 1825, at Courtland in Lawrence County, Alabama, and died on April 12, 1878, at Tuscumbia in Colbert County, Alabama (Find a Grave Memorial Number 96203773). He is buried in Oakwood Cemetery at Tuscumbia in Colbert County, Alabama.

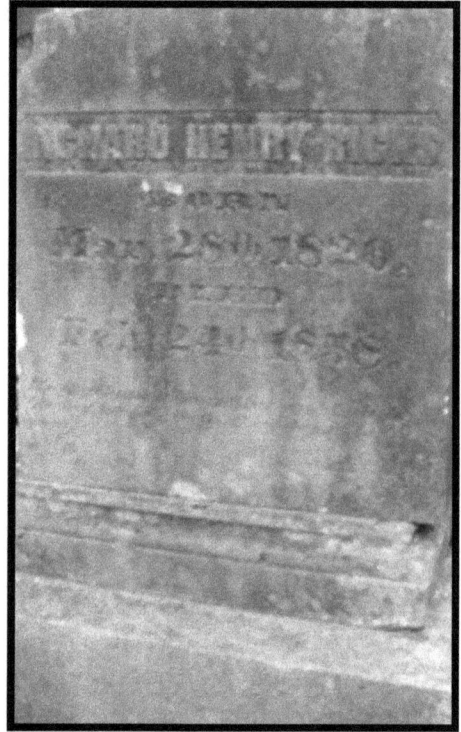

Abraham Ricks came to Alabama in a wagon train with all of his family, possessions, and approximately 50 black slaves. According to Bertie Ricks, her grandmother Mrs. Abraham Ricks said they moved to The Oaks Plantation on November 3, 1818. The land records indicate the same time since Abraham's first tracts of land were entered on November 3, 1818. In addition, the 1820 census lists Abraham Ricks and his family in Franklin County, Alabama.

Abraham may have visited the property that he entered before making the move with his family from Halifax County, North Carolina, to Franklin County, Alabama. On November 3, 1818, Abraham Ricks entered 480 acres in Township 4 South and Range 10 West in Franklin County, Alabama (Cowart, 1985).

According to the 1820 Franklin County, Alabama Census, Abraham Ricks owned 49 black slaves. Five people were living in his household in 1820 and included one white male five to ten, two white males 10 to 15, one white male 30 to 40, and one white female 30 to 40.

The Abraham Ricks' family was at Courtland in Lawrence County, Alabama, on December 18, 1825, since Abraham Jr. was born there on that date. However, Richard Henry Ricks was born on March 28, 1820, in Halifax County, North Carolina; therefore, Abraham and Charlotte Ricks moved after March of 1820. Supposedly, they moved by wagon train to Alabama with some thirty other families, bringing all their possessions including slaves. They lived on property they purchased in Lawrence County, Alabama, for a while, and then moved to Franklin County before the 1820 census.

About 1825, Abraham Ricks began construction of The Oaks Plantation house. Next to the site where their home was being built was a small log cabin which was a Cherokee home just prior to the land being taken by the Turkey Town Treaty of 1816. The Cherokee Indians occupied the area from the 1770 to 1816.

The Oaks Plantation House
Rear view, 3/28/1935, Alex Bush
Library of Congress

The Abraham Ricks family lived in the Indian cabin until their house was finished, but they kept and used the log home as part of the plantation quarters. Abraham Ricks added to the Cherokee log cabin that was built by the Indians; the little cabin was attached to the big house. In 1832, the main plantation house was completed and still stands today as an example of an early plantation home. The Oaks Plantation home was located on the flat plain that lies along north edge of LaGrange Mountain in Colbert County, Alabama. The Oaks was added to the National Register of Historic Places on November 7, 1976, and was assigned reference number 76000319. The architectural style of the home is Georgian.

From November 3, 1818, through June 21, 1839, Abraham Ricks entered 960 acres in Township 4 South and Range 10 West in present-day Colbert County, Alabama. From August 22, 1831, through June 21, 1839, Abraham Ricks entered 200 acres in Township 5 South and Range 10 West in Colbert County, Alabama (Cowart, 1985).

Abraham Ricks was one of the principal owners of the Tuscumbia, Courtland, and Decatur Railroad which was the first railroad west of the Appalachian Mountains. The railroad was some forty miles long and ran from

Old Slave Quarters-The Oaks
3/28/1935, Alex Bush
Library of Congress

174

Tuscumbia Landing in Colbert County, Alabama, to Rhodes Ferry at Decatur, Alabama. The railroad was used by the wealthy planters to transport cotton around the Elk River Shoals, Big Muscle Shoals, and Little Muscle Shoals on the Tennessee River. These three upper shoals were basically impassable most of the year. The rail line ended at Tuscumbia Landing on the west and at Decatur on the east end.

According to the 1850 Franklin County, Alabama, Slave Census, Abraham Ricks had 700 acres of improved land and 1,000 acres of unimproved land worth $45,000. He owned $500 worth of farm equipment and $3,500 worth of livestock.

Some say that Abraham Ricks owned about 10,000 acres of land, some of which was part of the original land grant to Lemuel Sledge. However, the 1850 agricultural census of Franklin County gives a total of 1,700 acres, and he entered only 1,160 acres.

Abraham Ricks died in 1852, and his slaves were probably divided among his heirs. Some say that Abraham Ricks owned 300 black slaves; however; according to the 1860 Franklin County, Alabama, Slave Schedule, Abraham Ricks, Jr. owned 132 black slaves, Abraham Sr.'s wife Charlotte Bryan Ricks is listed as owning 58 black slaves, and his son William Fort Ricks owned 86 black slaves. Three immediate family members of Abraham Ricks owned 276 black slaves. Since Richard Henry Ricks died in 1858, his share of the slaves was probably divided among the living heirs; therefore, the total number of black slaves could have very easily exceeded 300.

Abraham Ricks died on November 23, 1852, in Franklin County, Alabama (Find a Grave Memorial Number 15484592). Abraham is buried in LaGrange Cemetery. The cemetery is within a few miles southeast of The Oaks and on top of LaGrange Mountain; LaGrange is a French word that means "The Place."

By far, the largest monument in the LaGrange Cemetery is that of Abraham Ricks Sr., the owner of The Oaks Plantation. It took 16 yokes of oxen three days to transport the Italian marble from the Tennessee River to the top of LaGrange Mountain to construct Abraham Ricks' tombstone and monument.

Abraham Ricks Tombstone

George Ricks-Slave of Abraham Ricks of The Oaks

Abraham Ricks was said to have treated his slaves very well. Abraham provided for the slaves on his plantation an opportunity to develop spiritually and to worship God without hindrance from outsiders. Abraham Ricks was a member of the Church of Christ which was started by Alexander Campbell. Campbell broke from the Presbyterian Church in 1812 adopting baptism by immersion. Abraham Ricks wanted his black slaves to be converted to Christianity and to go to the Church of Christ. He allowed his slaves to be taught catechisms which were bible verses. Many of his freed slave descendants taught their children and grandchildren bible verses in the same tradition of the catechisms taught to their slave ancestors.

Sometime around 1825, Abraham Ricks built his slaves a log church about a quarter mile south of his plantation home on the little dirt road that passed just east of the main house. He provided his slaves land where the original church was built; being one of the first black churches in the area, it was called the Mother Church. The church was established as a Church of Christ, and in addition to being called the "Mother Church," it was also known as "Christian Home."

One of the black slave families of Abraham Ricks that attended the Mother Church was that of George Ricks. George Ricks was born in 1838 and died on Christmas day, December 25, 1908 (Find a Grave Memorial Number 20804543). Parson George Ricks was a preacher at the Mother Church and helped set up other black Churches of Christ in the area. During George's time, all black preachers were called parson.

Some claim that George Ricks was from Liberia, Africa; however, in 1808 slave trade from Africa was outlawed by the United States. Therefore, most of The Oaks Plantation slaves were probably descendants of those who had been in America prior to the stopping of African slave trade from Liberia, but they could have been descendants of Liberian slaves.

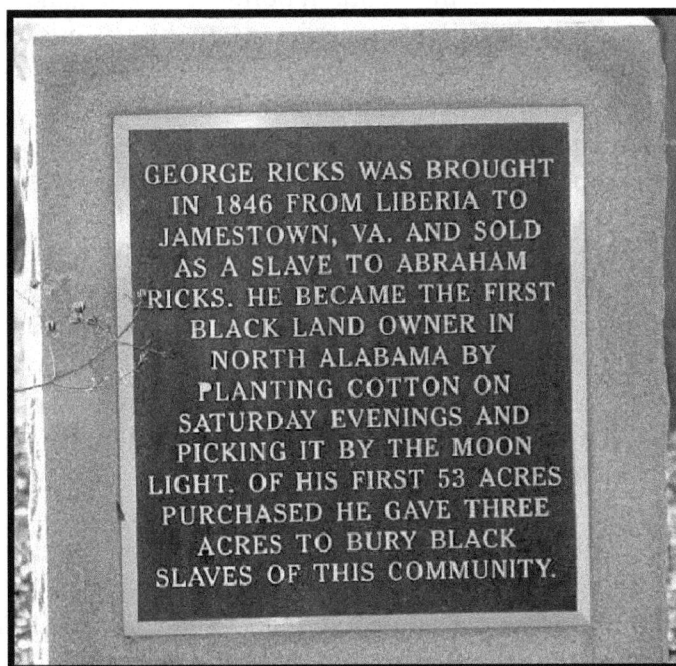

GEORGE RICKS WAS BROUGHT IN 1846 FROM LIBERIA TO JAMESTOWN, VA. AND SOLD AS A SLAVE TO ABRAHAM RICKS. HE BECAME THE FIRST BLACK LAND OWNER IN NORTH ALABAMA BY PLANTING COTTON ON SATURDAY EVENINGS AND PICKING IT BY THE MOON LIGHT. OF HIS FIRST 53 ACRES PURCHASED HE GAVE THREE ACRES TO BURY BLACK SLAVES OF THIS COMMUNITY.

By 1846, George Ricks would have been only 10 years old and Abraham Ricks would have been 55 years old and well established on his plantation at The Oaks. By the time Abraham died in 1852, George Ricks would have been only 16 years old. If Abraham wanted to purchase black slaves, he probably would not have made the trip to Jamestown, Virginia, when he could have purchased slaves locally.

The Mother Church was also used as a black school which was within a few hundred yards south of plantation house known as The Oaks. Activities for the black slave children were actually held at their church. The black Ricks ancestors were more than likely taught at the Mother Church. Many of the black families of Colbert County are descendants of the some 300 slaves and servants of Abraham Ricks. These black families were first listed in the Colbert County census of 1870.

Today, the third church building is still standing at the site of the original church. Many black children went to school in the second building that was on the site. Material from the second church was used in the construction of the third building and included the original pews of the second church. The first church was a log building which was built about 1825.

The second church building was used until 1937 when it was torn down and replaced in 1940 with the block building that is still at the site today. The roof on second building was replaced by Colonel Arthur Graves who paid for materials and labor for the roof that is on the Mother Church that stands today.

Fred Ricks, Parson George's grandson, carried on preaching at the Mother Church and later moved to Leighton, Alabama, some ten miles from The Oaks. All the black churches in the area would go to the old original church one Sunday per year to have service.

The great, great, granddaughter of Parson George was Lois Long; she died some years ago in her 70's. Prior to her death, Lois and her husband revived the weekly services at the original Mother Church. Grant

178

Ricks, Parson George's grandson, was the father of Nellie Mae Ricks Long who was Lois Long's mother; Nellie Mae Ricks married Isaac Long who had land on the Jackson Highway in Sheffield, Alabama.

The black cemetery of the Ricks Family is located just west of the Mother Church. Parson George bought 320 acres of land around the church and gave one half acre for the graveyard. The majority of the deceased black folks buried in the cemetery are the descendants of Abraham Ricks' slaves.

Abe Sledge Home

The Abe Sledge home behind the Oaks Plantation house is another old black landmark in northeast Colbert County, Alabama. The home of Abe Sledge, a direct descendant of the black slaves of The Oaks Plantation, is still standing; Abraham Ricks owned Abe Sledge's ancestors. Abe's old home appears to be in good shape and looks to be occupied today.

Abe Sledge Home

Abe Sledge's grandmother was Emma Ricks Sledge; she was born a free black woman at the end of the Civil War. She was known as Momma Emma, and she was the cook on the former slave plantation. Momma Emma Sledge was also a midwife that delivered both black and white babies. Emma was born on November 7, 1866, and died on May 7, 1954. In the 1930's, United States government officials and workers of the Library of Congress interviewed Emma Sledge.

Abe was born on The Oaks Plantation in the house where he later died. Abe Sledge was a black man; the Miles brothers repaired his old house which is located between The Oaks and the original black Mother Church. The Sledge name came from the white family of Lemuel Sledge, a white man who owned half a section of land in the area.

Sherrod, William C.-Locust Grove Plantation

On August 17, 1832, William Crawford Sherrod was born at the Cotton Garden Plantation at Courtland in Lawrence County, Alabama. He was the son of Colonel Benjamin Sherrod and Talitha Goode Sherrod. The Sherrod family originally came from England and settled in North Carolina. Colonel Benjamin Sherrod was a large cotton planter and owner of some 700 black slaves. Colonel Sherrod lived in Lawrence County, Alabama; he was the primary promoter and builder of the Decatur and Tuscumbia Railroad, the first railroad built in Alabama and west of the Appalachian Mountains.

According to the 1850 Franklin County, Alabama, Agricultural Census, the Locust Grove Plantation of William Crawford Sherrod consisted of 1,100 acres of improved land and 1,600 acres of unimproved land worth $40,000. He also had $1,200 worth of farming implements and machinery and $7,500 worth of livestock. According to the 1850 Franklin County, Alabama, Slave Schedule, Sherrod owned 84 black slaves.

In 1852, William Crawford Sherrod completed his education at the University of North Carolina at Chapel Hill, North Carolina. After college, William ran his "Locust Grove Plantation" in Franklin County, Alabama, and managed the Cotton Garden Plantation in Lawrence County, Alabama, that belonged to his father Colonel Benjamin Sherrod. He also owned a cotton plantation on the Arkansas River in Desha County, Arkansas.

On October 21, 1856, William Crawford Sherrod was married to Amanda Morgan at Nashville, Tennessee. Amanda was the daughter of Colonel Samuel Dodd Morgan and Matilda Morgan. Amanda was born on January 17, 1833, and she died January 24, 1921. She is buried in plot block F, lot 234 in the Riverside Cemetery at Wichita Falls in Wichita County, Texas (Find a Grave Memorial Number 59921528). Amanda Morgan Sherrod was one of the women leaders of Florence who raised funds to erect the statue of the Confederate soldier on the grounds of the Lauderdale County Court House.

William and Amanda's children were:
1) Adelaide Sherrod (1857-1864);
2) Charles Morgan Sherrod (1860-1926);
3) William Crawford Sherrod, Jr. (1863-1946);
4) Lillian Sherrod (1864-1951);
5) St. Clair Sherrod (1866-1954);
6) Benjamin W. Sherrod (1870-1953);
7) Eugene ("Big Daddy") Sherrod (1874-1963);
8) Lucille Amanda Sherrod (1879-1936).

In 1859 and 1860, William Crawford Sherrod served in the Alabama House of Representatives. In 1860, he was a delegate to the Democratic National Convention from Alabama.

William Crawford Sherrod

On April 12, 1861, at the start of the Civil War, William moved his black slaves to Texas to try to keep ownership and prevent them from escaping his control. During the war, he served as a Cavalry Colonel under the command of General Nathan Bedford Forrest. William Crawford Sherrod's record of military service in the Civil War is found in the Alabama Department of Archives and History.

According to the History of the Congress of the United States, William Crawford Sherrod wrote the following notes about his involvement and service during the Civil War. "At the beginning of the war I was engaged in special service the most of the time. I was in the last battle East of the Mississippi River which was fought after both Lee and Johnson surrendered. General Forrest, with whose command I was attached, fought General Wilson with about four thousand Confederates; the Federals having ten thousand as fine cavalry as ever followed any command in the line of battle. The last command that I ever received came from General Bedford Forrest in person at the battle of Selma which was to have all the dry grass removed from the breastworks; that it would catch on fire whenever the fire became hot, and smoke us out."

On May 9, 1865, at the end of the Civil War, Colonel William Crawford Sherrod returned to Lawrence County, Alabama, and resumed his occupation as a cotton planter, conducting his operation on an extensive scale. From March 4, 1869, to March 3, 1871, William Crawford Sherrod served in the Forty First United States Congress as a representative from Alabama. He wrote about his Congressional record as follows, "My (Colonel Benjamin Sherrod) father lived ahead of his time. He was the originator and builder of the line of Railroad from Decatur to Tuscumbia around the Muscle Shoals, predicting at that early day that a railroad would be built from the Mississippi River to the Atlantic Ocean, and that his line of road would be a portion of the trunk line, all of which prophecy has been fulfilled. When I was elected to Congress I concluded I would take up his work where he left it off, and conceived the idea of connecting the oceans by railroad over the line built by him, consequently I devoted the whole of my Congressional career to securing the passage of the Texas and Pacific Railroad bill, having the entire charge of that bill, the passage of which has done more to build up the Southern Country than any measure passed by Congress since the war." William Crawford did not run for re-election in the United States Congress, but returned to his business interests in Alabama

In 1875, William Crawford Sherrod was elected to serve in the Alabama Senate. In 1879, he represented the Second Senatorial district in the Alabama State Legislature, and as a member of the finance committee, he assisted in framing the revenue bill that got the state out of its indebtedness.

In June 1883, William Crawford Sherrod moved to Florence for the purpose of schooling his children. He was one of the originators of the Florence Land and Mining Company; the W.B. Wood Furnace Company of which he was Vice President; the Florence Coal Coke and Iron Company; the Florence Tuscaloosa and Railroad Company; the Tennessee and Alabama Railroad Company; the Alabama, Florence and Cincinnati Railroad Company; and, the Florence and St. Louis Railroad Company. He was a member and served on all of the several boards of directors of these companies.

In 1893, William Crawford Sherrod moved to Wichita Falls, Texas. According to the Wichita Falls Daily Times, May 3, 1910, "Owing to the constant decline in the price of cotton, which together with a destructive overflow finally swept away his entire fortune, he removed to Texas with his family in 1893, and soon after made Wichita Falls his home where he hoped in the Southwest his children might have a better showing than in Alabama. While in Wichita Falls he engaged in farming and ranching. In 1899, he was elected Mayor of Wichita Falls but the corporation being declared invalid did not serve. For years, he was a member of the Executive Committee of the Democratic Party in Wichita County and has also served as county chairman and chairman for the Congressional District. A strict party man, and usually identified with the wing of the party, he has always insisted on the rights of the people to rule untrammeled by bossism and dictation. While from his age not taking of late years as active a part as formerly, he is a man whose counsel is sought by party leaders. While a gentleman of the Old South with all its courtly manners, he never for a moment brooded over the losses of the war, but has been actively identified both in Alabama and Texas with the new order of things, and is a great believer in the future of the South. Now nearly 79 years of age, and probably the sole survivor of the Charleston Convention of 1860, having served in almost every civil capacity from road overseer up to member of Congress, and still interested in everything which affects the welfare of Texas

and the South. A typical Southerner and yet, broad enough to rejoice that the wounds of the war are practically healed, and that North and South can meet on equal ground in love for the flag of a common country. Wichita Falls has no citizen who better represents the true patriot than W.C. Sherrod."

William Crawford Sherrod died at the age of 85 on March 25, 1918, at Wichita Falls in Wichita County, Texas. He was buried at Riverside Cemetery at Wichita Falls in Wichita County, Texas, Plot Block F, lot 234 (Find a Grave Memorial Number 8649022).

Shine, John G.

John G. Shine was born about 1802 in North Carolina. Based on census records, it appears that John G. Shine was married two times. In 1850, Mary Shine was listed as 40 years old which means she was born about 1810. In 1860, Nancy Shine is listed as 48 years old which means she was born about 1812. These two women appear to be the wives of John G. Shine.

From September 6, 1849, through April 20, 1855, John G. Shine entered 361 acres in Section 29 of Township 5 South and Range 10 West in Colbert County, Alabama.

According to the 1850 Franklin County, Alabama, United States Census, John G. Shine was listed as a 48 year old white male born in North Carolina. Living in his house number 957 was Mary Shine a 40 year old female born in North Carolina, and Mary J. Shine an eight year old female born in Alabama.

According to the 1850 Franklin County, Alabama, Agricultural Census, John G. Shine owned 724 acres of improved land and 350 acres of unimproved land worth $20,000. He owned $1000 worth of farm implements and machinery and $3000 worth of livestock.

According to the 1860 Franklin County, Alabama, United States Census, John G. Shine was listed as a 58 year old white male of age born in North Carolina. Also listed is Nancy Shine a 48 year old female born in North Carolina, Anne Shines an 18 year old female born in Alabama, and C. Roberts a 27 year old male born in Alabama. According to the 1860 Franklin County, Alabama, Slave Schedule, John G. Shine owned 72 black slaves.

According to the 1870 Franklin County, Alabama, United States Census, John G. Shine is a 67 year old male born in North Carolina. Listed in his house number 32 is Nancy Shine a 59 year old female born in North Carolina, John Cooper a 33 year old male born in Alabama, Ann Cooper a 28 year old female born in Alabama, William Cooper a two year old male born in Alabama, and Langston Cooper an infant born in Alabama.

John G. Shine was a soldier in the Confederate States of America. He officially received amnesty in 1865-1867 under the United States Civil War Confederate Applications for Pardons.

Thompson, Lawrence

Lawrence Thompson was born about 1786 in North Carolina. He married Rebecca Bringham the daughter of Joseph Bringham (1764–1842) and Rebecca Haynes Bringham (1770–1853). Based on census records, Lawrence and Rebecca had the following children: Sarah R. Thompson, Lawrence Thompson, Mary Thompson, Anna C. Thompson, Joseph Thompson, and Rebecca Thompson.

From October 20, 1820, through June 1, 1835, Lawrence and Joseph Thompson of Williamson County, Tennessee, entered some 1,540 acres in Townships 2, 3 South and Ranges 12, 13 West in Lauderdale County, Alabama (Cowart, 1996). However, in 1830, Lawrence Thompson is listed in the Franklin County, Alabama, United States Census on page number 53.

On September 10, 1841, Lawrence Thompson entered 642 acres in Sections 26 and 27 in Township 4 South and Range 13 West in Colbert County, Alabama (Cowart, 1985). The land was west of Cane Creek in the previous Chickasaw Nation until their removal in 1837.

According to the 1850 Franklin County, Alabama, United States Census, Lawrence Thompson was a 64 year old white male planter born in North Carolina. Also living in his house number 426 is Rebecca Thompson a 42 year old female born in Massachusetts, Mary Thompson a ten year old female born in Alabama, Anna Thompson a nine year old female born in Alabama, Joseph Thompson a six year old male born in Alabama, Rebecca Thompson a four year old female born in Alabama, and Ellen M. Tyler a 19 year old female born in North Carolina.

According to the 1850 Franklin County, Alabama, Slave Census, Lawrence Thompson owned 59 black slaves. There were four more slaves listed under the last name Thompson but with no other name; these may have been his also.

According to the 1850 Franklin County, Alabama, Agricultural Census, Lawrence Thompson owned 550 acres of improved land and 1,320 acres of unimproved land with a cash value of his farm being $26,000. The value of his implements and machinery was worth $370 with $1,220 worth of livestock.

In 1855, Lawrence Tompson was listed in the Alabama State Census of Franklin County, Alabama, on page 28. According to the 1860 Western Division, Franklin County, Alabama, United States Census, Lawrence Thompson was listed as a 75 year old white male born in North Carolina. His spouse was Rebecca Bringham Thompson (1807-1856). Also living house number 65 was Anna C. Thompson an 18 year old female born in Alabama, Joseph Thompson a 16 year old male born in Alabama, and Rebecca Thompson a 14 year old female born in Alabama.

According to the 1860 Franklin County, Alabama Largest Slave Owners, Lawrence Thompson owned 73 black slaves. On November 4, 1864, Lawrence Thompson died at age 79 years in Colbert County, Alabama. He is buried in the Thompson Cemetery north of the Town of Cherokee near the south bank of the Tennessee River.

According to WPA records the following was found on his tombstone, "Lawrence Thompson, Sr., Birth: 1786, North Carolina, Death: Nov. 4, 1864, Colbert County, Alabama, Aged 79 years. Being one of the early settlers of Northern Alabama, he was well known to a large circle as a model man, possessing clear and comprehensive mind. That elevation of character of which exalted him above every mean artifice in his intercourse with the world. Judicious in his counsels, benevolent in his character, whereat in his donations to gospel, institutions. Calm as he descended life, delivery was peaceful in the home of death" (Find a Grave Memorial Number 94843749).

Lawrence Thompson's wife Rebecca Bringham died on February 24, 1856, and she was buried in the Thompson Cemetery in Colbert County, Alabama. The WPA records give the following, "Rebecca Bringham Thompson, Birth: Aug. 28, 1807, Sudbury, Middlesex County, Massachusetts, Death: Feb. 24, 1856, Colbert County, Alabama, Age 48 yrs, 6 mos., Wife of Lawrence Thompson, Daughter of Joseph Bringham (1764–1842) and Rebecca Haynes Bringham (1770–1853)."

Lawrence Thompson, Jr. was buried in the Thompson Cemetery in Colbert County, Alabama. The WPA records give the following, "Lawrence Thompson, Jr, Birth: unknown, Death: Sep. 17, 1847, Age 12 yrs., 10 mos., 8 days. Son of Lawrence Sr & Rebecca Thompson" (Find a Grave Memorial Number 94843828).

Sarah R. Thompson was buried in the Thompson Cemetery in Colbert County, Alabama. The WPA records give the following, "Sarah R. Thompson, Birth: unknown, Death: Jun. 29, 1845, Age 8 yrs., 9 mos., 4 days. Daughter of Lawrence & Rebecca Thompson" (Find a Grave Memorial Number 94843808).

Toney, Charles Augustus

Charles Augustus Toney was born on June 10, 1824; his parents were Charles A. Toney and Matilda Bondurant Toney. According to the 1820 Franklin County, Alabama Census, the elder Charles A. Toney owned 51 black slaves. In the 1840 census, the elder Charles A. Toney listed between 70 and 80 years old; therefore, he was born between 1760 to 1770. Charles Toney, Sr. was buried at Oakwood Cemetery in Sheffield, Alabama (Find a Grave Memorial Number 94757476).

Matilda Bondurant Toney was born on May 7, 1787, and died on July 23, 1874. She is listed in the census up to 1870 as living in the household of her son Charles. Matilda is buried next to her husband Charles Toney in the Oakwood Cemetery in Sheffield, Alabama. Both parents of young Charles A. Toney were born in Virginia. Charles Augustus Toney was probably a brother to Edmund Bondurant Toney of Madison County, Alabama; Edmund was also a slave holding plantation owner in Madison County where his parents had settled.

From November 2, 1818, through December 10, 1830, Charles Toney, Sr. of Madison County, Alabama, entered 640 acres in Sections 25, 28, and 29 of Township 3 South and Range 10 West in Franklin (Colbert) County, Alabama (Cowart, 1985). Charles Toney, Sr. owned land was just west

189

of present-day Ford City and just south of the River Road. On November 14, 1854, Charles A. Toney entered 40 acres in Section 22 of Township 5 South and Range 10 West in Colbert County, Alabama.

Charles A. Toney married Mary Ann Madding Toney, who was born on July 10, 1828. Charles and Mary Toney had the following children:

1) Charles E. Toney (born in 1849);
2) Eliza Toney (born 1851);
3) Lida Toney (1852-1938);
4) Matilda C. Toney (born 1853);
5) Edgar Toney (born 1856);
6) Mary Toney (born 1858);
7) Allen Toney (born 1861);
8) Cornelia Toney (born 1863);
9) Mary A. Toney (born1865);
10) Frank Toney (born 1872).

According to the 1840 Franklin County, Alabama, United States Census, Charles A. Toney's household is listed as follows: White Males: 10-15: 2, 15-20: 2, 20-30: 1, 70-80: 1, White Females: 10-15: 1, 15-20: 1, 40-50: 1, Slaves: Males: 23, Females: 23, Total Slaves: 46.

According to the 1850 Franklin County, Alabama, Slave Schedule, Charles A. Toney owned 41 black slaves. In the 1860 slave schedule, Charles was listed as the owner of 64 black slaves.

According to the 1850 Franklin County, Alabama, United States Census, Charles A. Toney was a 26 year old male born in Alabama. Also in his house number 737 was Mary A. Toney a 20 year old female born in Alabama, Charles E. Toney a one year old male born in Alabama, and his mother Matilda Toney a 69 year old female born in Virginia. In 1850, the value of Charles A. Toney's estate was given as $16,000.

According to the 1860 Franklin County, Alabama, United States Census, Charles A. Toney is listed as a 36 year old white male born in Alabama. Also listed is Mary A. Toney a 30 year old female born in Alabama, Charles E. Toney a 11 year old male born in Alabama, Eliza Toney a nine year old female born in Alabama, Matilda C. Toney a seven year old female born in Alabama, Edgar Toney a four year old male born in Alabama, Mary Toney a two year old female born in Alabama, Matilda Toney a 73 year old female born in Virginia, Maria Toney a 30 year old female born in North Carolina, Georgia Roberts a 17 year old female born in Alabama, Septimus R. Longbottom a 30 year old male born in New York.

In 1860 census, Charles A. Toney's real estate value was $40,000. and the value of his personal property was $63,000. According to the1860 Franklin County, Alabama, Slave Census, Charles A. Toney owned 64 black slaves.

According to the 1870 Colbert County, Alabama, United States Census, Charles Toney is a 46 year old white male born in Alabama. Also listed in the household is Mary A. Toney a 40 year old female born in Alabama, Charles E. Toney a 20 year old male born in Alabama, Eliza Toney an 18 year old female born in Alabama, Matilda Toney a 16 year old female born in Alabama, Edgar Toney a 14 year old male born in Alabama, Allen Toney a nine year old male born in Alabama, Cornelia Toney a seven year old female born in Alabama, Mary A. Toney a five year old female born in Alabama, Matilda Toney a 78 year old female born in Virginia, Silla Toney a 35 year old black female domestic servant and cook born in Alabama, Adam Toney a nine year old black male born in Alabama, and Elizah Toney a five year old black male born in Alabama. There is no listing for value of estate or personal property in the original census document.

According to the 1880 South Florence, Colbert County, Alabama, United States Census, Charles A. Toney was a 56 year old white male farmer born in Virginia. His father and mother's place of birth was listed as Virginia. Also listed in his household was Mary Ann Toney the 50 year old wife born in Alabama, Eliza Toney a 28 year old daughter born in Alabama, Allen Toney a 19 year old son born in Alabama, Camilla Toney a 17 year old daughter born in Alabama, Mary Toney a 14 year old daughter born in Alabama, Frank Toney an eight year old son born in Alabama, James Bynum a 20 year old male tenant born in Alabama, and Mollie King a 30 year old female tentant born in Alabama. There is no value listed on estate.

Charles Augustus Toney died on November 18, 1886. He was buried in the Oakwood Cemetery at Sheffield in Colbert County, Alabama (Find a Grave Memorial Number (94758468). His wife Mary Ann Madding Toney died on November 17, 1907, and she was also buried in the Oakwood Cemetery at Sheffield in Colbert County, Alabama (Find a Grave Memorial Number 94765453). Their daughter Lida Toney (1852-1938) was buried at Elmwood Cemetery at Memphis in Shelby County, Tennessee (Find a Grave Memorial Number 132528514).

Vinson, Drury

On March 4, 1788, Drury Vinson was born in Johnston County, North Carolina. On December 26, 1811, Drury Vinson married Mary "Polly" Curtis when she was nineteen years old. Mary Polly Curtis was one of four sisters who came with their husbands and children from Wake County, North Carolina, to Franklin County, Alabama. Mary Curtis was the daughter of John Curtis (1760-1816) and Mary Shaw (1765-1794), both of Wake Co, North Carolina.

Drury Vinson supposedly came to Alabama in 1826, but according to the 1820 Franklin County, Alabama Census, D. Vinson owned 31 black slaves. Also, the tombstone of his son says they were in Alabama by 1824. In addition, other families who supposedly came with the wagon train had children born in Courtland in 1825.

Many believe that around 1826, Drury Vinson was with a large wagon train coming 650 miles from Wake County, North Carolina. The wagon train arrived in North Alabama carrying several prominent cotton planters, their families, black slaves, household furnishings, livestock, and farming equipment.

Some of the individual planters included in the wagon train were Edward B. Delony, Colonel James Fennell, Henry King, Hartwell Richard King, Thomas Lyle, Elisha Madding, Aldridge Myatt, Richard Preuit, John Rand, Abraham Ricks, and Drury Vinson.

From November 3, 1818, through October 17, 1854, Drury Vinson entered some 802 acres of land in Townships 4, 5 South and Range 10 West in Colbert County, Alabama. On November 14, 1854, Fletcher C. Vinson entered 322 acres in Township 5 South and Range 10 West in Colbert County, Alabama (Cowart, 1985).

Drury Vinson Home-front view
Library of Congress
Alex Bush-March 27, 1935

According to the 1850 Franklin County Alabama Slave Schedule, Drury Vinson owned 107 black slaves. According to the 1850 Franklin County,

Alabama, Agricultural Census, Drury Vinson owned 2,400 acres of improved land and 1,400 of unimproved land worth $68,000. He owned $2,000 worth of farming implements and equipment and $10,300 worth of livestock.

Drury Vinson Home-rear view
Library of Congress
Alex Bush-March 27, 1935

According to Colbert County, Alabama, cemeteries, Vinson Cemetery is near Leighton and is listed as the "Vinson Private Yard." The cemetery includes the following:

1) "Vinson, Fletcher C., 3 Jan 3, 1822, Mar 25, 1879." His date of death on his military marker indicates he died on March 5, 1879. According to

inscription, "Born in Johnson Co. NC; Came with his parents to this state, 1824 and graduated with distinction at LaGrange College, Ala., June 14, 1841. While young he joined the Masonic Lodge & in later years he connected himself with the M. E. Church. Departed this life 25 Mar 1879 regretted by many who had been the recipients of his favors. When the crown is won at last who will count the trials past. Erected by his last wife and younger children, Dec 1880" (Find a Grave Memorial Number 39393335).

2) "Vinson, Drury, 4 Mar 1788, 31 Mar 1862 In Memory of; was married to Mary Curtis daughter of John & Mary Curtis Dec. 26th, 1811, professed

religion and gained the M. E. Church in 1811 & continued a faithful & exemplary to the end of his life. He moved to this state in 1826 & died 31 Mar 1862."

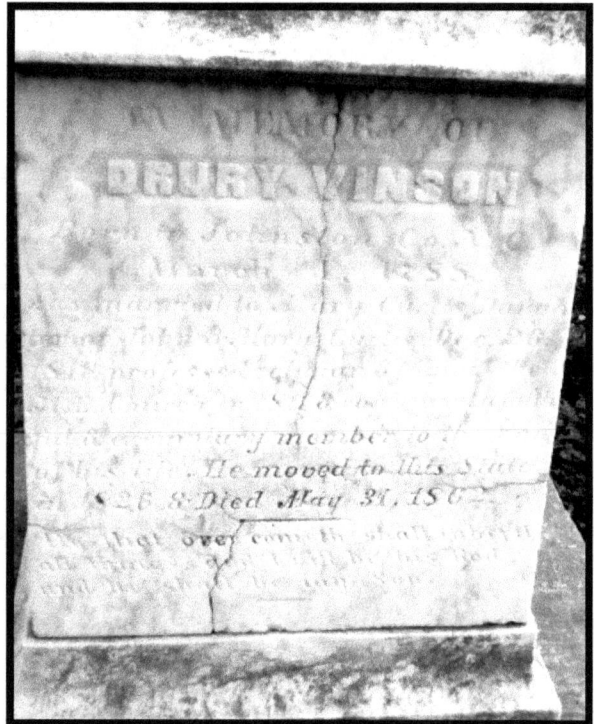

3) "Vinson, John Wesley, 20 Dec 1812, 5 Aug 1841 Father; Sacred to the Memory of; son of Drury & Mary Vinson born in NC and emigrated to this state in 1826. The degree of Bachelor of Arts was conferred on him in LaGrange College, June 4, 1834. Was married May 16 1837 and died at his residence in Lawerence County, Ala. Aug 5 1841 in the 29th year of his age. Every joy earned by noble principles the closing scene of his

life was marked by more than ordinary patience. Friend after friend departs who has not lost a friend."

4) "Vinson, Fletcher Curtis, 6 Nov 1845, 11 Feb 1846, Sacred to the Memory of; son of Fletcher C & Mosley Vinson."

5) "Vinson, Katie, Jul 1862-Oct 1862 dau of F. C. & M. A. Vinson."

6) "In Memory of Rand, Molsey Ann, Daughter of John & Martha Rand, Born in Wake Co. N.C. May 29, 1824, married to F. C. Vinson January 6, 1842, Died September 14, 1862, The Mother of ten children, seven of whom in their infantile purity at the call of their Heavenly Father, had already preceded her to the Home of the blessed" (Find a Grave Memorial Number 39393317).

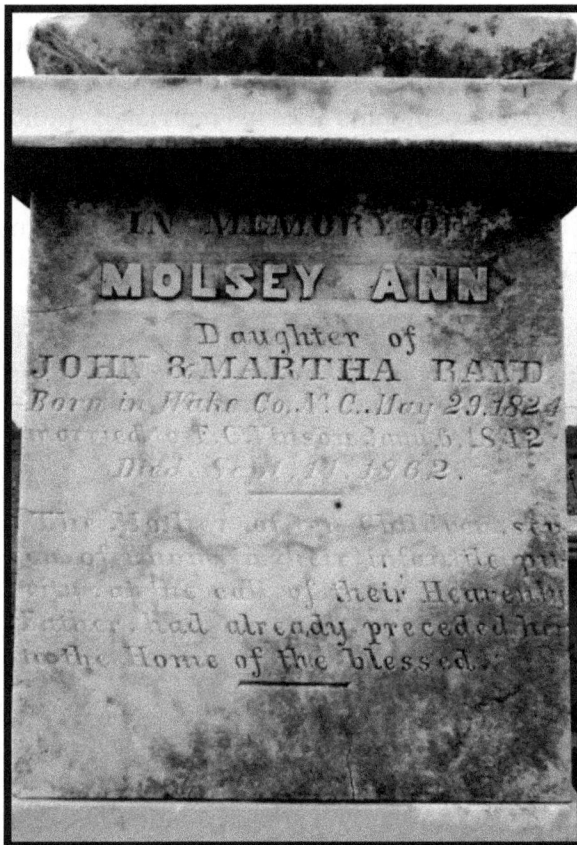

7) Martha Ann Vinson was born July 3, 1815, and died October 13, 1830. Her tombstone reads, "Sacred to the Memory of, dau of Drury & Mary Vinson, born in NC, Educated at LaGrange, receiving the highest honors of LaFayette Academy June 17, 1830, and died Oct 13, 1830 with a rising nation that accorded with her former profession."

8) "Gargis, Henry d 13 April 1912 aged 69 yrs 6 mos 28 days."

Drury Vinson died May 31, 1862; he was buried in the Vinson Cemetery at Leighton in Colbert County, Alabama (Find a Grave Memorial Number 39393373). His wife Mary "Polly" Elizabeth Curtis died on September 12, 1877. She was buried in the Vinson Cemetery at Leighton in Colbert County, Alabama (Find a Grave Memorial Number 101113231).

Winston, Captain Anthony Jr.

Captain Anthony Winston, Jr., was born in Hanover County, Virginia, on November 15, 1750, and died in 1828. He married Keziah Jones on March 11, 1776; a few months after his marriage, Anthony served as a captain during the Revolutionary War. In 1801 to claim bounty lands for his service during the war, Anthony and Keziah moved from their Hunting Towers Plantation in Buckingham County, Virginia, with their family to settle near Lebanon in Wilson County, Tennessee.

The migration to Tennessee and eventually Alabama included Anthony's sons and his brothers-in-law Joel, John, Samuel, and Arthur Jones, and their families, household goods, and black slaves. The wagon train probably consisted of several wagons with the members of the family, their black slaves, all their belongings, and farming equipment. About 1804, the Winston family moved to Nashville in Davidson County, Tennessee, and they settled on a plantation next to Andrew Jackson's Hermitage.

In 1811, the Winston family moved south from Davidson County, Tennessee, to Madison County, Alabama. The main southern route from the Nashville area to Huntsville and Madison County was the Great South Trail which became the Old Huntsville Road. In the Turkey Town Treaty of September 1816, the Cherokee and Chickasaw Indians ceded their land claims which included Franklin, Lawrence, Lauderdale, Limestone, and the southwest half of Madison County, Alabama. Shortly after these new cotton lands west along the Tennessee River opened to settlement, Anthony Winston's family moved to the Big Spring area of the newly created Franklin County, Alabama.

Anthony and Keziah had seven sons and two daughters as follows:
1) Anthony Winston
2) John Jones Winston

3) William Winston
4) Joel Walker Winston
5) Isaac Winston
6) Edmund Winston
7) Thomas Winston
8) Alice T. Winston (Pettus), and
9) Mrs. Jesse Jones.

Many of the Winston family were buried in the family cemetery located on the plantation of their son Anthony Winston in Tuscumbia, Alabama. According to the 1820 Franklin County, Alabama Census, the Winston family owned 437 black slaves.

Anthony Winston

Anthony Winston was born on December 5, 1782, in Buckingham County Virginia. He was the son of Anthony Winston who was born in Hanover County, Virginia, and Keziah Jones. On September 27, 1806, Anthony Winston IV married Sarah Ann Watson Winston, the daughter of John and Elizabeth Jones Watson. Sarah Ann was born on March 19, 1791, in Prince Edward County, Virginia. She died on July 24, 1843, in Sumter County, Alabama. Sarah Ann was buried in the Winston Family Cemetery at Gainesville in Sumter County (Find a Grave Memorial Number 32319473).

Anthony and Sarah had the following children: William Overton Winston (1809-1894); John Lewis Winston (1813-1878); Anthony Augustus Winston (1815-1897); Mary Dandridge Winston Steele (1819-1904); and, James McDonald Winston (1826-1905).

From September 10, 1818, through September 16, 1818, Anthony Winston entered some 2,400 acres in Townships 3, 4, 5 South and Ranges 8, 9 West in Lawrence County, Alabama (Cowart, 1991). Some of the land he entered was adjacent to former United States President James Madison's property. A large portion of the land was between Courtland and the Tennessee River with 160 acres west of Town Creek in present-day Colbert County, Alabama.

On October 23, 1820, Anthony Winston purchased lots 228, 229, and 230 in the Town of Cold Water (Tuscumbia) in present-day Colbert County, Alabama. On October 28, 1820, Anthony Winston purchased lot 423 in Cold Water. The record stated that Anthony Winston was from Limestone County (Cowart, 1985).

According to the 1820 Franklin County, Alabama, Census, Anthony Winston owned 89 black slaves. In 1820, Anthony Winston owned more black slaves than his siblings as follows: John Jones Winston owned 46 slaves; William Winston owned 32 slaves; Joel W. Winston owned 41 slaves; and Isaac Winston owned 31 slaves.

From March 28, 1825, through July 30, 1830, Anthony Winston entered some 1,400 acres in Townships 3, 4 South and Range 11 West in present-day Colbert County, Alabama (Cowart, 1985). Since the father of Anthony IV is also Anthony who died in 1828, it is not clear if Anthony III or Anthony IV entered the land prior to 1828.

On March 20, 1837, Anthony Winston IV entered some 3,870 acres in Sumter County, Alabama. Anthony Winston IV died on September 24, 1841, in Sumter County, Alabama. He is buried in the Winston Family Cemetery at Gainesville in Sumter County, Alabama (Find a Grave Memorial Number 32319413).

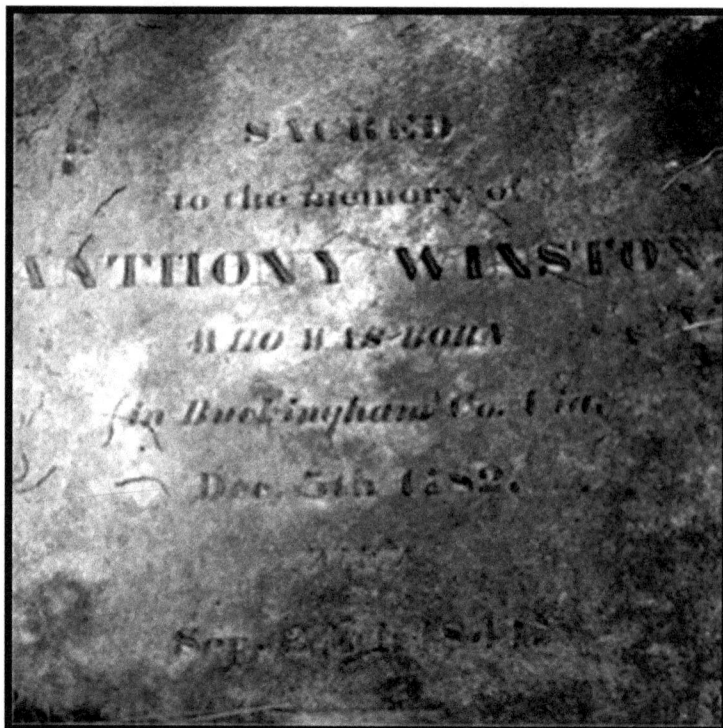

Colonel John Jones Winston

John Jones Winston was the second son of Captain Anthony Winston and Keziah Walker Jones. He was born on May 31, 1785, in Buckingham County, Virginia. John migrated with his family from Virginia, to Tennessee, and Alabama. He first married his first cousin Mary Walker "Polly" Jones in Williamson County, Tennessee, on January 17, 1807. John Jones Winston and Polly Jones Winston had the following children: 1) John Milton Winston (1808-1847) married Lucy Norfleet Smith; 2) Minerva West Winston (1810-1882) married William Winter Payne; 3) Elizabeth E. Winston (1816-) married Dr. Peter Whiting and William E. Morgan; and 4) Mary Francis Winston (1817-1843) married Dr. Madison Bruce Posey.

After migrating with his family to Madison County, Alabama, John Jones Winston was selected as cavalry captain of a company serving under General Andrew Jackson during the War of 1812. The Winston brothers also served in the company under John's command. Their company was attached to the Second Tennessee Regiment of Volunteer Mounted Gunmen under the command of John Coffee. John Winston's Company fought in the Battles of Tallushatchee, Talladega, and Horseshoe Bend where John was wounded. Later, John's company defended General Jackson's left flank at the Battle of New Orleans.

After returning from the War of 1812, John Jones Winston acquired thousands of acres of the Indian land cessions of 1816. On March 7, 1818, John Jones Winston entered 320 acres in Township 2 South and Range 11 West near Florence in Lauderdale County, Alabama (Cowart, 1996).

About 1818, John Jones Winston moved with his family to Franklin County, Alabama. According to the 1820 Franklin County census, Winston is listed with some 46 black slaves. From March 4, 1823, through October 3, 1825, John Jones Winston entered 1,760 acres in Township 4 South and Range 11 West around Tuscumbia in present-day Colbert County, Alabama (Cowart, 1985).

About 1819, John's first wife Mary Walker "Polly" Jones Winston died leaving him with four children. After Polly died, John Jones Winston married Susan Johnston a 19 year old from Duplin, North Carolina. On April 20, 1820,

John and Susan were married in Nashville, Tennessee. They had the following children:

1) Anthony Winston (born in 1823) and married Catherine E. Moseley;
2) George White Winston (1825-1827);
3) Anne C. Winston (1829-1860) married Stephen Parks Winston;
4) Lafayette Winston (1834-1919) married Rebecca Catherine Cooper Moseley;
5) Fountain Winston (1832-1905) married Christina Rebecca Moseley.

In 1833, the John Jones Winston migrated from Franklin County, Alabama, to Greene County, Alabama. He was elected for a term to the Alabama House of Representatives (1835-36) while living in Greene County. John's oldest son John Milton Winston and his daughter Mary Francis Posey died in Greene County, Alabama.

John Jones Winston died of an apparent stroke on April 5, 1850 (Find a Grave Memorial Number 33065221). In 1852, most of his children migrated to Texas. In 1858, John's wife Susan Winston died at Columbia in Brazoria County, Texas; she was interred in the Cedar Lake Cemetery (Find a Grave Memorial Number 130329272).

William Winston

Colonel William Henry Winston was born on March 24, 1789. He was the son of Captain Anthony Winston, of Hanover County, Virginia, and Keziah Jones. William first married Mary Bacon Cooper on August 21, 1811, in Davidson County, Tennessee. In 1822, William married the second time to Judith McCraw Jones; Judith was born on March 10, 1806, in Buckingham County, Virginia.

William Winston fathered the following children first with Mary:

1) Governor John Anthony Winston was born on September 4, 1812, in Madison County of Alabama Territory. In 1832, he married Mary Agnes Walker. In 1834, he established a cotton plantation in Sumter County, Alabama. Mary died in 1842.

On October 18, 1843, John Anthony Winston married Mary "Polly" W. Longwood, but the marriage ended in divorce granted by the legislature in 1850. After catching his wife and Dr. Sidney S. Perry having an affair, John Anthony Winston shot Perry to death, but his action was ruled justifiable homicide.

John Anthony Winston was the first native born Governor of Alabama. He

Alabama Governor
John Anthony Winston
9/4/1812-12/21/1871

203

served as fifteenth Governor of Alabama from 1853 to 1857. Governor John Anthony Winston died on December 21, 1871, in Mobile, Alabama. He was buried in the Winston Cemetery at Gainesville in Sumter County, Alabama (Find a Grave Memorial Number 10326608).

2) William Henry Winston was born about 1814 in Alabama. He first married Mary W. Watts, and on May 18, 1840, he married Sarah A. Winston, the daughter of Anthony and Sally Watson Winston. William married the third time to Mary E. Jones.

3) Pamelia Virginia Winston was born about 1815. Pamelia married her first cousin Governor John Jones Pettus; she died after April 1857.

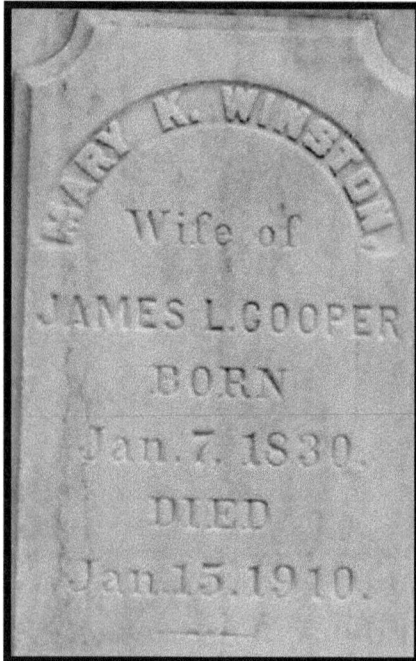

William fathered the following children with Judith:

4) Stephen Parks Winston was born in 1829. He married his first cousin Catherine Winston and moved to Brazoria County, Texas. Later, Stephen married the second time to Sallie Jones.

5) Mary "Polly" K. Winston Cooper was born on January 7, 1830, at Tuscumbia in Colbert County. She married James L. Cooper, and she died on January 15, 1910, at Huntsville in Madison County, Alabama (Find a Grave Memorial Number 39605901).

6) Sarah Miller Winston was born on February 2, 1832. Sarah married Governor Robert Burns Lindsey, and she died on October 7, 1905.

7) Martha Bacon Winston was born on April 30 1834, at Tuscumbia, Alabama. On April 3, 1856, Martha married John Anthony Steele; she died on January 25, 1895.

8) Thomas Early Winston was born on February 6, 1836. He married Iowa Merredith; he died on August 24, 1869.

9) Susan E. Winston was born in 1837 and died in 1840.

10) Judith McCraw Winston was born in Tuscumbia on May 21, 1841. On March 28, 1860, Judith married John Bolton Sherrod; she died on May 13, 1921.

11) Rosa Octavia Winston was born in 1844 and died in 1845.

12) Anna Helen Winston was born on May 6, 1846, and she died on April 22, 1860 (Find a Grave Memorial Number 129811466).

13) Edmond Cooper Winston was born on September 29, 1849. On December 28, 1896, Edmond married Mary McKiernan Jackson, the daughter of James and Sallie Moore Jackson of the Forks of Cypress. Edmond died in October 1902.

According to the 1820 Franklin County, Alabama, census, William Winston owned 32 black slaves. William was not as aggressive as his brothers in acquiring large tracts of land and acquiring a large number of slaves.

On October 8, 1824, William Winston entered 160 acres in Section 26 of Township 4 South and Range 11 West in Colbert County, Alabama. On February 18, 1828, William Winston entered 160 acres in Section 27 of Township 4 South and Range 11 West in Colbert County, Alabama.

According to the 1850 Franklin County, Alabama, Agricultural Census, William Winston owned 650 acres of improved land and 350 acres of unimproved land worth $1,300. He owned $500 worth of farm equipment and $3000 worth of livestock. His estate consisted of 1,000 acres of land which was valued at only $1.30 per acre.

William Winston died on April 27, 1857; he is buried in the Winston Family Cemetery at Tuscumbia in Colbert County, Alabama (Find a Grave Memorial Number 129811403). Judith McCraw Jones Winston died on November 22, 1874, at Tuscumbia in Colbert County, Alabama. Her death was the result of a tornado that struck Tuscumbia in 1874. Judith is buried in the Winston Family Cemetery in Tuscumbia (Find a Grave Memorial Number 129811432).

Judith McCraw Jones Winston
3/10/1806-11/22/1874

In 1824, construction began on the plantation era home of William Winston, father of Alabama Governor John Anthony Winston; the house was completed in 1833. The house was a Georgian style dewelling and is the largest slave era home in Tuscumbia, Alabama. The home features a winding staircase, eight fireplaces, and ten original closets. At the northwest back corner of the house is a log kitchen that was used for cooking in order to avoid having fire too near to the house; the log kitchen no longer exists.

While members of the Union Army were occupying the home during the Civil War, a note was written on the basement wall probably by a Yankee soldier that says, "It is a damn shame to destroy this mansion." Somehow, the William Winston House survived the Yankee occupation of the Civil War.

The William Winston House and property was the location of the new Deshler High School campus. The Winston house serves for school functions as a museum and a site for special events.

William Winston House-front view
W. N. Manning, 3/8/1934

The original Deshler High School was located on property several blocks south of the William Winston House. The property for the first school given by

Major David Deshler in memory of his son, Brigadier General James Deshler of the Confederate States of America. On September 20, 1863, General James Deshler was killed leading charge at Battle of Chickamauga.

On April 15, 1982, the William Winston House was placed on the National Register of Historic Places with reference number 82002005. The Winston home is located on North Commons Street in Tuscumbia, Alabama. Restoration of the William Winston House began shortly before being placed on the National Register.

Joel Walker Winston

Joel Walker Winston was born on December 5, 1792, in Hanover County, Virginia, to Captain Anthony Winston, of Hanover County, Virginia, and Keziah Jones. On January 16, 1817, Joel married Mrs. Elizabeth Easley Jones Atkins in Madison County, Alabama.

According to the 1820 Franklin County, Alabama Census, Joel W. Winston owned 41 black slaves. On June 10, 1820, Joel Walker Winston purchased lot number 160 in the Town of Coldwater (Tuscumbia) in present-day Colbert County, Alabama. From September 4, 1824, through July 4, 1825, Joel W. Winston entered some 320 acres in Sections 23 and 27 of Township 4 South and Range 11 West.

From March 20, 1837, through August 28, 1838, Joel Walker Winston entered 1,044 acres in Townships 21, 22 North and Ranges 1, 3 West in Sumter County, Alabama. Joel Walker Winston died in 1840 in Sumter County, Alabama.

Isaac Winston-Belle Mont Plantation

Isaac Winston was born on January 22, 1795, at New Store in Buckingham County, Virginia. Isaac was the son of Anthony Winston (1750-1828) and Keziah Jones (1760-1826). He moved with his family from Virginia, to Tennessee, and then to Madison County, Alabama. From Madison County, Isaac Winston moved to Franklin County, Alabama. According to the 1830

Franklin County, Alabama Census, Isaac Winston owned 31 black slaves, and by 1860, he owned 114 slaves.

Isaac married Catherine Baker Jones (1798-1884), the daughter of Arthur Jones. They had the following children:

1) Mary Susan Winston Armistead (1822-1879);
2) Isaac Winston Jr. (1829-1863);
3) Infant son (1830);
4) Catherine Baker Winston Burt (1832-1876);
5) Elizabeth Jane Winston Bowling (1834-1892);
6) Infant daughter (1836);
7) Madora V. Winston (1839-1852); and,
8) Ella Walker Winston Thornton (1836 or 1840-1904).

All the names and dates are from the Winston Genealogical Chart compiled from 1980 through 1985 by Marie Rauschenberg Rice except for the dates for Eliza Jane which came from Find a Grave Memorial Number 134790231.

Isaac Winston
1/22/1795-8/13/1863

Isaac Winston's son Isaac Winston, Jr. was also a cotton plantation and slave owner. Isaac, Jr. lived in Lawrence County, Alabama, which was the county east of his father. According to the 1850, Lawrence County, Alabama, Agricultural Census, Isaac Winston, Jr. owned 1500 acres of improved land and 500 acres of unimproved land that was valued at $30,000. He had $1,000 worth of farm equipment and $4,454 worth of livestock. In the 1860 Lawrence County, Alabama, Slave Schedule, Isaac Winston, Jr. owned 80 black slaves. From September 8, 1854, through January 2, 1855, Isaac Winston Jr. also entered 360 acres in Section 3 of Township 5 South and Range 11 West in Franklin County, Alabama.

In 1833, Isaac Winston, Sr. and Catherine Winston acquired the Belle Mont Plantation from Alexander Williams Mitchell; Alexander grew up in Louisa County, Virginia, only 25 miles from Jefferson's home at Monticello. Belle Mont which means "Lovely Mountain" is located just west of present-day United States Highway 43 about one mile; the old plantation mansion site is between Littleville and Muscle Shoals at 1569 Cook Lane, Tuscumbia, in present-day Colbert County, Alabama.

According to the 1830 Franklin County, Alabama, United States Census, Alexander Williams Mitchell owned 115 black slaves and was one of the largest slave holders at that time. Living in his house hold was one white male over 21, one white male under 21, one white female over 21, and five white females under 21 for a total of eight white inhabitants.

On March 3, 1823, Alexander Williams Mitchell entered lot number 10 including 40 acres in Section 4 of Township 4 South and Range 11 West in Cold Water (Tuscumbia) after moving to Franklin County, Alabama. According to a map dated March 6, 1820, and signed by John Coffee, surveyor, the southwest ¼ of Section 4 and the northwest ¼ of Section 9 in Township 4 South and Range 11 West was laid off for the Town of Cold Water. From March 4, 1823, through December 30, 1833, Alexander entered another 1,440 acres Townships 4, 5 South and Range 11 West in present-day Colbert County, Alabama.

Dr. Alexander Williams Mitchell, a graduate of the University of Edinburgh in Scotland, was a physician, cotton planter, and owner of black slaves. Alexander Williams Mitchell started construction of the Belle Mont Plantation Mansion about 1828 and completed the home by 1832. By 1833, Alexander sold the mansion and plantation to Isaac Winston in 1833.

In 1832, he remarried after his first wife died, and he put Belle Mont Plantation up for sale. In addition to the home, the advertisement included 1,760 acres on the plantation that were planted in clover, grass, corn, cotton, and an orchard. On December 30, 1833, Alexander entered land 40 acres in Section 2 of Township 5 South and Range 11 West. According to the 1840 Franklin County census, Alexander is listed as owning nine black slaves. He eventually moved to Philadelphia, Pennsylvania.

Both Alexander Williams Mitchell and Isaac Winston's family were originally from Virginia. They were also from wealthy plantations families that utilized a black slave labor to plant, maintain, and harvest their cotton crops.

Isaac Winston bought and operated Belle Mont Plantation primarily for the production of cotton. As other cotton planters of his time, Isaac used black slave labor to plant and harvest the cotton. According to the 1850 Franklin

County, Alabama, Agricultural Census, Isaac Winston owned 2,000 acres of improved land and 1358 acres of unimproved land worth $30,000. He owned $1500 worth of farm implements and machinery with $10,000 worth of livestock. According to the 1860 Franklin County Census records transcribed by Tom Blake, Isaac Winston Sr. owned 114 black slaves.

The picture above is a dog trot log cabin that was used as slave quarters. On August 5, 1935, one of the dog trot log homes of the slave quarters of Belle Mont Plantation was photographed by Alex Bush of the Library of Congress. On the hilltop setting near the historic Belle Mont Plantation house, a number of slave homes were used to house the 114 black slaves of Isaac Winston.

After Isaac and his wife Catherine died, Belle Mont mansion became the home of their daughter Ella Winston Thornton. The family eventually sold the entire Belle Mont Plantation in 1941.

Isaac Winston died at his Belle Mont Plantation home on August 13, 1863, in Colbert County, Alabama. Isaac Winston was buried in the Winston Family Cemetery at Tuscumbia in Colbert County, Alabama (Find a Grave Memorial Number 37663589). His wife Catherine lived at the home until her death on July 25, 1884 (Find a Grave Memorial Number 37663624). She was buried in the Winston Family Cemetery at Tuscumbia in Colbert County, Alabama.

Through the history of the Belle Mont Plantation Mansion, the home has been known as the Isaac Winston House. Belle Mont is listed as Belmont in the National Register of Historic Places. The plantation house is also known as the Henry B. Thornton Plantation House in the Historic American Buildings Survey; Henry Thornton was married to Isaac's daughter Ella Walker Winston.

Catherine Baker Jones Winston
12/15/1798-7/25/1884

The Belle Mont Plantation house is a brick structure similar to the Saunders, Hall, Goode Mansion in Lawrence County, Alabama; the Saunders, Hall, Goode Plantation Mansion is in bad shape and has not been restored like Belle Mont. Both the plantation era homes were of Palladian-style similar to those designed by United States President Thomas Jefferson, who was also an architect. The mansions are no more than 30 miles apart, but to prove that President Thomas Jefferson had a direct role in their design is difficult.

In addition to the brick Belle Mont Plantation home, the John Johnson Plantation home, and John T. Abernathy Plantation home in Clobert County were also early brick plantation houses in the area. The Abernathy plantation home is gone and half of the John Johnson Home has been destroyed; the rest of the Johnson home probably will not last much longer.

213

The 188 year old Belle Mont Plantation home is currently owned by the Alabama Historical Commission. In 1983, the Belle Mont Plantaion home and 35 surrounding acres were donated to the State of Alabama by Fennel family owners.

By the time the home was donated, it was falling in disrepair and ruin. The old mansion was turned over to the historic commission that eventually saved the architecturally significant plantation home.

The Alabama Historical Commission continues phases of restoration of the home as State funds allows. Volunteers from the Colbert County Historical Landmarks Foundation assist with special events and participate in fund raising activities. A "Plantation Christmas at Belle Mont" is held annually the first Sunday in December and features period costumed interpreters, decorations, refreshments, and entertainment.

Beginning in 2006, the Colbert County Historical Landmarks Foundation assumed operation of the museum for the AHC, which still owns the mansion. Belle Mont is open to the public for tours Wednesdays through Saturdays from 10:00 a.m. through 4:00 p.m. It is also available on other days by appointment for tours of 10 or more people. The historic home is often the scene of special events including weddings. For more information on the Belle Mont Plantation Mansion contact 256 381-5052 or www.ahc.alabama.gov/properties/bellemont.

214

Thank you From Rickey Butch Walker

      I am extremely honored and humbled by the many people who read my books. I greatly appreciate the readers that enjoy truthful historical stories of the Warrior Mountains and the great Tennessee River Valley. I send all the followers of my books a heartfelt thank you; without people who love local history about North Alabama, all my research and work would be in vain. I graciously request that each of you who acquire one of my books from Amazon to please post an honest review. A short two to three line evaluation of my books would be greatly appreciated. Again, thank you to all who take the time to read a book by Rickey Butch Walker.

References

1820 Franklin County, Alabama, United States Census

1830 Franklin County, Alabama, United States Census

1840 Franklin County, Alabama, United States Census

1850 Franklin County, Alabama, Agricultural Census

1850 Franklin County, Alabama, United States Census

1860 Franklin County, Alabama, United States Census

1860 Franklin County, Alabama Slave Schedule, Transcribed by Tom Blake, May 2001

Ancestry.Com

Cowart, Margaret Matthews, "Old Land Records of Colbert County, Alabama," 7801 Tea Garden Road Southeast, Huntsville, Alabama, 1985.

Cowart, Margaret Matthews, "Old Land Records of Lawrence County, Alabama," 7801 Tea Garden Road Southeast, Huntsville, Alabama, 1991.

Cowart, Margaret Matthews, "Old Land Records of Franklin County, Alabama," 7801 Tea Garden Road Southeast, Huntsville, Alabama, 1986.

Dailey, Freda S., "Riverton, How This Heritage Came To Be," Lambert Book House, 2014.

DeLand, T.A. and A. Davis Smith, "Northern Alabama Historical & Biographical," Donohue & Henneberry Publishers, Birmingham, Alabama, 1888.

Find a Grave, www.findagrave.com

Foreman, Grant, "The Five Civilized Tribes," University of Oklahoma Press, Norman, Oklahoma, 1934.

Leftwich, Nina, "Two Hundred Years at Muscle Shoals," The American Southern Printing Company, Northport, Alabama, 1935.

Malone, Henry Thompson, "Cherokees of the Old South: A People in Transition," University of Georgia Press, Athens, Georgia, 1956.

McLoughlin, Wm. G., "Cherokee Renascence in the New Republic," Princeton University Press, Princeton, New Jersey, 1986.

Owen, Thomas M. and Marie Bankhead Owen, "History of Alabama and Dictionary of Alabama Biography," S. J. Clarke Publishing Company, Chicago, Illinois, Volume 3, 1921.

Powell, John Wesley, Matthew Williams Stirling, Jesse Walter Fewkes, Frederick Webb Hodge, William Henry Holmes, "Annual Report", Volume 5, Parts 1883-1884, Library of American Civilization PCMI Collection, Smithsonian Institution, Bureau of American Ethnology, Government Printing Office, Pennsylvania State University, page 272, 1887.

RootsWeb.com

Royal Anne Newport, "Letters from Alabama 1817-1822," University of Alabama Press, Tuscaloosa, Alabama, 1969.

Saunders, James Edmonds, "Early Settlers of North Alabama," Willco Publishing Company, Tuscaloosa, Alabama 1961.

"The Heritage of Colbert County, Alabama," Heritage Publishing Consultants, Clanton, Alabama, 380 pages, 1999.

Wallace, Harry E., "History of the Shoals," Times Daily, Lauderdale County, Alabama, Thursday, February 25, 1999.

Index

Moore, Molsey Rand, 162
Monoah Hampton
    Hampton, Monoah, 34
Moorefield's Plantation, 103
Moorefields Plantation, 104
Morgan, 1, 11, 14, 15, 57, 62, 72, 81,
    112, 113, 118, 120, 127, 140, 141,
    147, 155, 159, 160, 181
Morgan County, Georgia, 70
Mother Church, 177, 178, 179, 180
Mount Holly Cemetery, 55, 60
Mt. Olivet Cemetery, 129
mulatto, 70, 132
Mulberry Creek, 143, 145
Muscle Shoals, 1, 2, 11, 12, 13, 15, 16,
    31, 32, 52, 62, 97, 128, 154, 165, 175,
    183, 210, 217
Mushhetubby, 9
Mustang Greys, 88
Myrtle Hall Plantation, 80
Nancy Ann Blackwell Malone
    Malone, Nancy Ann Blackwell, 121
Nancy Brigham
    Brigham, Nancy, 90
Nancy C. Martin
    Martin, Nancy C., 147
Nancy Caroline Peden
    Peden, Nancy Caroline, 154
Nancy Harris
    Harris, Nancy, 92, 93
Nashville, 15, 16, 58, 59, 72, 91, 108,
    129, 130, 131, 132, 134, 181, 198,
    202
Natchez District, 10
Natchez Trace, 7, 8, 17, 51, 82, 114, 143
Nathan J. Huston
    Huston, Nathan J., 102
Nathaniel A. F. Ragland
    Ragland, Nathaniel A. F., 168

Nathaniel Hutson
    Hutson, Nathaniel, 101
Nathaniel J. Pride
    Pride, Nathaniel J., 82, 159
Nathaniel Jones Pride
    Pride, Nathaniel Jones, 155, 159, 160
Nathaniel Ragland
    Ragland, Nathaniel, 169, 170
National Register of Historic Places, 56,
    174, 208, 213
Nellie Lane
    Lane, Nellie, 119
Nellie Mae Ricks Long
    Long, Nellie Mae Ricks, 179
Nelson Dickson Gun Factory, 69
New Orleans, 32, 128, 130, 201
New York, 101, 102, 153, 191
Newport Plantation, 142, 143
Nicholas Johnson
    Johnson, Nicholas, 77
Norman Farrell
    Farrell, Norman, 128, 129
North Carolina, 10, 11, 14, 18, 39, 40,
    42, 43, 52, 54, 59, 62, 63, 67, 69, 72,
    81, 82, 83, 85, 86, 87, 88, 89, 93, 95,
    96, 98, 99, 101, 102, 103, 105, 107,
    108, 110, 111, 112, 118, 119, 120,
    121, 122, 123, 135, 136, 138, 139,
    142, 149, 150, 152, 153, 154, 155,
    156, 157, 159, 160, 162, 164, 165,
    170, 172, 173, 180, 185, 186, 187,
    191, 193, 201
Oakwood Cemetery, 64, 72, 80, 84, 96,
    98, 126, 149, 158, 167, 172, 188, 189,
    193
Oates Cemetery, 144
Oats Plantation, 143, 146
Oats, Samuel
    Samuel Oats, 142

www.ingramcontent.com/pod-product-compliance
Lightning Source LLC
Chambersburg PA
CBHW050458110426
42742CB00018B/3300

9 781949 711080